Memories that the wind brings

PSYCHOGRAPHY OF
Mônica De Castro
BY THE SPIRIT
LEONEL

Translated into English by:
Carolina Higinio Bernal
Lima, Perú, February 2021

Original title in Portuguese:
"LEMBRANÇAS QUE O VENTO TRAZ"
© MÔNICA DE CASTRO 2007

Revision:

Renato Marcelo Gil

Natalie Zegarra Bartolo

World Spiritist Institute

Houston, Texas, USA

E- mail: contact@worldspiritistinstitute.org

MÔNICA DE CASTRO

My love for literature has existed since my childhood. I always liked to read and write, in verse and prose, and it was in Manoel Bandeira's poems that I further refined my soul's sensitivity.

I liked writing poems, stories, different texts, and I even won a poetry contest at the age of thirteen, here in the city of Rio de Janeiro, where I was born in 1962. At the same time, my mediumship was awakened and I adopted Spiritism as a balm for my heart.

My desire was always to be a writer, but life takes us down different paths, always for our benefit, and I ended up graduating in law and passing a competition for the Public Labor Ministry.

Years later, after my son was born, I felt the first inspiration. It was a strange thing.

A voice was in my head, repeating that name: Rosali, and the idea of making a romance immediately came up. I rejected the idea and thought, "Who am I to write a novel?

On the other hand, the same voice also told me: "It never hurts to try. The worst that can happen is not to get anywhere." I accepted the suggestion of the invisible, believing it was my thought, and went to sit in front of the computer.

At the same time, the inspiration for "Una historia de ayer" came spontaneously, and I began to write, a little bit every day. Until then, I didn't know I was doing psychography.

It was only when I finished the novel that I received Leonel's psychography, which opens my first book, where he introduces himself and gives his name. But it took a lot of detachment to write, without questioning and accepting the interference of the Spirit. Today I can say that Leonel is a fundamental part of my life.

I do not write for a living. I write because I like it and because I think I am doing something good for people. And it is this feeling that makes me want to write more and more. It is for people that it is worth writing.

For readers who are looking for something, beyond the here and now, and who believe in the power of faith, self- knowledge and love, as safe paths to the transformation of self.

I believe that we can all work for the moral improvement of humanity to build a better world.

Visit the writer's website:
www.movimentoecrescimento.com

LEONEL

Leonel is a very dear spirit in my heart. In our first novel, he gave me an idea of what he would have been like in his past life: a writer.

I know that he was born and lived in England in his last incarnation, as well as in previous ones. In *"Secrets of the Soul"*, he tells a little of his story, along with that of the woman who was the great love of his life. He was not a famous writer. He was a bohemian, but someone with such dignity who soon woke up with the true values of the spirit, and today is able to transmit messages of optimism and love. I realized this in almost daily contact with him and in the communications he transmits, always in a mental way.

Some time ago, he let me know what he looked like. Leonel showed himself to me in the spiritualist house, in a moment of deep memory and reflection.

Physically, he is a handsome boy. Black hair, full, with delicate features and blue eyes. Medium height, slim, he came dressed in pants and a white robe, barefoot and with calm air. He had such a serene face that he transmitted it to me. There, he told me things that changed forever my way of seeing certain aspects of life.

His proposal is the growth and diffusion of love. That's what he works for, that's what he believes in and makes me believe too. Without hope and certainty in the consolidation of love, life has no reason to be. And the instrument he found for the realization of that purpose, at this moment, was psychography.

Like me, Leonel writes for himself and his neighbor.

Memories that the wind brings

I consider Leonel another fighter of the invisible. A spirit with enormous wisdom and an unparalleled capacity to love. An evolving being who knows the growth path and knows where the source of discernment and morality lies. A soul that grows through self- effort, the recognition of its imperfections, and the unceasing search for self- mastery. And this, above all, is where its value lies.

Mônica de Castro

PREFACE

This is the end of the trilogy that began with the book "Eeeling in One's skin" passing through "Love is not to be played with" until arriving at this one, "Memories that the wing brings" that closes the history of the Sales from Albuquerque and the slave Toña, who was linked to them by ties of love and hate from the past.

The sequence of events, which began 200 years ago, ends in Cabo Frio (Cape Cold), the birthplace of my grandfather Edmundo, who introduced Leonel to the real characters, in spirit, so that he could bring his story as an example to us all. But the story is not his, nor was he the one who lived it. His characters are people he once knew, even though he had no closer relationship with any of them. Those were things of small towns, at the end of the 19th century, where everyone knew each other, at least by name or when they found out about it.

As my grandfather told me, they are a family like many others, but whose truths we do not know. No one ever knew about the drama that took place in that house, and, for the city's inhabitants, they were just people who lived there, halfway through everything and everyone. Quiet and unimportant people, who did not attract anyone's attention.

But the death of the body awakens these truths and then is when we see that they will never be unimportant.

Mônica de Castro

Feeling in One's Skin

At the age of ninety-seven, Toña witnesses the abolition of slavery and refuses to leave the hacienda where she lived most of her life. Called to intervene, Clarissa and Luciano, the young sons of the lord of those lands, cannot convince her to leave. At great cost, Clarissa convinces her father to let Toña stay in a small room, where she tells her story...

In the early 19th century, Toña came from Africa on a slave ship to serve as a birthday gift for a rich farmer's daughter. Sold by his tribal chief, it is taken from her mother's arms and dragged by force, until she arrives in Brazil and, after brief teachings, she is ready to be presented to Aline, her new owner.

Aline, the rich white girl, eventually becomes attached to Toña and begins to question her father's attitudes, opposing the way he treats the slaves. The two girls grow up together, Toña always under Aline's protection until they meet two young men, Ignacio and Cirilo, with whom they fall in love.

Aline and Cirilo soon become engaged, while Toña is forced to live a hidden romance with Ignacio. From then on, events happen and Toña began to feel on her own skin the same type of treatment that she had inflicted on the humblest one when she was Cláudia, a rich and useless girl who, in another life, had despised the true values of the spirit.

Until destinies intertwine and life takes over to show each one the value of respect and forgiveness.

Love is not to be played with

Toña, now an elderly woman, continues to serve the same family, but is forced to endure the displeasure of Palmira, mother of the twins Fausto and Rodolfo.

Physically identical, however, the twins differ in temperament. While Fausto is upright and honest, Rodolfo is envious and cunning, and plans to force a relationship with Julia, who is engaged to his brother, causing these immense jealousies.

But destiny reserves other paths for them, and Rodolfo ends up meeting Marta, the daughter of the foreman of the hacienda, who falls in love with him and will do everything possible to win his heart. At the same time, other characters are emerging, such as Camila, Palmira's daughter, and her sons, Dário and Túlio, who are involved in pleasures and crime.

At the same time, on the neighboring farm, a Jewish family suffers from the prejudices and illnesses of their only daughter, who has tuberculosis. But the spiritual world draws much bigger plans for them, and help comes in the form of a priest who knows the hidden things, and Marta, a healing medium who helps in the patient's recovery.

Many intrigues and lies arise in the course of the history, while life puts Fausto and Rodolfo in front of situations that call them to experience and overcome their more difficult feelings. For Rodolfo, hate. For Faust, jealousy.

CHAPTER 1

As soon as the birds started chirping outside, Clarissa woke up in disgust, stretched out, rubbed her eyes, and looked out the window.

One more day of boredom at the San Jeronimo hacienda, another day with nothing new to do. Except for her brother Luciano and her cousin Jerusa, there was no one else to talk to. The older sister, Valentina, was an authoritarian busybody and was too busy with the baby.

Clarissa heard a loud knock on the door and said, without much interest:

– You may enter.

The door opened and the mother entered, greeting her with a smile:

– Good morning Clarissa.

– Good morning, Mom. Any news?

– Why do you ask?

– For you to come to my room early in the morning, sure, something new has happened.

– You are very smart.

– Is Dad back from the capital yet?

– Not yet.

– Then what is it?

She looked at his daughter with amusement and announced:

– Your order has just arrived...

Memories that the wind brings

She didn't even have to listen to the rest. Clarissa jumped out of bed and threw her shawl over her shoulders, went downstairs and ran into the living room. As soon as she entered, she saw a large box by the window and began to jump for joy. Completely intoxicated, she started untying knots and pulling boards, trying to open the box as fast as she could.

But the wood was hard, and she couldn't. Immediately, she began to scream:

– Luciano! Luciano! For God's sake, come help me!

Hearing those screams, the brother seemed breathless, followed by the other sister, who was carrying a month- old baby.

– But what is happening here? – He asked indignantly.

– Look at Luciano! – exclaimed Clarissa, pointing to the box- . Dad kept his promise and sent me what I asked for! Come on, help me open it!

Flora, the mother, stood behind, while the son helped Clarissa to open that huge box. It was very well tied and fastened, and it was necessary to find some tools to loosen the screws. A few minutes later, the boards began to give way, and Clarissa was pulling them, full of excitement. A new harpsichord appeared amidst the pieces of sawn wood, and Clarissa clapped happily, smoothing the keys with her long fingers. Immediately, the strings inside resounded and a soft melody invaded the room. It was wonderful!

– Where did Dad get the money to buy that? – Valentina asked contemptuously.

– Don't be a spoilsport, Valentina, her mother reproached her. Didn't your father promise? So? He kept his promise.

– We all know that our situation is not the best. Yesterday we didn't even have enough money for expenses, and today I have this harpsichord here from the capital, which must have cost a small fortune. Look at these keys. They're ivory!

– What's the problem?" answered Clarissa. I bet you're jealous.

– I don't know why I would be jealous of you, silly girl.

– Because you don't know how to play. You never managed to learn.

– And who says I want to learn?

– Enough, girls, Flora ordered. There is no reason to fight. What matters is that your father bought the harpsichord, right? And he certainly didn't have to steal or extort from anyone. Or do you think your father suddenly became a thief, Valentina?

– I don't think so – answered Valentina reluctantly. – I just think Dad spoils that girl too much. He does all of Clarissa's bidding.

– And what happens? – Clarissa said, in a very defiant way. The girl in the lap of Valentina began to cry, and Flora considered:

– Valentina, my daughter, I think it's time to feed the baby.

Reluctantly, Valentina left the room and went into the room to take care of her daughter. After she left, Clarissa and Luciano began to mount the harpsichord, adjusting the body to the feet. All set, Clarissa took out the stool and sat down to play. It was in tune, and she intended to prepare a concert when her father returned.

She would return the gift with another one, playing it to cheer his ears up. Flora sat down on the couch and admired her daughter. She was beautiful and sweet, though a little stubborn and even daring, and how she loved music!

Clarissa had approached her.

When Flora married Fortunato, he allowed her to take the harpsichord that had been her mother's, and as soon as the children were old enough to learn, she set out to teach them.

But Valentina did not give way with a ball. She hadn't listened, she wasn't interested in learning. Luciano, on the other

Memories that the wind brings

hand, was very restless and didn't have the patience to spend long hours sitting down, which made it difficult for him to concentrate.

Only Clarissa was interested. The girl, from an early age, demonstrated an innate musical gift and spent hours and hours entertaining herself with music, without even remembering the games.

There were times when the cousin from the Oro Viejo hacienda came, and then they had beautiful meetings, with her and her daughter taking turns with the harpsichord. But, unfortunately, about a year before, someone had left the window of the room open, under which the instrument was, just as they were traveling to the capital, to witness the marriage of a distant relative. It was a rainy season and a storm hit the region. Through the open window, it poured on the furniture, carpets and also the harpsichord. When they returned from the trip, all the furniture was damaged, the carpets stained and the harpsichord wood swollen and smelled musty. Clarissa and Flora came to cry in disgust. In addition to the damage, the loss of the beloved instrument seemed irreparable. But Fortunato had promised them: as soon as he could, he would order an instrument from the capital, more beautiful and more sonorous, the latest model in Europe.

Clarissa was full of hope and looked forward to receiving her gift. However, the situation at the haciendas had become worrying. The entire last harvest had been lost due to a fatal plague that had attacked the plantation. No matter how hard they tried, the farmers could not contain it, and in a short time, the devastation was total. Her father had lost practically everything, as well as her relatives at the Oro Viejo hacienda and some of the closest farmers.

It was said that the carelessness and neglect of Mr. Américo, owner of a neighboring hacienda, ended up bringing the plague, which soon spread to the surrounding lands. At great cost, they managed to exterminate it, but the losses, besides being incalculable, were also irreversible.

Memories that the wind brings

After the plantation was destroyed, all they had to do was start over. But how? Fortunato had lost almost all of his coffee beans. Money was needed to buy new seeds, plant them and wait for them to grow and bear fruit. All this took time, and the money they had would not be enough to support that much. Finally, convinced that his reserves would not be enough to pay for the planting and subsistence until the new harvest, Fortunato went to the capital, in an attempt to obtain a loan from the bankers.

The situation was precarious, but Fortunato enjoyed prestige, which would undoubtedly make it easier for him to obtain the loan.

Upon seeing the harpsichord that her husband had sent to Clarissa, Flora concluded that she had obtained the money and began to make some expenses. She was happy, yes, but thinking about it, maybe Valentina was right. Would it be wise to spend so much money on a harvest that didn't exist yet? A shadow of concern crossed her mind. The husband, besides being an excellent businessman, was a prudent and sober man, and he would never count on something that was not really his. Where, then, would that money have come from? Had he sold any property? It was possible, but all his assets were found there, in those two haciendas, in addition to some buildings in the capital, whose income from rent was not enough to cover all his expenses. They were used to luxury and wealth, and it was not easy to settle for a life of savings and deprivation.

Young and dreamy, Clarissa did not realize all this. The family's financial problems did not concern her. If her father had sent her the harpsichord, he had certainly gotten the money in an honest way.

Besides Valentina, Luciano was also surprised. He loved his younger sister very much and didn't want to ruin her joy, but he was very worried about that luxurious harpsichord. However, he chose not to say anything. The mother also seemed happy, and he did not want to stain so much happiness.

Memories that the wind brings

* * *

Early the next morning, after breakfast, Valentina got up, handed over the baby to the maid and asked her:

– Did you bring the flowers I asked for?

– Yes, ma'am. They are in the vase on the living room table.

– Excellent. Now take the child to sunbathe. But be careful, don't forget that outside.

– You can be calm, Ms. Valentina, I do not forget, no.

Valentina got up, went into the living room and picked up the flowers. She returned to the breakfast table, where the others remained, amused in lively prose, and asked:

– Aren't you coming?

– Where to? – replied Luciano.

– Today, grandfather Rodolfo passed away two years ago.

– Didn't he? – continued the brother.

– That's right. I'm going to the cemetery to bring him some flowers. For him and Grandma Marta, may God have them.

– You do very well.

– Aren't you coming with me? It is the family's duty to watch over the memory of their ancestors.

– I don't think I should cry over my grandparents' grave to remember them – Clarissa objected. – And, if you really want to know, Grandpa Rodolfo wasn't even that good.

– You are a brazen and impolite girl, Clarissa, and you should be ashamed of talking that way about our grandfather, who did everything for us.

– What did he do for us apart from reproaching us? I don't remember anything he did to please us. Grandmother Martha, no. She was sweet, loving, friendly...

Valentina gulped and replied:

— You are ungrateful, that is, and it is better even if you don't go —. And, turning to her brother, she asked him: — And you, Luciano, aren't you coming?

— Who me? Ah! No, don't count on me. I have more things to do. I agree with Clarissa. We don't need to stop at her grave to remember that he existed.

— You two are impossible. No wonder you get along. You are the same: selfish, rude, disrespectful…

— Okay, Valentina, that's it — said Flora. — Leave your brothers alone. I will go with you.

Flora took the shawl and left with her daughter. She didn't like her father-in-law either. He had been a boring and irascible man and was always ranting and cursing.

The mother-in-law, however, was different, and everyone liked her. Marta had been a good and pious woman, and had lived a selfless life with her husband, always ready to help him and do everything for him. Only she could control him. Rodolfo had always had a terrible temper, and his wife was the only one he listened to.

But if Valentina liked her grandfather, what could she do? After all, they had the same blood, and she looked a lot like him. She always had been. The same temperament, the same beliefs, the same ideals. It was for no other reason that she had always been her grandfather's favorite, unlike Clarissa and Luciano, with whom he lived to tease and scold.

* * *

That night, when she went to sleep, Clarissa smelled a slight perfume of roses in the air and remembered Toña. Toña had been a slave on her hacienda since she was very young, when she was brought there from Africa on a slave ship, to serve as a birthday present for Aline, her grandfather's older sister, who had died at an early age. While Aline was alive, Grandma Toña had enjoyed certain freedom. But after she died in a fire, Toña was brutally punished and thrown to senzala, until luck greeted her, and she was called to serve as a wet nurse for her grandfather and twin brother. Since then, she returned to live in the big house and raised most of the children born on the hacienda. Shortly after the abolition of slavery, Toña died, after almost a hundred years of struggle and suffering. Toña had always been a friend of Clarissa. She had seen her born, helped in her upbringing, taught her to embroider and prepare delicacies like no one else. Even as an old woman, she did what she could, and Clarissa was delighted with the stories she told of her people, her land, her culture.

Clarissa loved the religion of the blacks and from an early age had learned to recognize and identify all the African gods. Toña told her about the association they made with Catholic saints, and Clarissa was delighted. She knew that there were slaves coming from different regions of Africa, who also had different languages and cultures.

Then, the peoples began to mix, and the Yoruba culture ended up predominating over the others, even imposing its Orixás, replacing the darkness that Toña talked about so much. But she said that the gods were all the same, and it didn't matter what they were called. The important thing was that both the Orixás and the Inkices were deities that represented the forces of nature and that could be invoked in any situation of life. The image of the slave did not come out of his head. About a year after Toña's death, Clarissa began to dream about her, which always seemed smiling, dressed in white or blue.

He gave her news of his life in the invisible world, talked to her about things she did not know, and used to warn her about some dangers or difficulties. Although Clarissa did not remember everything she dreamed of, she always managed to preserve in her memory the impressions of what Toña spoke to her, impressions that used to arise at the most opportune moments, in the form of intuition or sensations.

Memories that the wind brings

That night, it was no different. As soon as she fell asleep, Clarissa's fluid body separated from her physical body and found Toña there, standing by her bed, waiting for her. Clarissa smiled and took her hand, speaking sweetly:

– Hi, Grandma Toña, did you come to visit me?

– I came to pick you up for a walk. Let's walk a little in the moonlight.

The two of them went out into the garden. It was a beautiful night, covered with stars, and they were lying on the soft grass, enjoying the starry sky above their heads. After a few minutes, Clarissa asked:

– So, Grandma Toña, what are you talking about this time?

Without looking away from the sky, Toña shook Clarissa's hand and replied:

– I needed to warn you. To tell her that you will soon make a long journey to a distant and unknown land.

– How so?

– When the time comes, you will know.

– Is something going to happen to me on this trip? Am I going to die?

– You will not die, but you will go through a very difficult period in your life, full of conflicts and anguish. I will always be by your side, and if you stand firm in your purposes of growth, you will be able to free your spirit from the guilt it carries from the past.

– What guilts? I never hurt anyone.

– Haven't I told you that we have many lives and that often, using our free will, we adopt attitudes that put the harmony of life and the universe out of balance? And then, wanting to improve, we choose certain paths and situations that will put us face to face with the opportunity to give back to life what we took from it?

– Yes...

– So? Everything is just the possibility that the universe is giving you to restore to the world the part of balance that you took from it, at another time when you lived in another place and occupied another body of flesh.

– I don't remember any of that.

– When the time comes, your memory will activate your hidden records and you will relive moments of extreme importance to understand some episodes that will unfold in your current life.

– Couldn't you tell me something? If the worst happens, I don't want to be unprepared.

– Nothing will happen to you, and your soul knows what it needs to live. Trust in God and have faith. Think of the Orixas. They can help you too. And remember that it was your choice.

After that, Toña gave Clarissa a soft kiss on the forehead and took her back to her room, helping her return to her body. The girl sighed while sleeping, turned to the side and continued to sleep peacefully. The next day, when she woke up, she only had a vague memory that she had dreamt of Toña and, in her dream, she told her something about travel, choices and balance. What would it be? She couldn't remember. When the cousin arrived to drink coffee, she was there too. It was Sunday and Jerusa had come to invite her to go to church together. The girls were not close cousins. Jerusa was the daughter of Laís, the firstborn of Dário, who became the nephew of his grandfather Rodolfo. Grandfather Dário, as he used to be called, was still alive, as was his wife, Grandmother Sara, who, despite not being in very good health, survived the years with faith and confidence.

– Good morning, Clarissa, said Jerusa happily.

– Good morning, she replied. Am I late?

– No. It's just that Mom wanted to be early. She said she needs to talk to the priest about a Mass of Thanksgiving for her grandmother's improvement. She almost died after the last flu.

– That's right. But Grandma Sara is a very strong woman.

– That's right. Who knew she would live so many years, right?

When Luciano came down and saw his cousin, he rushed to her. Luciano and Jerusa, for some time, were in love for the happiness of both families.

– I'm glad you came early, Jerusa, she melted and kissed him on the cheek.

– Mother's things, she answered, blushing.

After the mass, everyone went to the hacienda of San Jerónimo, where Sunday lunch would be served. The young people were extremely close and friendly, and they used to walk around the hacienda together, going to the stream to wet their feet or to fish. After lunch, Clarissa sat down with the harpsichord, playing, filling the house with her joyful and well-executed melody.

It was almost three o'clock and she wasn't tired. She loved music, and playing the harpsichord was what gave her the most pleasure. The notes amused her when a booming voice came from the direction of the door:

– Good afternoon!

Everyone turned around and Clarissa released the harpsichord, ran to the newcomer and exclaimed euphorically:

– Dad! Dad! Why didn't you say you were coming?

The father picked her up in his lap, as he always did, kissed her on the cheek and placed her back on the floor, going towards the woman and kissing her respectfully and in a measured way. With him came his son-in-law, Roberto, Valentina's husband, who always accompanied him on his travels.

He then greeted the others and began to distribute the gifts he had brought. There were gifts for everyone, and Valentina was the first to ask:

– Dad, where did the money for all this come from?

Memories that the wind brings

Fortunato was about to answer when a "hum... hum..." interrupted his speech. Immediately, everyone turned around, facing a mature, tall, thin and slightly bald man. The stranger looked at them and made a ceremonious gesture, to which the others responded, without fully understanding what it was all about. More than quickly, Fortunato introduced the visitor to the group:

– Flora, I would like to introduce Mr. Abílio Figueira Gomes, our guest. – Flora looked at him in surprise. She didn't expect to receive visitors, much less staying, and was extremely upset.

However, good manners commanded her to welcome the newcomer, and she spoke kindly:

– Nice to meet you, Mr. Abílio, and welcome to this house.

– Thank you, madam – he replied, kissing her hand formally and looking Clarissa out of the corner of his eye.

The girl felt a chill and shivered. She had not sympathized with this guy, and the way he looked at her as if he were studying her, left her confused. Fortunato continued the introductions and then told the woman:

– Flora, Mr. Abílio came from the capital to stay at our house for a while. We have important things to do, and I want your stay here to be as pleasant as possible.

– Of course, Fortunato – Flora turned to Abílio and continued: – I ask you to forgive me, Mr. Abílio, but we were not expecting your visit. So, if you will excuse me, I would like to retire and have decent accommodations prepared for you.

– At ease, madam – he replied. – But you need not worry. I am a simple man and I do not insist on luxury.

After Flora left, Laís also excused herself to go with her daughter. It was getting late and they had to return. She had left her husband at the hacienda, in the company of her parents, and a

Memories that the wind brings

lot of time had passed. They thanked those present and were preparing to leave when Luciano asked:

– Couldn't Jerusa stay? I will take her home later. Jerusa looked at her mother anxiously, but she did not agree:

– No, my daughter, I don't think this is the right time.

– Oh! please, Aunt Laís, come on – insisted Clarissa – . Jerusa can stay and sleep with me, in my room.

– No, my children, I don't think it is appropriate. We don't want to get in the way, do we?

– You can let her stay," interrupted Fortunato. Jerusa is a good girl and won't bother anything. And tomorrow, Luciano can take her home.

Laís still hesitated for a few minutes, but when she saw the air of anxiety and pleading of Jerusa and Clarissa, she ended up accepting:

– Well, if that's the case, that's fine. But have some manners and obey Aunt Flora.

– Don't worry, Mom.

Laís said goodbye and left. Jerusa looked at Luciano, who winked at her, and at Clarissa, who smiled at him. In fact, Clarissa had a strange feeling, and did not want to be alone. It was something that she did not know how to define, but she felt that she was about to fall into an endless abyss, and Jerusa's presence gave her certain security. The woman was like her sister, and Clarissa would feel stronger and more courageous in her presence. During the rest of the day and part of the night, Fortunato remained locked in his office with Abílio, without giving any further explanation to the family. Until then, no one even knew where the money for the harpsichord and the gifts had come from, nor did they suspect the reason for Abílio's presence there. If it was a business that this man had to deal with Fortunato, it was better not to bother them, as they should be discussing the future of the hacienda and their own lives.

Memories that the wind brings

It was only at dinner time that they left the library. Abílio seemed to be a quiet and serious man, and Fortunato had a cloud of sadness in his eyes. The dinner took place almost in silence, which was only interrupted by the casual conversation of Jerusa and Luciano. Flora did not understand very well what was happening, but she knew it was serious, or her husband would not let that expression of disgust show. At the end of dinner, she got up and went back to the library, in the company of Abílio. Only this time she called Flora to join them. The young people did not understand and did not ask any questions. Only Valentina, after retiring, asked her husband:

– Dad is very strange. Do you know what happened, Roberto? – The husband shrugged his shoulders and responded:

– It's business.

– And do they have to do with the fate of the hacienda?

– In a way, yes. They can solve the fate of the hacienda – . She looked at him perplexed, raised her eyebrows, and then continued:

– Do you know what this is about?

– Yes, I know, but I can't talk.

– Not even to me? I am your wife, and there must be no secrets between us.

– Your father asked me not to say anything.

– Come on, Roberto, you can tell me. I won't say anything to anyone. Roberto looked at the woman hesitantly and nodded. After all, she was his wife and deserved his trust. And then, soon, soon, everyone would know what kind of business the father-in-law was in.

CHAPTER 2

The next day, Clarissa was woken up by her mother, who came to call her for an important conversation. In the next bed, Jerusa was still sleeping and Flora instructed her daughter not to wake her up. Clarissa got out of bed, washed, dressed and went downstairs.

– What is this all about? – she asked, anguished.

– You'll find out.

Flora fell silent and followed her in silence. Her swollen eyes revealed that she had cried, and her hands pressed together nervously. At every moment, she let out sighs and looked up, struggling desperately to hold back her tears. Unable to contain her curiosity, Clarissa asked again:

– Mom, what happened?

They came to the office. Flora knocked slightly and slowly opened the door. Inside,

Fortunato was waiting for them with Abílio, who looked at the floor and said nothing.

– Sit down, my daughter, the father began to speak. What I have to tell you is extremely important and can seal the fate of all of us here in this house forever.

Without understanding anything, Clarissa sat down and looked at her father. She had no idea what was happening, she was just a child. How could she contribute to the fate of the family? The father cleared his throat, looked at Flora, who did not look back, and continued:

– Mr. Abílio here is a friend of Commander Travassos, who introduced us – . Clarissa said nothing, and he continued: – Mr.

Memories that the wind brings

Abílio told me that he has been looking for a long time for a girl from a good family, demure, who he would like to marry...

At that moment, as if she understood what was happening, Clarissa jumped up and exclaimed in amazement:

– Daddy!

– Wait, my daughter, let me finish. As I was telling you, Mr. Abílio is looking for a wife, and since he is an honest and upright man, I was wondering if it would be a good combination for you and...

Clarissa didn't let him conclude. Indignant and hurt, she ran to the door and, with her eyes bathed in tears, decreed:

– What you are saying is an affront! How can you think of marrying me without even consulting me? This man is a stranger, and I have no intention of marrying him, ever!

Fortunato looked at her with deep disgust and declared, his voice almost gone:

– I'm sorry, my daughter, it's already decided.

Clarissa turned away from him, horrified. She could not believe this was happening. Why was her father punishing her like this? Why did he want to get rid of her? What would she have done? She quickly went upstairs and locked herself in the room. When the door slammed shut, Jerusa awoke with a shock and saw her cousin standing there with her back to the door, crying and asking in anguish:

– Clarissa! What happened to you?, my God, You look like you've seen a ghost! – The girl ran to her cousin's bed and threw herself into her arms, crying copiously.

Jerusa, not understanding anything, straightened her hair, trying to calm her down. After a few minutes, joining forces, Clarissa expressed:

– Oh, Jerusa, you cannot even imagine the monstrosity my father wants to make on me!

– Don't say that! Since when is your father a monster? He likes you a lot!

– He doesn't like me. If I liked him, I wouldn't think of marrying with that... With that... – she didn't end up, collapsing in the lap of the other and crying nervously.

– What's going on, Clarissa? You're scaring me.

There was a knock at the door and Jerusa reached Clarissa to the side and stood up to answer.

– Please don't! – Don't open that door, for God's sake, or it will be my end!

– What are you talking about?

– Clarissa! – It was the mother's voice, calling her from outside the room.

Clarissa, my daughter, open that door, please, and let's talk.

– No! No! She shouted from inside – . All of you are cowards, cruel. I don't want to see you, I don't want to!

– Clarissa, open...

Jerusa, who did not understand anything, heard her aunt's voice, opened the door without Clarissa noticing, and Flora entered with her eyes still wet, squeezing her hands nervously.

– Aunt Flora, said Jerusa, what is it?

– Please, Jerusa, leave us alone, okay? Pick up your clothes and go change in the guest room.

Without asking, Jerusa did what her aunt had ordered. Quietly, she picked up her clothes, threw a robe over her nightgown and left, closing the door carefully. After she left, Flora went over to the bed, sat down and put her daughter's head in her lap, stroking her hair. Clarissa collapsed into more meaningful crying and questioning in the midst of sobbing:

– Why... why, Mom... why did you do that... to me? Why do you hate me so much...?

– How can you think that we hate you?

– What do you want me to think? My own father gave me in marriage to a stranger, much older than me...

– A very rich stranger.

Clarissa raised her head and looked at her hesitantly. What do you mean by that?

– ¿And?

– And, well, it's a complicated story.

– I would love to know. Please, Mom, what's going on?

– I want you to know my daughter, that I was against what I am going to tell you now. However, your father...

– What's wrong with him? Please tell me! Tell me what I already suspect, but refuse to believe.

– You know that our situation at the hacienda is almost chaotic, don't you? – Clarissa nodded – And you also know that your father went to the capital to ask the bankers for a loan to save not only our land, but also the land of the Oro Viejo hacienda, which also belongs to our family, don't you?

– Please, Mom, stop spinning and get to the point.

– Well. The bankers did not refuse to grant the loan, but they demanded guarantees that your father considered, for example, excessive.

– What guarantees?

– A mortgage on the two haciendas. Do you know what a mortgage is?

– I don't know what a mortgage is.

– As his father explained to me, a mortgage is a business for which the debtor, in this case, your father, offers a property as security for the payment of a debt. If the debt is not paid, the bank, through an unknown legal process, takes the property to auction and keeps almost all the money. If that happens to us, we may be left with nothing, and it is a very big risk for your father to take. Clarissa thought for a few minutes and said

- Okay, Mom. But that risk will only exist if Dad doesn't pay the debt, right? - She agreed. So? If Dad takes the money and invests in the plantation, he will surely recover everything he lost and be able to pay back the loan. Our farm has always been productive, we have always had good coffee crops. I don't see any reason for concern.

- What happens if a new pest emerges?

- Don't you think that's unlikely?

- No, I don't think so. And then, there is the question of interest... They are exorbitant. Clarissa sighed dejectedly and considered:

- Exactly where do you plan to go?

- In the face of these difficulties, her father was almost discouraged. Despite the risks and the fear of losing everything, he was going to accept the loan, until he met Commander Travassos.

Talking to him, he found out about his friend, Mr. Abílio, who went to the capital in search of a new wife.

- Have he ever been married?

- Yes, Mr. Abílio was married, but the woman died about a year ago, leaving him two children...

- Stop it, Mom, I don't want to hear anymore! Besides wanting to marry a stranger, they still want me to face two children who aren't even my own! It was just what I needed

- It's not those kids. Your father told me that Mr. Abílio has a couple of children, who are now twelve and seventeen years old.

- I'm sorry if I disappointed them, but I'm not willing to bury my life and youth by taking care of the children of an old, scowling husband. I'm sorry, but I have better plans.

- It turns out your father has already compromised his word...

Memories that the wind brings

– So come back. I'm not getting married, and he can't make me. And if you insist, I'll kill myself.

– Dear God, Clarissa, don't even say that, not even as a joke!

– Seriously, Mom, I'm not kidding. I'd rather die than marry that horrible, disgusting man.

– He's neither horrible nor disgusting. He's just older. But he's not ugly...

– I'm not going to marry him!

Flora took a deep breath, held her daughter's chin lovingly and watched:

– You know, Clarissa, when your father told me what he had done, I cried a lot and even thought about leaving here. And don't think he convinced me, that's not all. But he is my husband and I owe him obedience. So do you.

– He is not my husband.

– But he is your father. That's why I agreed to come here and talk to you. As a daughter, you must resign yourself to your fate and follow your destiny.

– The fate my father chose.

– In any case, you cannot refrain from obeying him.

– Mom, you don't understand. It's not about obeying an order or not.

It's about my happiness.

– But it is necessary. We all have to give our share of sacrifice.

– This is a very large share of sacrifice. And what good would it do me to marry this man? What does he promise in return?

– He gave your father the money to rebuild the haciendas.

– What?! – Clarissa was amazed – my dad sold me to that old man?

– No, he didn't.

– Now I understand. The harpsichord, the gifts. It was all a fix, right? It was to ease his own conscience that my father gave me that harpsichord, thinking of redeeming himself. I wanted to pretend to be good and generous, while he stabbed me in the back. How stupid and naive I was, thinking that he hadn't forgotten his promise to me.

But no. What he really wanted was to trick me, to get rid of the guilt while selling me to a stranger!

– That's not what this is about...

– What is it about? A business? After all, he was the one who said he was in business with that man. Now I understand everything. He sold me, he sold his own daughter to the first person who showed up offering good money.

– You're getting it all wrong. Of course, your father didn't sell you. He accepted Mr. Abílio's proposal because he knows he is a good man and will take good care of you.

– Should I thank him for his consideration?

– You don't have to be sarcastic. Your father did what he did for the good of all.

– Is everyone good or is he himself? He's selling me out! Don't you see? And then I, who always loved him and thought he loved me.

– Your father loves you very much and is very sad about everything. Believe me, Clarissa, if there was another solution, I would have preferred it.

– That's a lie! There was another solution. He could have accepted the terms of the loan, he could have sold his houses in the capital, the furniture, the artwork, the jewelry. We're rich, Mom. Why did he only have to get rid of her daughter?

– Things are not as you think. The houses we have in the capital wouldn't give us much money, and the rental income is still useful to help us.

Memories that the wind brings

As for our valuables, her father thinks they wouldn't make a good profit.

– How could they not? We have art objects...

– That's not worth that much.

– How does he know? Has he evaluated it?

– Your father knows the value of everything we have, and if he says it's not enough, it's because it's not.

– I doubt it. He doesn't want to get rid of his relics, his treasures. He's attached to his treasures, but he's not attached to his daughter!

– Don't you understand that your father would never have done this if he had a choice? That is the price of your sacrifice for the family.

– I'm sorry, Mom, but it's too high a price to pay.

– Okay, you're the one who knows. Your father can't force her to marry against her will.

But think carefully. Would you like to be responsible for the ruin of our family?

Believe me, my daughter, your father would not resist. He would either die of heartbreak or commit suicide.

Clarissa buried her face in his hands and began to cry again. It was too heavy a burden to ask. Suddenly, she remembered the dream she had had with Toña and felt a chill running down her back. He looked at his mother and asked her, already knowing the answer:

– You said that Mr. Abílio went to the capital in search of a wife. Where does he live?

Trying not to look nervous, Flora responded:

– In Cabo Frio.

– Where does he live?

– Cabo Frio is a small town on the coast of Rio de Janeiro.

Memories that the wind brings

– I know where it is.

– They say it is a beautiful place, with many beaches...

– Please, Mom, you don't have to try to impress me, I'm not a child. If I accept, I must go with him, right?

– That is the condition. You have to go with it.

– Why doesn't he hire a housekeeper?

– Because he wants a wife, with all the duties that a wife should respect.

An indescribable fear took hold of Clarissa. Her desire was to escape from there and hide anywhere no one could find her, at least until Abílio left. However, Toña's words the other night came vaguely to her mind, and a certainty sprang up in her heart.

It was necessary to accept that marriage because it was her destiny.

For a few moments, Clarissa still hesitated, fearing for her future, but the certainty within her was too strong to be ignored, and she looked at her mother dryly, responding resolutely:

– Okay, Mom. If it's to save the family, tell Dad I accept.

The news provoked astonishment and indignation in almost the whole family. Except for Valentina, who even rejoiced at her sister's departure, everyone mourned the fate of poor Clarissa. Luciano, as soon as he heard, burst into his father's office, shouting in anger:

– Dad, you can't do that!

Fortunato looked at his son with air between penalized and angry, and answered:

– I'm sorry, but there's no other solution.

– This is cruelty...

– No, Luciano, it's desperation. I can't lose everything.

– But we can work. I'm young, so is Roberto.

– You don't understand. Without Mr. Abílio's money, we can't even try. The era of slavery is gone. Now we have employees, settlers to whom we owe wages. How do we pay all these people?

– We will find a way. We can talk to them, ask for their cooperation. They will understand.

After all, you've always been fair to them. You never delayed their wages and, unlike other farmers in the region, you never looted them or forced them to buy from your warehouses. We don't even have warehouses.

– It's no use. And then, everything is fixed. Mr. Abílio and I are already providing everything for the wedding.

– I can't believe you're doing this. You're going to send your daughter into exile, married to a stranger, to live in a strange land, among strange people? Think about it, Dad. Clarissa is a child. How is she going to react? Fortunato let out a long sigh, hid his face in his hands and remained for a few moments without saying anything. He didn't even like that idea. But it was the only way. Either that, or ruin.

And then, Mr. Abílio was a rich and decent man. Commander Travassos himself had said so. He was upright, honest, correct. And he promised he would take good care of his girl.

Fortunato looked at Luciano and finished:

– I may seem insensitive at this moment, Luciano, but believe me, I am very worried about Clarissa's fate. However, Mr. Abílio is of the highest distinction and will do everything possible to make your sister happy. He promised me.

– How do you expect her to be happy away from her family?

– She will have a new family.

– A family you don't even know? Well, Dad, frankly, I really think that Clarissa will end up becoming some kind of fancy maid for this Abílio.

– You are wrong. He promised me... And now, please. Don't bother me anymore with this subject. This situation is also very painful for me.

The matter was closed and there was nothing more anyone could do. In her room, Clarissa was venting her anger on Jerusa, already resigned to the fate that had been reserved for her.

– I don't even know what to say, said Jerusa, deeply saddened. If I could, I would do anything to help you.

– I know you would. Don't be sad. I am not.

– How can you not be? This is really an eyesore. If I were in your shoes, I would run away.

– You think it didn't cross my mind? But what good would it do to run away? Run away to where? Live on what? If this is my destiny, I have to conform.

– But it is cruel, bad...

There was a knock at the door and Clarissa spoke mechanically:

– Come in.

It was the mother who came to call her for a meeting. Certain details had to be worked out, and Fortunato requested her presence in the cabinet. Clarissa looked at Jerusa with a certain melancholy, got up and left with her mother. In the office, Father and Mr. Abílio were waiting for them. When they entered, Abílio stood up and bowed, greeting them with formality. Fortunato, uncomfortable in that role of Cupid from hell, told his daughter:

– Clarissa, I sent for you because we need to resolve certain issues...

– What issues?

– Actually, I'm not exactly the one who wants to talk to you. And Mr. Abílio... He asked me to talk only to you, and I thought it was fair.

Clarissa looked at the man and felt a great disgust. It's not that he was really ugly or disgusting. It wasn't that. If it weren't for the situation in which she met him, she would have found him attractive. He had a certain distinction in his eyes, an elegant demeanor, vestiges of a classic beauty marked by the wrinkles that the years tried to impress him with.

He must have been in his early forties, which was a contrast, compared to nineteen- year- old Clarissa. After the parents left, she remained silent, waiting for him to say something. Abílio, however, clearly embarrassed, could not find the right words, until, joining forces, he whispered:

– Miss Clarissa, I would like you to try not to hate me.

That request was a source of amazement, and Clarissa looked at it. Abílio was nervous, rubbing his hands together with exaggerated tension, walking around the room.

I'm not sure what answer to give, Clarissa simply said:

– I don't hate you.

– No?!

– No.

– Will you be able to understand me?

She hesitated for a few moments, until she answered, as sincerely as possible:

– Understand, I don't understand. But I don't hate you.

– Very well. I will not ask you to like me. I am a stranger, much older than you, and I do not intend that one day you will really become attached to me.

I would simply like you to respect me, as I will respect you.

– Or...

– There is no or. Soon you will be my wife and you will only have to obey. Treat me well and I will treat you well. Mistreat me and I will treat you the same.

– Mr. Abílio, are you threatening me?

He blushed and, with his cheeks burning with shame, answered:

– No, not at all. I am a gentleman and I would never threaten a lady.

– Then I don't understand what you mean.

– What I mean is, if you are nice to me, I will be nice to you and we can achieve a harmonious relationship in our home. Otherwise, we will live like two strangers.

But I will never mistreat you. I am an honorable man, not a scoundrel.

– If you are as honorable as you say, why did you propose this immoral business to my father?

– Because I need a wife and he needs money, he answered promptly.

– And do you think that's right? Do you think this is moral?

– I'm not here to talk about rights or morals. It's a game of interests.

– I understand. And you and my father decided to play with my life as if it were a toy.

– I'm sorry you feel that way, but the agreement was completed with your acquiescence, wasn't it?

She hesitated, but ended up confessing.

– It was. But don't think I'm happy about it. If I accepted, it was only to save my father from ruin.

– Because if I set out to save your father from ruin, it was only because he promised me a wife.

– Why do you need a wife?

— To take care of my house.

— I understand... And to take care of your children, right?

— Also. To take care of everything, like a good wife should take care — . He raised his hand in an irritated gesture and concluded:

— And now, if you'll excuse me, I have to go. I don't think I have anything else to say. — He turned on his heels, opened the door and left, leaving Clarissa in deep discouragement.

That Abílio must be crazy, and she was the main victim of his madness.

About two months later, Clarissa left with him for a new life. In her heart, an indescribable fear of the unknown, a feeling of abandonment, a sense of regret like never before experienced.

For those who remained, it was not nostalgia that tortured them. It was the pain of loss, of betrayal, of humiliation. Clarissa had left as a slave, sold to her new master, who had paid a good price for her. Seeing her leave, Fortunato had a strange feeling. It was as if she was doing to her daughter exactly what she had done many times before with the blacks. He bought and sold them to whoever offered the best price, without even worrying about the friends and families they left behind.

Luciano, horrified by the fatality, was full of hate against his own father. He wanted to go with her sister, but she wouldn't let him. It was her destiny, and she didn't need anyone to share it with her.

Inconsolable, Luciano did not want to stay to say goodbye and early in the morning he went to the Oro Viejo hacienda, there alone, in the company of grandfather Dário and grandmother Sara, Laís, her husband and daughter had left very early to say goodbye to Clarissa. They were very sad, especially Jerusa, the friend of the heart. Jerusa had promised to visit her as soon as she could and asked her not to stop writing.

After the carriage disappeared at the bend in the road, Fortunato arrived home devastated. In silence, he went through all the rooms, always followed by Flora. He stopped at the door of the daughter's room, opened it and looked. It was empty, that room, which for almost twenty years had come to life with Clarissa's joyful laughter, now seemed dead, lifeless, like a mausoleum. She closed the door and entered the living room, with Flora always behind her without saying anything. The harpsichord he had given his daughter lay inertly beneath the window, accusing him of treason.

Fortunato approached the instrument, sat down on the stool and tested the keys. The uneven sound filled the room, and it seemed to him that his daughter, at any moment, would seem to recriminate and correct him. Suddenly, unable to bear the pain and guilt any longer, he collapsed on the keyboard in a convulsive and sincere cry, and Flora ran to him, hugging him from behind. He, sobbing, still found the strength to let off steam:

– My daughter! Oh! My God, forgive me! I sold my daughter, my own blood! My only treasure! I traded my daughter for a cheap ambition!

And he was distressed, he did not even listen to the woman's plea, who begged him not to torture himself so much. But Fortunato could not forgive himself and wondered if it would have been worthwhile to exchange his daughter for money he no longer considered so important.

CHAPTER 3

In Rio de Janeiro, Abílio and Clarissa stayed in a hotel so the next day they could take the boat to Cabo Frio. The city was difficult to access, there were no roads and the best way to get there was by sea. At the reception, he asked for a room and, after accommodating Clarissa, he went out for a drink. The girl was left alone with her thoughts. Everything was very new and she was scared.

She did not know what would happen to her from now on and was afraid of herself. She had never traveled by sea before and suddenly she was afraid.

Night came and Abílio did not come. Clarissa had spent the whole day practically alone.

She went down to lunch and tea, without her husband appearing. She was now his wife and knew her duties. If he loved her, she would submit to him with resignation and obedience.

Abilio, however, had only sought her out on his wedding night. He had been cold and indifferent, but had not treated her harshly or brutally. On the contrary, he had tried to do everything calmly and serenely, trying not to hurt her in the least. And then, when it was all over, he just asked:

– Do you feel good? – turning to the side and then sleeping.

It was late at night when Abílio returned and she pretended to sleep. Although she didn't know where he had been, she could sense from the smell that he had been drinking, he didn't look drunk.

He entered quietly, undressedand lay down on the bed next to her. Clarissa felt like running away, but she stopped and remained silent, afraid that he would touch her. In a few minutes, however, Abílio fell asleep, snoring loudly and preventing Clarissa from falling asleep as well. It wasn't exactly the sound of snoring that prevented her from sleeping. It was the sadness that was beginning to take hold of his spirit.

At seven o'clock the next morning, they arrived at the port's dock. It was a dirty and crowded place, where the most diverse goods and the strangest passengers passed by.

On their ship, there was more cargo. Bags of food, furniture, cattle and even some black people, hired to work in the salt mines and fishing. There were very few travelers.

Clarissa remembered what her father had said: Abílio was a rich goldsmith, owner of several jewelry stores in Rio de Janeiro, but when his wife became ill, he retired from society and took refuge in Cabo Frio, leaving the business to a representative. They had two children: Vicente, the oldest, was now seventeen, and the youngest, Angelina, had just completed twelve years.

Abílio's wife's illness was not known. It was said that she suffered from chronic rheumatism and that the doctor had prescribed frequent sunbathing by the sea.

However, Fortunato learned from the Commander that there were suspicions that the woman had contracted leprosy, that she had been taken to Cabo Frio because of an alleged leper camp that was said to be there. All this, however, was conjecture. No one could prove anything. Abílio was a discreet man and the family lived in isolation. Even the children spoke little. They attended school, but did not have many friends.

All that was known was that, one day, Leonor, that was the name of Abílio's wife, took an extreme step. She could no longer bear the pain and isolation, went into the sea one morning and disappeared among the waves, leaving her husband a desperate note. In it, she said she could no longer live that way, hindering the lives of her husband and children, and that death would be the best cure for her illness. Therefore, if God did not decide to call her, she herself would go to meet him or the devil and make the sea her eternal tomb.

She asked everyone not to cry for her or mourn her departure. What she did, she did it with conscience and determination, and she suffered more from seeing her own suffering than from the threat of death.

Her body was never found, despite the efforts of Abílio and some fishermen. He was on the verge of despair, but the men tried to calm him down by telling him that the strong ocean currents always ended up returning to the same place, and the drowned bodies were often returned to the beach. Leonor's body, however, did not reappear, which made Abílio even more upset. Was she still alive? But it was impossible that, at that moment, she was still alive. Most likely she had been eaten by the fish. There were many rays and sharks in some areas, and they probably ended up eating your body.

Abílio was not satisfied and stayed on the beach, waiting for her to appear. Until one afternoon, about three days after she disappeared, a fisherman discovered her dress on the beach, all torn and tattered. Called out in a hurry, Abílio confirmed his painful suspicions: the woman had actually committed suicide, because that was the dress she was wearing the morning she left her house, saying she was just going to walk on the sea. Abílio's sadness and disappointment were indescribable. At least I wanted to give him a decent burial, with a grave where he could cry and take flowers.

Clarissa's eyes filled with tears as she remembered that story. It was really sad, and Abílio must have suffered a lot. She felt sorry for him, but she also felt some pity for herself, because she went to share a life with him that she didn't feel belonged to her. And what would the children say? Certainly, they knew about her departure. But would they approve?

From the railing of the boat, Clarissa remained watching the movement, and the boat was gradually loading. Abílio preferred to stay in his cabin. He had no one to say goodbye to, and he did not like noise or crowds. As he looked at the dock, he saw a black woman, with a small daughter in her lap, crying and waving a handkerchief at someone. Following the direction of the woman's gaze, Clarissa saw that she was saying goodbye to a man, still young, who waved in response. At the same time, her heart sank. The man left, leaving his wife and daughter, perhaps to try his luck in a distant and unknown land.

At one point, a cabin boy approached and reluctantly said something to the black man, who walked away, following the other into the basement. It was there that he would travel, together with the cargo. Although the blacks were no longer slaves, they had no money to pay for a decent trip and bought tickets in the basement because they were cheaper and sometimes even free, as long as they paid with small services rendered on the ship.

Suddenly, after almost four hours of waiting, the sailors began to move, loosening their moorings, hoisting sails, lifting the anchor, and the ship whistled and left for the horizon; Clarissa grimaced. Why did that seem so familiar and saddened her so much? Remembering Toña, she asked the former slave not to abandon her and to give her courage and bravery.

During the whole trip, Abílio barely spoke to her. He treated her with courtesy and deference, he was gentle, gentlemanly, but as cold as a glacier, and the words he exchanged with her were mechanical and impersonal. Nothing to show that he cared or was concerned about her. Abílio did not seem to want to know about her feelings or her fears.

At one point, the color of the sea became greenish, changing from dark blue to light green, and high, steep, rocky cliffs appeared, lined with trees to the top.

At the top, a thick fog covered the mountain, making it difficult to see from the top.

Memories that the wind brings

Down the slope, a white sand beach, where gigantic and terrifying waves broke. Clarissa found this beautiful stone giant and asked to a sailor who was passing by:

– What is that?

– That? Oh! It's the island of Cabo Frio, ma'am.

– It's a beauty!

– Yes, very beautiful.

– Is that where we're going?

– No. That's the island, which has the same name as the Cape, but it's not the Cape. We're going to the mainland, a little further.

There are strange phenomena in those parts that shake and agitate the sea, bringing many boats to the coast in a few minutes. One of these phenomena is the resurgence, a cold current that, when it emerges, causes a sudden drop in temperature and the sea breeze freezes to the bone. Another phenomenon, much more frequent and dangerous, is the strong winds that plague the region, like the northeast wind.

The winds near the island of Cabo Frio tend to be extremely cold and strong, and the northeast, in particular, makes it difficult for ships to arrive from Rio de Janeiro, because it blows in the opposite direction, pushing them back and thus prolonging the travel time.

Together with the northeast, the flows, also in opposition to the course taken by the ships, contribute to their being forced backward, and the ships cannot cross the promontory and enter the bay of Cabo Frio. For experienced sailors, the northeast can be easily detected, and there are some alternatives that, if taken in time, can prevent the ship from sinking.

Clarissa knew nothing about that. She didn't know anything about navigation and was even enjoying that trip. The port of Rio de Janeiro was not far from Cabo Frio, and the trip was not too strenuous or unpleasant. I was admiring the beauty of the region

Memories that the wind brings

when, suddenly, the air started to get cold and there was a tremor in the boat. It shook and shrank, feeling that the gentle breeze blowing on the sails suddenly seemed to have changed direction, blowing in the opposite direction and making it difficult for the boat to enter the bay. At one point, a strange commotion erupted on the deck. Sailors were rushing back and forth, going down to the captain's cabin. Soon the captain appeared and tested the air. From where Clarissa was, I could hear their conversation, and the boatswain said:

– Sir, it's the northeast...

– Hum... – said the captain. I don't think so. This looks more like a resurgence.

– No, Captain, we are in the northeast, I'm sure. We need to go back.

– Did you go crazy? We're almost there.

– Captain, added another – who seemed to be his companion – this is your first trip in these parts, but we know this sea like no one else. And I can assure you that it is the northeast that is beginning to explode.

– And? replied the captain, grumpy. It's weak. We will have time to go up and dock.

– I must insist, Captain. We have to go back.

– We cannot. The land is near.

– We cannot enter the sea. And even if we did, we couldn't windward[1] to mount the tripping line[2].

- (1) N.A.: Windward, advance the ship in the direction from which the wind is blowing.
- (2) N.A.: Tripping line, a cable attached to the stone and pulled manually, to help ship enter the channel.

The captain looked at the still dubious boatswain and considered:

– What do you suggest I do? Going back is impossible.

– We can try to take refuge in Massambaba.

– No way! Massambaba is a dangerous and treacherous sandbank, with high waves and numerous sandbanks. Do you want us to run aground and get knocked over by the waves?

– Then, sir, I see no other way out but to go back. Otherwise, the one that will knock us down will be the northeast.

– You are exaggerating. I know that the northeast wind is strong and capable of turning boats.

However, I believe that we will succeed.

– Sorry, Captain, the boatswain insisted, but if you take this boat forward, you will be solely responsible for your accident.

– Enough, man! Be brave and obey my orders, or we'll have a mutiny here. Come on!

Under the captain's orders, the crew had no choice but to obey. They did not want to be accused of rioting, they were not prepared to face any court- martial.

Clarissa was alarmed. Were they really shipwrecked? Terrified, she ran to her cabin and found Abílio sitting at the table, reading quietly. The ship was already beginning to rock, but, until then, he had not worried. He thought that the captain was experienced and that there would be no risk in the voyage.

When he saw Clarissa standing at the door, white as wax, Abílio asked with concern:

– Did something happen?

– Mr. Abílio, tell me, what is the northeast wind? – Abílio put the book in his lap and looked at her seriously:

– Where did you hear that from?

– I heard the captain, just now, talking to his men, and they say that the northeast is on its way and...

Abílio didn't give her time to finish. He also knew those seas and he knew that, with the northeast, they wouldn't have any chance to windward and enter the bay. Long before that, the wind

Memories that the wind brings

would throw them against the rocks of the island of Cabo Frio and cause them to be shipwrecked. It would be madness.

By the time Abílio reached the deck, where the captain was standing at the helm, it was too late. The ship, at great cost, reached the tip of the promontory, and the sea began to shake, with giant waves rising over the ship. It was a general uproar. Sailors ran from the stern to the bow, trying to hold ropes and sails, while the boat was launched from side to side, as if it were out of control. The wind was blowing mercilessly, and the boat was flapping like a sheet of paper. At that moment, they heard the voice of the captain, who cried out in desperation:

– We are going back! We are going back!

There was no time. The northeast had hit them hard, rocking the ship as if it were made of cardboard. Suddenly, a mast broke free and fell into the water, taking away some men who were screaming in terror. Other sailors tried to throw them a rope, but it was useless. The waves had swallowed them up, taking them to the bottom of the sea.

Clarissa, terrified, went up on deck and stopped in horror. It looked more like a hurricane. The ship suddenly began to roll. The force of the wind and the waves had pushed it aside, and the water began to cascade down. The lifeboats were thrown overboard, and the men began to jump into the water. Clarissa was terrified. She couldn't even swim. Suddenly, someone pushed her, and she too fell into the water, feeling an immense liquid mass covering her head.

Desperately, she tried to fight her way back to the surface, but in vain. She was about to faint when she felt hands grabbing her and pulling her up, and she was thrown into a small boat by the powerful hands of Abílio. Inside, some men used their strength to row, propelling the boat to the beach, in a desperate struggle to cross the channel that separated the island from the continent.

Memories that the wind brings

The lifeboat was small and could not withstand the rain. Driven by the wind, already in the middle of the channel, it entered something that seemed to be a whirlpool and almost turned as well.

Abílio, at the height of his anguish, grabbed Clarissa by the waist and pushed her again, jumping at the exact moment when the small boat succumbed. He began to swim desperately, fighting with all his strength to keep Clarissa's head out of the water, when something like a mast came to his encounter and hit him on the forehead. Despite the pain and the blood that was beginning to flow, Abílio managed to catch it and, throwing Clarissa's torso over it, he pulled the mast against her, trapping her between him and his own body.

Almost breathless, clinging to the mast and Clarissa, Abílio began to swim, thinking of nothing, looking neither forward nor back. He just kicked his legs, trying to push forward that stick, providentially thrown in his path, always with Clarissa caught in his embrace. Realizing his effort, Clarissa clung even more to the mast and began kicking her legs. She swallowed water and coughed, sometimes even slipped, but Abílio did not let go. He seemed to be possessed by a strange force that made him believe in life and was not willing to give up so easily. Fighting against the waves and the flow, which insisted on taking them back, Abílio swam like a madman, holding Clarissa's almost weak body between the mast and her body.

At the height of the exhaustion, Abílio felt that the sea was beating less strongly and that the currents were decreasing in intensity. Suddenly, his feet touched something soft, and he realized that he was already beginning to touch the sand at the bottom. In the waves, he could sometimes step on the ground, and escaping became less difficult. Soon after that, he could stand up. He had reached the beach.

Almost fainting, Abílio dropped the stick that had served as his salvation, lifted Clarissa's almost lifeless body and with it came out of the water. Coughing and vomiting water, unable to endure the fatigue and shortness of breath, Abílio knelt on the cold, wet sand, still holding the woman in his lap, falling.

Then, on the ground, his face sank into Clarissa's lap, crying and feeling the cold of the wind manifesting all life force on her.

– No, please don't! – cried the man, in desperation. – Please have mercy! That voice, spoken in a strange language, echoed in Clarissa's head like a curse. In front of an old man, a man begged for forgiveness and, beyond that, anchored the ship that would take him into exile. He was a tall, sturdy black man, who had in his eyes the terror that the sight of that ship caused him. Clarissa participated in the scene as a spectator, but she could feel the pleasure of the old man, the pride of power, which allowed her to decide on the destiny of the people.

She remained there, impassive, seeing the desperation of the man in the face of the inevitable. Suddenly, a white man came and tied shackles to his feet and hands, pulling him violently. The black man shouted desperately, while the white man, without paying attention, dragged him through the center of the village, toward the place where other blacks were, all in chains. The old man turned his back on him and entered a kind of hut.

Clarissa woke up scared and sweating. It had been a dream but it looked so real! However, it was not real. She had slept and had a nightmare. But where would it be? When she opened her eyes, she tried to see in the twilight around her and could see that she was in some kind of mud hut. She was lying on a mat and on the other side of the room, there was something similar to a chest. Where was it? What could have happened?

The cold, damp air came in through the open window, and she shuddered. Suddenly, she remembered everything. The cold, the wind, the boat, the waves, the shipwreck. She had lived a

Memories that the wind brings

nightmare, but now she was awake. Was she dead? Was this place part of hell? Joining forces, she called, almost in a whisper:

– Mr. Abílio! Mr. Abílio!

Immediately, Abílio appeared, and she sighed with relief. In spite of everything, she felt great satisfaction in seeing him alive and well. Abílio stopped in front of her, put on his hands at the waist and he asked:

– Do you feel good?

She shook her head, feeling a little dizzy, and responded:

– Yes... I think so... What happened?

– Don't you remember?

– We sank, didn't we?

– Yes, we did.

– And the others? Are they dead?

– Almost all of them. And we almost died too.

She looked at him, trying to remember how it all happened. She knew the ship had sunk, but she had trouble remembering how it happened. Fixing her eyes on Abílio, she began to remember. He had thrown her overboard and then pulled her out of the water, swimming and fighting the waves and the current. Clarissa remembered that on several occasions she had almost sunk and taken him with her, but Abílio had not let go. Not one minute had she felt that he would let her go. On the contrary, she knew that if she succumbed, he would succumb with her. He had saved her from the waves, he had fought against everything, he had done everything possible to keep her alive. She lowered her eyes and began to cry softly, saying in a low voice, full of emotion:

– Thank you.

– There's nothing to be grateful for – he replied sharply.

– I've already lost one wife in those waters. I didn't intend to lose the second one.

She swallowed her saliva and was about to defend herself. Despite having saved her life, Abílio was sharp and rude. When she opened her mouth to speak, he cut her off and ordered her:

– If you feel well enough to travel, get ready. We need to leave.

– Where are we going?

– Home.

– Aren't we home?

– No. This is the cabin of a fisherman who, seeing our situation as a castaway, received us kindly.

– Didn't we get to Cabo Frio? – she said, perplexed and horrified – Do we have to take another boat? For God's sake, I couldn't stand it...

– You don't need to worry. We are already in Cabo Frio, yes, but in a town far from our home. Although the boat sank near the entrance to the bay, we couldn't get in. Now come on, let's go the rest of the way by car. – Clarissa sighed again with relief. Never again, while she was alive, did she intend to get back on a boat. It had been her first and last experience at sea.

She got up and felt slight dizziness, supported by Abílio, who insisted:

– Are you feeling well? Are you sure?

– I am very grateful. A little dizzy, but fine.

– Will you be able to go on?

– It is necessary, isn't it? If this is not our home, we must leave immediately. The sooner we get there, the better.

– Very well. Then let's go.

– Wait. What about my belongings?

– You don't have any more belongings. Everything is under the sea.

– Did I lose everything? Clothes, jewelry, everything?

– Yes, Clarissa, it's all gone.

– And now?

– Don't worry. We will ask for everything you want from the capital. Now come on, hurry up. I want to enjoy the daylight.

It was only then that Clarissa realized that she was dressed only in a rough but very clean nightgown, and she blushed. Abílio, realizing his shame, turned his back on her and left, and a woman entered, smiling at him. Clarissa smiled in response, and the other one asked her:

– How are you, miss?

– Well, thank you...

Near the mattress on which she had been lying, there was a small dresser, and on top of this, a piece of mirror, probably the remains of some piece taken from the sea.

Clarissa raised the mirror and looked at herself. It was horrible.

– I brought your clothes – said the woman, stretching out her skirt and blouse, washed and ironed.

Although clean, the clothes were torn and frayed, but they would have to be. Clarissa thanked her with a look and began to dress. Then the lady of the house handed her a brush and some hairpins, and she pulled her hair up to style it in the best possible way.

Afterwards, Clarissa accompanied her in search of Abílio, who was in a room that could be called the living room, talking to an old man.

– Well – he said, as soon as Clarissa entered, now we have to go. I thank you for your generosity and welcome. If necessary, just call me and I will do everything in my power to help you.

They said goodbye and left. Outside, a cart pulled by a pair of oxen were waiting for them. Abílio helped Clarissa up and went up after her, sitting next to her. He held the reins, greeted the couple

Memories that the wind brings

and started the oxen. As they followed him, Clarissa admired the landscape. Seeing huge white mountains, she asked curiously:

– What is that?

– That one? – Abílio answered, pointing to the place she had indicated. It's dunes. Mountains of fine white sand.

She didn't say anything. On another occasion, she would have even stopped to admire the landscape. The land was of an incomparable and indescribable beauty, but her state of mind did not allow her to enjoy all that majesty. She was still very downcast and upset. He had been taken from her land by a strange man, carried to a strange land and, moreover, had almost died, a victim of a shipwreck. A shipwreck... When, in her life, would she had imagined herself in a similar situation?

Grandmother Toña remembered it. The slave had told her about her adventure aboard a slave ship, almost a hundred years before, and Clarissa had found that story very sad. And now it was she who was going through a similar situation. She had practically given herself to a stranger and had traveled by ship, suffering horrors on the way. They were different horrors than Toña's, it was true, but they were still horrors. Toña had almost died in the basement of a *tumbeiro1* and was almost killed, thrown into the treacherous sea by a sinking ship.

(3) N.T. *Tumbeiro*, minor draught slave boat

Clarissa remembered the dream she had that morning. How strange! She had never seen those men before, but she was sure she knew them, and the situation was extremely familiar. However, she knew it couldn't have happened. The only blacks she had ever met were the slaves on the hacienda, and she had never gone near the sea or ship with any of them before. So, what was that? Nothing, she thought only a dream. A dream, nothing more than a dream.

By her side, Abílio was silent, guiding the animals along the sandy path. It was a beautiful day, but the heat was cooled by the gentle breeze blowing on their faces. Nor did it seem those hours before they had faced a storm at sea.

– Does the weather here change so quickly? – She asked casually.

– Yes. We hardly have any rain, because the winds take away the clouds.

She fell silent and turned her attention to the road, and Clarissa was already upset with her near- mutism:

– You really don't like to talk, do you, Mr. Abílio? – He looked at her sideways and agreed:

– No, when I have nothing to say.

She shut up. She was not prepared to listen to the man's rudeness. She turned her face away and pretended to enjoy the view. But the rocking of the car, along with the enormous tiredness she still felt, put her to sleep. Her head ended up falling on Abílio's shoulder, and she fell asleep almost instantly.

He tensed all her muscles and even shook her, but she was so tired that she did not wake up.

Abílio decided not to bother and continued the rest of the way with Clarissa asleep on his shoulder. Every once in a while, the car shook, Clarissa's head fell from side to side, and Abílio supported her. He didn't want her to fall. Some time later, a buzzing sound was heard and she woke up. She rubbed her eyes and, realizing that she had fallen asleep on Abílio's shoulder, blushed. She straightened up on the bench, smoothed out her wrinkled and torn clothes, and asked:

– Where are we?

– In the city. In the Calle de la Playa, the main street.

It was a fairly wide, gravelly street where most of the local commerce seemed concentrated. Flanking it, something that looked like a river, with green and crystalline waters that shone in the sun.

– What is that place? – she asked, curious.

Memories that the wind brings

– It's the Itajuru channel. This is where the port is.

– Where is it?

– Here – she finished, pointing to the boats stopped in the middle of the channel.

In fact, there was no port at all. What Abílio called a port was nothing more than the canal itself, where ships entered and anchored. She stopped the cart in front of a kind of shop, jumped in and, without saying anything, went back in, returning shortly afterwards with a large bag on her back, full of fabric so that she could sew some clothes.

Then they continued and she asked:

– Isn't it here yet?

– No.

– May I know where we are going?

– You will see.

She shut up again. There was no point in trying to talk to that man. He simply answered her questions, but didn't make any comments, didn't ask her questions, and didn't explain anything.

Soon after, the ox cart began to enter a more deserted area. The houses were left behind and the sandy soil began to become more pronounced. Soon they entered a beach, with no streets or roads, only a small path, through which the ox cart advanced. It was already getting dark, and the wind was now blowing more strongly, picking up the sand and entangling Clarissa's hair. She tried to catch them, but the force of the wind made them loose and flutter, free and unmanageable.

She was afraid. The wind was cold and fast, and howled as if he were being whipped. She looked at Abílio, and he, seeing the fear in her eyes, said calmly:

– Don't be afraid. The wind is only dangerous at sea.

He continued to touch the animals, until they reached a kind of place, covered with thin, low vegetation, where you could see the sand, leaving between grasses. Further on, some bushes and trees were growing in closed forests. It was almost dark, but you could still see the silhouette of a large house built in the bushes, with several windows on both floors. Everything was made of stone and lime, the windows and door were painted blue, flanked by bushes and almond trees. Some trees cast the whitish shade of the moon over it, blinking in a ghostly dance. All around, the forest.

There were no walls or fences to isolate it, only the undergrowth, and the main gate was reached by a white sand road, lined by kerosene lamps, at that time, still outside. In the distance, the sound of the waves gave the scene a certain aura of melancholy and sadness. She breathed deeply and the pleasant smell of the sea air hit her hard, making her feel some pleasure.

The house, however, did not please her. It felt like something out of a horror story, and she was afraid again. When Abílio stopped the car, right in front of the house, the front door opened and a black man, about sixty years old, appeared and waved:

– Mr. Abílio! Is it really you?

– Yes, Tiago, it's me. I'm home. Finally, at home.

CHAPTER 4

Once established, Clarissa fell into a deep sleep. She was exhausted and slept a dreamless night, only to wake up the next morning. When she woke up, it was still very early and there was no noise in the house. The room that had been reserved overlooked the sea, and she went to the window to look. She was delighted! The house was high up on a kind of dune, and the beach was reached by a narrow path, open between the grasses.

The sea had a fantastic color, ranging from deep blue to emerald green, ending in small waves of white foam that extended to the beach of fine white sand. In the distance and left, a small fortress, built on a hill of stones, which Clarissa later discovered was the fortress of San Mateo, built to defend the city from enemy attacks, which invaded the land in search of the forest of Brazil. Further on, on the right, a large extension of white sand, which ends in another hill, miles away, called Pontal. Further on, the island of Cabo Frio, which seemed an extension of the land, where the ship had been shipwrecked. The view was beautiful and Clarissa was delighted.

Despite all that had happened, she could not deny that the place was a paradise and she thanked God for being able to count, at least, on the comfort of nature.

She was so ecstatic when she heard a knock on the door, and Abílio walked in, wearing skirts and blouses, that they were already out of fashion.

– Good morning – she said, trying to look more pleasant. – Did you sleep well?

– Very well, thanks.

– Excellent. I brought you these clothes, so you can wear them while yours aren't ready.

Can you sew? – She shook her head negatively, and he considered: Well, then we'll have to ask Mrs. Maria to make more clothes.

– Who is Maria?

– She is a seamstress. She lives there by the Pass, but she won't bother coming here, in exchange for some good pennies.

He laid out her clothes, which she took and asked him:

– Whose clothes are these?

– They belonged to my first wife.

Clarissa felt a chill but picked them up without saying anything.

– Well – Abílio concluded – I'll let you get ready. Don't delay, we'll wait for you to have a coffee.

About half an hour later, Clarissa came down the stairs, Abílio was sitting in the living room, in the company of his children, and he got up when she came in, taking her to sit at the table.

Discreetly, Clarissa looked at the rough and dirty cloth that covered the table, and was surprised by the tin cups that served as mugs.

Abílio made her sit down and said:

– I don't know if you like it. After my wife's death, my daughter took over some tasks, and you know how it is...

– Don't worry about it.

After sitting down, Abílio made the necessary introductions:

– My children, I want you to meet your new stepmother, Mrs. Clarissa. Clarissa, these are my children, Vicente and Angelina.

– How are you? – replied Clarissa, uncomfortable under the eyes of the stepchildren.

– Come on, – encouraged Abílio, – say hello to your stepmother.

– We're fine, stepmother – responded Vicente with irony.

She looked at him with disgust and objected, trying to imprint a tone of warmth in his voice:

– I wish you wouldn't call me that.

– Do you want us to call you Mom? – he continued, visibly trying to irritate her.

– Vicente! – scolded the father. Have more respect.

He looked at his father angrily and lowered his head, mumbling:

– I don't know why we need her here.

Abílio hit the table and everyone was shocked. Clarissa felt like running away from there. It was obvious who was not welcome and who did not have the courage to try to impose himself on those children. Deep down, she could understand Vincent's reaction. She was a stranger, who had married her father in his absence and had left to replace her mother. He had every reason not to do as she did. Suddenly, Abílio's voice was heard:

– I will not tolerate disrespect in my home. Vicente, go to your room!

The boy got up and left, not before casting a hateful glance at Clarissa, who looked at him sympathetically. After he left, she confronted Abílio and spoke in a tone of censure:

– You didn't have to do that.

– Clarissa, you must never interfere with the education I give my children. – She suddenly stood up, outraged. That was too much. Until then, she had been supporting everything in silence, as a duty of conscience, but now he was already pushing the limits, he would not admit that he would disapprove of her in that way, especially in front of his daughter, still a child. Shooting, Clarissa looked at him and shot:

Memories that the wind brings

– Listen, Mr. Abílio, until now I have been tolerating your bad mood in consideration of my father. But don't think that you will treat me like a slave or an object, because I am not. If you want my respect, and more, if you want your children to respect me, start by respecting me.

Examples are still the best way to teach! – she said.

Abílio looked at her puzzled. She had a foul-tempered sort, and he would have to work to tame her. Looking at her a little more pleasantly, he said:

– Calm down and sit down. I didn't mean to offend you.

– But I was offended. I'm not used to being treated that way.

– I beg your forgiveness. It's just that you are not used to Vincent and you don't know how he is.

– Likewise. That's no reason to talk to me like that.

– Again, I ask you to forgive me. And now, please sit down and finish your coffee

– . Somewhat uncomfortable, she sat down again and could see the discreet look of admiration that Angelina gave her. Clarissa had never eaten such a simple and insipid breakfast before, but she did not complain. The meal continued in silence, and when everyone finished, Abílio called Tiago and ordered:

– Go call Vicente. I don't want him to be late for school. – The servant left and soon after, Vicente appeared, holding the folder with the school books in his hand.

He passed by the room, mumbled a goodbye, and left with Angelina. When they left, Clarissa asked:

– Don't you think it's cruel to send him to school without eating breakfast?

He looked at her in dismay and felt like scolding her again. However, recalling the previous scene, he responded briefly.

– No, I don't think so.

He got up and prepared to leave, but Clarissa stopped him with her hand, speaking meaningfully:

– Listen to Abílio, I didn't want to be rude either. But I would like you to remember that I am here against my will, and that it is not easy to be treated harshly when all you want to do is help.

He sighed, looked at her a little kindlier and responded:

– I understand. However, you are my wife, and it is a wife's duty to obey her husband. – Clarissa bit her lip and responded:

– I did not ask to be your wife, Mr. Abílio, and I must also remind you that I almost stopped being one. If it hadn't been for your... generous offer, I would still be in my home and would never have experienced the terror of that disaster.

She was trying to make him feel guilty, and he knew it. Trying not to be tough again, Abílio argued:

– However, Clarissa, despite your discomfort, you married me. So I hope you will obey me and no longer question my orders.

He turned his back on her and walked out the door. She didn't know where she was going, but she didn't care. She even thought it was good that he had left. Only then would she not have to endure. After he left, she stayed there, not knowing what to do. She looked at the coffee table, still set, and wondered who would pick it up and wash the dishes. Abílio had told her that Angelina was in charge of some tasks. Didn't they have servants? Clarissa shrugged her shoulders and returned to the room. This was not his problem.

Having nothing to do, she started packing the clothes he had given her and looked around. Now, in the light, she could see.

It was a little dirty and messy, and she wondered what time he would get to the maid.

However, time passed and no one came. Tired of waiting, she put on her shoes and walked down the stairs. After all, she was now the owner of the house, and if Abílio hadn't introduced her to the staff, she would try to do it herself and continue giving orders. When she arrived downstairs, she noticed the dirt in the house. There was dust on the furniture, the sofas and carpets had to be brushed and the curtains had to be washed. The silver was also black, and the few pictures were covered with cobwebs. And the breakfast table? It hadn't even been raised. That house really needed a woman to fix it. Certainly, after the woman had died, the employees were left without direction, and everyone ended up doing what they wanted. It was really necessary to order the place.

Overseeing general cleaning, ordering towels and dishes exchanged, but where were the servants?

In the kitchen, Clarissa was surprised. It was empty. No fire lit, no peculiar food smell, nothing. The wood stove looked dirty and abandoned, and the floor was so dreary from blue to dark gray. Too much. On the other wall, there was a closed door, and Clarissa opened it, facing a courtyard full of trees that swayed in the wind. In the background, a little white house, which she had not seen when she arrived. Curious, she went there, but saw no one. She heard a noise on the other side and surrounded the house, meeting the black Tiago, who was busy cutting wood. She approached and greeted him:

– Good morning, Tiago.

He dropped the axe and looked at her, responding:

– Good morning, siñá.

– Where is everybody?

– All of them?

– Yes, the servants, where are they?

– Servants? There are no servants here, ma'am. Only me.

– Only you?

– Yes. I am the caretaker.

– Inside the house? And who looks after the house?

Memories that the wind brings

Tiago looked at her without understanding, raised his shoulders and, grimacing, scratched his head and answered:

– He scratches his head and answers: "You scratch it, huh?

– Me?! – she said, between astonishment and horror.

– Isn't that why you came here, to take care of the house?

– Is that what your boss told you? That I came to take care of the house?

– Wasn't it?

– No, it wasn't.

Clarissa was indignant and offended, she turned on her heels and entered the house again, going to sit in the living room to wait for Abílio. When he arrived, it was almost noon, and he was surprised to see her sitting on the couch, looking with unfriendly face.

– What happened? What are you doing sitting there?

– Mr. Abílio, why did you bring me here?

– What did you say?

– I asked you why you brought me here.

– Well, but that question is completely out of line. So you're not my wife?

– I'm your wife, not your maid.

– I'm not understanding.

– I met Tiago outside and, from what I could see, you expect me to personally take care of your home.

– Isn't that a woman's job?

– No, Mr. Abílio. I came here to manage your home and I expected to find employees at your service. If not, I won't do the housework. I am not your maid, I am a lady.

– So? What's wrong with that? My first wife took care of everything practically alone and she never complained. And now, my daughter...

Memories that the wind brings

- I am not your first wife and I am not used to domestic service - Clarissa said. - And as for your daughter, she is still a child and should not be busy with these tasks. She should have been playing with dolls.

Abílio fell silent. He was already beginning to regret that business. He had agreed to give Fortunato the money in exchange for his daughter's hand, but he expected her to be more docile. He didn't have the time or patience for female friction and he blurted out:

- Although I am not willing to argue with you, I will give you some explanations that I think are necessary. I married you because I needed a woman, in every way. However, in order not to impose my presence too much on you, I have given you a separate room to use as you please. I don't want to bother you often, only when it is extremely necessary. I will give you everything you need. I called the seamstress to make you new clothes and I am providing someone to go to Rio de Janeiro to bring me some orders of fashionable dresses, shoes, hats, jewelry and everything necessary to satisfy a lady's pampering. But I hope that, in return, you will behave like a real wife, faithfully fulfilling your duties within the home - . Clarissa gave him a whitering stare and was going to retaliate angrily:

- Why don't you hire servants? Many black womenwant to work...

- No. The only servant I have at my service is Tiago. I don't need another one.

- And you expect me, alone, to do all the housework? Are you crazy?

- If you don't, you'll have to get used to living in filth and disorder, and eating fish soaked in flour. We've gotten used to it, but you...

Clarissa grimaced. Flour- soaked fish, only? It was too much. She, used to the delights of the farm, the softness of silks, the fragrance of French perfumes, having to get used to living in a pigsty? Never. It was outrageous. Completely amazed, Clarissa turned her back on her and walked up the stairs, walking at a steady pace, like a queen. She entered her room and collapsed on the bed, crying profusely. Why? Why had this happened to her? Why had the father committed himself to this injustice and cruelty, condemning her to a life and sacrifices without glory?

Why? Try as he might, she could not find the answers and wondered if it would not have been better if she had perished in that accident.

For the rest of the day, Clarissa did not leave the room and, by nightfall, her stomach hurt from hunger. But she would not go down. She would not give Abílio the pleasure of seeing her defeated and defeated, nor would she submit to a meal unworthy of her position. She had a minimum of dignity and was not willing to give up just to satisfy the will of that tyrant.

She tried to sleep, but hunger prevented her from falling asleep. Around nine o'clock, she heard a soft knock at the door, but did not respond. If Abílio had mocked her hunger, he was wasting his time. She wouldn't give him that opportunity. She turned her face to the window and closed her eyes, trying to ignore the insistent knocking on the door, until she heard a weak voice coming from the other side:

– Mrs. Clarissa, open up, it's me, Angelina.

Clarissa jumped out of bed. What would the stepdaughter be doing there at that hour? Silently, she opened the door and looked outside. Angelina was standing in the hallway, holding a tray with a piece of bread, some fruits, and a glass of milk in her hands. When Clarissa saw the food, she opened the door wide and pushed the girl inside, sitting her on the bed.

Memories that the wind brings

- I brought you this - said Angelina. - I thought maybe you were hungry...- Clarissa didn't even give her time to continue. She quickly grabbed a banana, peeled it and began to eat, then served herself a piece of bread.

Angelina, seeing the appetite with which she devoured that little meal, smiled and added:

- You know, I thought about bringing you some fish, but I thought you wouldn't like it. I don't even like it. Clarissa looked at her, still chewing the bread, already half- hard, and asked:

- If you don't like it, why do you eat it?

- Now, Mrs. Clarissa, if I don't eat it, I will die of hunger. We have nothing else.

- Why doesn't your father hire some servants? At least a cook?

She lowered her head, visibly saddened, and, with her eyes moist, answered:

- After mother left, no other woman entered this house. Until you arrived and...

- Please don't call me Mrs., just call me Clarissa. She looked at her hesitantly.

- Dad might not like it.

- But I like it and I'm asking. Still hesitant, Angelina continued:

- Well... Clarissa... as I was saying, no woman has come into this house in a long time. Until you came along, and Dad was hoping you could take care of us.

- And you, what do you expect from me?

Angelina looked at her with honey- colored eyes and shrugged her shoulders. She was confused and didn't know how to respond. She thought for a few minutes until she considered:

- I wish you could be my mother.

Memories that the wind brings

– Do you miss your mother?

– Uh, uh!

Clarissa was penalized. Angelina was still a child in need of her mother's care.

Thinking about it, she began to understand Abílio's attitude, marrying her. He wanted a kind and educated woman who would take care of his children as a real mother would. Not a housekeeper who treated them coldly and indifferently, tolerating them only because of the money. No. He wanted something warmer, more personal, more maternal. And only a wife could come close to his desire.

However, he had chosen the wrong methods to get a woman, and she couldn't help but feel a little angry when she thought about what he had done to her. And, besides, there was Vicente. The boy clearly had no sympathy for her. He had been hostile, had treated her badly and had let it seem that he didn't want her there. But there was the girl... Angelina was a sweet and kind girl, and she didn't deserve his contempt. Sitting next to her, Clarissa approached her and held her to her breast, and Angelina, trembling, began to cry. Clarissa, not understanding anything, was frightened and, turning away her wet face, asked, while she was wiping her tears:

– What happened Angelina? Did I do something wrong?

She, passing the back of her hands over her eyes, began to stutter with shame:

– No... it was... nothing... It's just that... your hug... reminded me a lot of my mother...

She started crying, clinging to Clarissa's neck and soaking her shirt collar with the tears. Clarissa, deeply dismayed, hugged her very tightly and whispered:

– Okay, honey, calm down. I am here and I want to be your mommy. Shh... don't be afraid.

She began to swing the child, who soon fell asleep in her arms. Afraid to wake her up, Clarissa put her in bed, covered her with the sheet and lay down beside her. Her stomach, relieved by the food Angelina had brought her, no longer bothered her, and she soon fell asleep.

The next day, very early, when Abílio woke up and went downstairs to have breakfast, he smelled a good smell of coffee coming from the kitchen and ran over there, thinking of finding his daughter by the stove. However, what was his surprise when he confronted Clarissa, who, at that very moment, was removing the oven from some rolls she had put in the oven to bake. Completely amazed, he spoke hesitantly:

– Well... good morning...

Clarissa put the tray with the rolls on the table, looked at it, and said coldly:

– Good morning.

Abílio thought of making a comment about her sudden change, but thought it was good not to say anything. He didn't know what had happened, but it was better not to provoke her, or she would be able to leave everything and lock herself in the room again. Then he lowered his eyes and mumbled:

– Excuse me.

When he turned his back to leave, Clarissa called out to him and, in a firm voice, declared:

– Mr. Abílio, I don't want you to think that I'm here obeying your orders. I am here for your daughter.

– My daughter?

– Yes. Last night I had the opportunity to get to know her a little better and I was surprised at what a wonderful girl she is. I am doing this for her, not for you. Angelina is a girl and she needs affection and care.

Abílio looked at her with emotion, but only responded:

Memories that the wind brings

– Thank you.

He went to the living room, to wait for her to serve the coffee, he was surprised by the whim she had set the table with. He had placed a linen towel, arranged cups and cutlery, and even placed wildflowers in a glass jar, long forgotten from a boring old buffet. When she arrived from the kitchen, holding the coffee tray in her hand, seeing the amazement in her husband's eyes, she considered:

– I hope you don't mind me placed the dishes, towel and jar.

– No, of course not. How did you find them?

– I went out and opened the drawers. Did I do wrong?

– No. This house, since we got married, has also become yours. You can do whatever you want.

Soon after, the children arrived for breakfast. Angelina, upon waking up, seeing that Clarissa was no longer there, went down to look for her and Vicente was in a bad mood as usual.

The two sat down and Angelina could not help but praise Clarissa's whim.

– Wow Clarissa! – she exclaimed. – You did the best you could, huh? Everything is beautiful!

– Girl! – scolded the father. – Is that the way to talk to your stepmother?

– Please, Abílio, – interrupted Clarissa. – I was the one who asked Angelina to call me by my name. And that works for you too, Vicente.

Abílio was going to compete, but prudence kept him silent. If she preferred it that way, he would have no objections. At least now it seemed that he was beginning to adapt. Try it, Angelina – she argued the delicacies Clarissa had prepared:

– They are delicious! I didn't know you could cook so well.

– A strange thing for a lady – Vicente joked.

– In fact, – answered Clarissa, pretending not to pay attention to the ironies of the child, – the one who taught me to cook was an old slave of the hacienda, Grandma Toña, who, even as an old lady, did not lose her hand to the delicacies. And the funny thing is that, at that time, I learned only by listening to the stories she told while teaching me, but I never thought I would cook. Who knew that someday your cooking classes would be of some use?

– But what's the use?" Vicente continued. – It even looks like you did a little too much.

– Vincent! – scolded Abílio. – Don't start again with your wicked mischief. That wasn't the education I gave you.

Vicente remained silent. He didn't want his father to tell him to leave the table. Not after all this time without trying a delicious breakfast like that.

– Let him, Mr. Abílio – said Clarissa – . If Vincent doesn't want to, he doesn't need to eat.

He glances over to her and didn't respond. He lowered his eyes and continued eating, and the father even laughed intimately, knowing that his son was enjoying the food and felt satisfied. At least something was right when he took Clarissa there. In the days that followed, Clarissa, helped by Angelina, tried to put the house in order. The two of them swept, dusted, washed, polished. The house was big and dirty, but, with goodwill and persistence, in a few days, they put everything in order. Angelina always helped Clarissa in any way she could and they soon became excellent friends.

On the rare stormy nights, Angelina would jump into Clarissa's bed and fall asleep hugging her. The child was terrified of lightning and thunder, and without her mother, she spent her nights thundering, afraid to even move. Until Clarissa appeared, and everything changed. Angelina felt safe and thanked God for sending her that loving and dedicated mother.

CHAPTER 5

– What are you doing, my son? – asked Flora, seeing her son bent over the desk, pen, and paper in hand.

– I'm writing a letter to Clarissa, – answered Luciano, in a good mood. – I want to invite her to my wedding and Jerusa's. Will she be able to come?

– I would very much like her to come. She left a long time ago, and it would be good if she took advantage of it and stayed for the Christmas holidays.

– I will suggest that too. But, if she doesn't come, Jerusa and I have decided that we will go there right after the honeymoon.

– Do you intend to go to Cabo Frio?

– Any objections?

– The objection, properly speaking, no. But the city is almost a town. They say there isn't even water.

– It seems you weren't too worried about this when you forced Clarissa to get married to Abílio. Why do you care now?

Flora looked hurt and said in a melancholy voice:

– It's not like that. I did not force her. Clarissa did the right thing.

– Okay, for whom?

She bit her lip and responded with uncertainty:

– For all of us...

– Then let me do the right thing too. I intend to visit my sister, and if she does not object, Jerusa and I will board a boat there shortly after our honeymoon.

– You know. I will not interfere. But I would prefer that she and her husband come and visit us here, to the farm.

– So do I, but if she can't, we're done. We'll visit, unless Mr. Abílio doesn't allow it.

The memory of Clarissa brought tears to Flora's eyes, who left in a hurry, so that Luciano would not see her crying, as she would like to see her daughter again, holding her in her arms, kissing her cheeks! She had doubts about whether his son-in-law would be willing to make that long journey again, and her heart sank. Anyway, she would also write to her. Perhaps, seeing her longing, Clarissa could convince him to go, in her company or not.

Clarissa received the letter with euphoria and emotion, and then Luciano and Jerusa finally decided to get married! It was wonderful news. With the letter in her hand, she went to look for her husband.

She knew what his response would be, but it didn't hurt her to try.

– I'm sorry, Clarissa, but we can't go, – he said. – It's a very long trip. I can't take the children and I wouldn't like to leave them alone again.

– I figured... Well, but if we can't go, Luciano said he'll come here with Jerusa. Is that possible?

– I don't think so, – he answered dryly, looking away from her.

– Why not?

– We don't have adequate accommodations.

– But what shamelessness! Such a big house, with so many rooms available.

– If you have noticed, the rooms are very simple.

– ¿And? We can fix them up. My brother and Jerusa aren't ceremonious. Oh, please, Abílio, let them. I'm left alone, I only have Angelina to talk to. And then, I miss them very much...

Memories that the wind brings

– All right, Clarissa, stop crying. I promise to think about it.

– Think? But I thought you would give me a definite answer by now. I need to write to Luciano. He needs to make arrangements...

– In two days, I'll give you the answer, okay?

– Two days? But why?

– Why? Because first I need to resolve some... issues.

– What issues?

– You are not interested. These are my issues, which do not concern you.

Clarissa felt her face burning and then blushed. She was angry and couldn't hide it. Clenching her teeth, she took her revenge:

– Mr. Abílio, I have never seen a man as rude as you. It is not for nothing that your wife committed suicide.

Abílio stood up, frothing with hatred, and raised his hand to hit her. Clarissa, frightened, shrank, waiting for him to slap her, but the slap did not come.

Instead, she closed her hand and struck the wall, looking at it angrily. The bloodshot eyes pointed at her with a finger and grunted like an animal:

– Never again, do you hear me? Never repeat that again, or I won't answer for myself! –

Abílio turned on his heels and left in an anguished race. She had crossed the line, and he almost lost his head and hit her. What if he had given her that slap? What face could she look at afterward? Worse. What face could he look at himself, knowing he was a coward, accusing himself of hitting a woman?

Annoyed, he went into the kitchen and ran out into the courtyard to Tiago's house. The wind was already beginning to blow, and he knocked violently on the door, shouting breathlessly:

– Tiago! Tiago! Open up! It's me, open up!

Memories that the wind brings

A few moments later, the door opened and Tiago let him in. He was scared, not understanding what had happened, and asked:

– Mr. Abílio, what happened? Abílio cried and sobbed, clinging to the black man's body.

– Mister, what happened? – repeated Tiago, who could not understand the reason that had led his boss to this lack of control.

Abílio, joining forces, separated from him, wiped his face with the back of his hands and breathed;

– Oh! Tiago, I don't know what to do. She... she... – and started crying again.

– Who is she? What happened? Was it Leonor? – Abílio stopped short and responded aggressively:

– Leonor can no longer do anything to anyone. – The former slave looked at him sympathetically and, shaking his head, considered:

– That is why. You should not cry like that for whom left.

He sighed deeply and listened to his ears, hearing the wind stirring against the windows from the outside.

– Why, Tiago, why did it have to be like this? Why did I have and lose her?

– I don't know. These are God's things. He's the one who knows.

– Is it? Sometimes I even doubt...

– You shouldn't talk like that.

– Oh! Tiago, forgive me! I know I promised, but I can't, I can't.

– Why don't you tell me what happened?

Abílio turned to the window, seemed lost in a small swirl of sand that was forming right in front of him, and responded discouraged.

– It was Clarissa.

Memories that the wind brings

– I told you not to bring a woman here. It couldn't work.

– You're right, but what could you do? I promised...

– It's not a promise you make. And what did she do, you ask?

– No. She wants me to let his brother come here. I promised to think, and she called me rude, accusing me of contributing to Leonor's suicide.

– She said what?

– Well, not exactly. But that's what she meant. And the worst thing is that I almost hit her.

– Sir! – Tiago was horrified – . God forbid such misfortune. You are not a man to defeat a woman.

– I know Tiago, and it was God who took my hand just in time to stop the blow.

Otherwise... – . he interrupted the speech and cried desperately again.

Tiago, approaching him, put his hand on his shoulder and caressed him like a father, and said tenderly:

– Don't think about it, he said, it's over. Fortunately, you held back just in time.

– I know Tiago. After that time, I promised I would never touch a woman again.

– And you kept your promise, didn't you?

– Yes, but today...

– Today you lost control, that was all. It's normal, it's human. But what matters is that nothing happened.

– Oh! Tiago, what would I be without you?

– You know I'm your friend, right?

– I do know. The only one I have.

– Now let's not think about those sad things anymore. Wipe away the tears and come home.

– I don't know if I can face Clarissa again, after what happened.

– Do you want some advice?

– I do want it.

– I know that you don't like strangers in the house, that Clarissa is already a stranger that the master had to accept. But if she is going to be happy, let the brother come. It is a way to make peace with her, and that she doesn't leave. You will be distracted.

– What if he finds out something?

– He won't discover anything. I'm here to watch over you and your family.

– You are my guardian angel Tiago.

– Black angel, master? – He answered in a good mood. – Uh– huh!

– You know I never discriminated against you because you're black man, right?

– I know, sir. I was only joking. I've never seen a man as good as you.

Too bad not everyone knows that.

Abílio smiled gratefully, took the black man's hand and kissed it. Tiago, embarrassed, withdrew his hand and turned his face to the side, trying to hide the tears coming down his cheeks.

He loved Abílio like a son. I had never known anyone like him. He had his quirks there, it was true. But after what happened to the woman, who wouldn't?

That night, the wind seemed desperate. It blew and swayed the windows, as if it wanted to come in. Clarissa had never seen or heard anything like it. It was scary, and she shrank, trying not to look at the window, afraid of the ghostly vision that the night's shadow cast on the walls. Suddenly, she heard a knock on the door and, thinking it was Angelina, she said in a low voice:

– You may come in.

When the door opened, she heard boots on the floor and knew who it was.

She lifted her startled body, trying to cover herself with the sheet, and exclaimed:

– Mr. Abílio! You didn't say you were coming.

– Don't worry, – he answered, waving his hand to her – "that's not why I came here.

– No? Then why did you come?

Abílio looked around and cleared his throat, a little uncomfortable. He wanted to apologize, but didn't know where to start. Full of courage, he announced:

– I came here to tell you that your brother can come if he wants to.

Clarissa wanted to jump on his neck and kiss him, but she stopped. She was so happy that she didn't even remember the previous discussion. All she could say was:

– Thank you very much, Mr. Abílio.

– There is no need to thank me.

Then, without even saying good night, he turned and left, carefully closing the door. Clarissa was so happy that she had even forgotten the fear the wind caused her. All she could think of was the joy she would feel having her brother and Jerusa there, very close to her.

Thinking about them, she fell asleep. Almost at midnight, she woke up with a strange noise, which seemed to come from the end of the corridor, and heard: uiuiuiui…

– But what is this?" she asked in alarm, immediately jumping out of bed. – Who is there?

Memories that the wind brings

When no one answered, she lay down again, covering herself with the sheet up to her head. It should be an impression. Or, who knows, did she not dream? Trying to control her fear, she closed her eyes to sleep, until the noise was heard again: uiuiuiui...

She opened her eyes, terrified. What would that be? Some ghost or demon? And the noise continued: uiuiuiui...Clarissa shrank as much as she could and began to pray, asking God to take her far away. She believed in the souls of another world. She remembered that Grandma Toña had told her many stories about ghosts and apparitions, and she was full of terror. She was still praying when she heard a knock again.

Afraid to respond, she covered herself again with the sheet, pretending she hadn't heard anything. Until, suddenly, the door opened and she saw the shadow of a nightgown approaching the bed, holding a small flickering candle in her hand.

– Angelina! – she exclaimed with relief. – What a fright you gave me.

– Sorry, Clarissa, I didn't mean to scare you. But the wind is blowing very hard, and I was wondering if you were afraid.

– Wind? So this horrible, terrifying noise is just the wind?

– That's right. Why? What did you think it was?

Clarissa laughed. She was a frightened fool; that is, to think there were ghosts in the house.

Seeing Angelina's inquisitive look, she responded:

– Forgive me, Angelina, I couldn't help it.

– What are you laughing at?

– I just thought I was a soul from another world.

– Good God, Clarissa!

– Yes. Now, look at this nonsense. And it was only the wind. But also, I've never heard anything like it. What a strange sound, it really sounds like a groan.

Memories that the wind brings

– It's always like that when it's loud. But there is no need to stop. I guarantee that there are no ghosts around here.

– Of course not.

– But if you want, I can sleep here with you. Clarissa thanked her with a look.

In spite of everything, she was afraid, yes, and Angelina's presence would help relieve the tension of those last moments. She stepped aside, leaving space for the girl, who lay down and settled under the sheets. It was cold and she cowered next to Clarissa. Then she blew out the candle and asked:

– Do you believe in ghosts?

– Do I? Well, I could say that.

– Do you?

– Not in ghosts like you hear, dressed in white, howling and dragging chains. But I do believe in spirits, in the afterlife.

– Do you?

– I believe so. In my land, grandma Toña told me many stories. I myself, after she died, already saw her near me.

– Oh really?

– Yes. There were few occasions when I saw her and, even so, at a glance. But I dream about her often.

– And how do you know what her spirit is? Can't it just be your memory?

– I can't say. But it is different. When I dream about Grandma Toña, it's very real. It's like she's right next to me.

– How strange.

– Yes, very strange. But sleep now. It's late, and I don't want you to be late for school tomorrow, or your dad will get mad.

In a few minutes, they went back to sleep. Clarissa was more comforted by Angelina's presence. The wind continued to howl, as if groaning through the halls, but Clarissa was no longer afraid.

However, she dreamed. Again she was in that unusual scene, as a spectator, looking at an old man and that black man begging:

– Please don't! Have mercy! Piety! I don't want to go, I'm afraid!

The old man, who looked cold, took his cane and turned his back on it, entering his hut. Suddenly, a white man appeared, who told him he needed a black girl. The old man thought for a few seconds, scratched his chin, and responded:

– Mudima

Then the scene changed, and she saw a little girl, nine or ten years old, being dragged by the white man under her mother's disconsolate cry. The elder, despite her pleas, waved his hand and shrugged. There was nothing he could do. It was business. The white man needed a black girl, the payment was good and Mudima served.

He was a slave there, and it was up to him, as chief of the tribe, to dispose of his fate. Clarissa watched, horrified, as the white man dragged the girl away screaming, and she began to cry, until she felt someone shake her, calling her by name:

– Clarissa! Clarissa! – It was Angelina – Wake up! You had a nightmare.

Clarissa, in a cold sweat and crying, opened her eyes. It was a dream, thank God it was a dream.

But how strange it had been!

– What had happened? – asked Angelina. "What did you dream? – Clarissa looked at the girl and caressed her hair, calming her.

– It was nothing. Go to sleep.

She turned to the side, but she could no longer sleep, that night had been full of surprises and shocks, and she was confused. Was this nightmare the result of the strong emotions that had happened hours before? She wasn't quite sure. However, she had

Memories that the wind brings

seen those men in other dreams, although she didn't know who they were. What about that little girl? Mudima was the name. Where has she heard that name before? Suddenly, Clarissa felt a chill. That was the name of Grandma Toña before she was brought from Africa, but what did it mean? Trying to concatenate the ideas, Clarissa went back to sleep, only waking up the next day when the sun was already high. Keeping in her memory the image of those people. She knew she knew them, but how, from where? She had to find out.

CHAPTER 6

The days in Cabo Frio were almost always mild, and even the summer heat was influenced by the coolness of the breeze and the winds, which made the land a pleasant place to live. It had not been the precariousness of the village, until Clarissa would have liked it. Not that the valley of Paraíba was very different. It was quiet and peaceful, but it was a prosperous place, with rich and educated people, farmers who sent their children to study in the capital or abroad.

The sea, in a way, fascinated her. It had a special charm, a touch of mystery, an unmistakable beauty, and Clarissa began to admire the waves breaking on the beach, thinking how sad it would have been if she had perished in that shipwreck, without the opportunity to know so much beauty. She thought of that land with dual feelings. If, on the one hand, she appreciated its charms and freshness, on the other hand, loneliness consumed her and she spent her days waiting for her brother's arrival.

It was ten o'clock on a Sunday morning and she had finished tidying up the house when, from the porch, she saw Vicente sitting on the white sand of the beach. Since she arrived there, Clarissa had not yet gone. Although she thought the sea was beautiful, she was a little afraid to go near it. She did not forget that she had almost been swallowed by the waves and was afraid that another accident would happen. However, when she saw her stepson on the sand, with his head thrown back and basking in the sun, she wanted to go to him. She washed her hands, straightened her hair, straightened her skirt and left. She walked slowly and continued along the road until she reached the beach and continued walking. As he approached Vicente, she noticed that his eyes were closed and touched him gently on the shoulder. He started opening his eyes, looking at her, standing against the sun.

- What do you want? - he asked aggressively.

- Nothing, - answered Clarissa casually, sitting next to him on the sand.

- I saw you here and wondered if you would like to talk.

- I have nothing to talk about with you. Go away.

- Why do you treat me like this, Vicente? What have I done to you? - He looked at her with disdain and said coldly:

- You are not my mother.

- I know. And I wouldn't even like to be. In fact, I couldn't, since I'm not much older...

- ¿And? One more reason I don't know what went on in my father's mind to bring a stranger here who might well be his daughter after all.

- Are you jealous?

- Jealous? You are crazy. I don't care what my father does with his life.

- Then why don't you like me?

- Since you're not my mother, you're not like her and you don't look like her.

- I have no intention of being like your mother. I didn't know her, but I respect her a lot...

- Why?

- Because she was a person, and all people are worthy of respect and consideration. But you, I don't know why you treat me that way.

- I didn't ask you to come.

- Neither did I.

- How so?

- Your father didn't tell you?

- What did he say?

Memories that the wind brings

– Didn't he tell you why I married him?

– Not why? Wasn't it because of the money?

– In a way, yes.

– Then, I don't understand what you mean. You wanted the money, he gave it to you.

– Things are not as they seem. I married your father because mine made a deal with him.

Vicente seemed to be admired, opened his eyes wide and asked:

– Deal? What kind of deal?

In detail, Clarissa told him how she got there. The fall of the farm and its near ruin, Abílio's opportunity to meet with his father and the offer he had made, offering a good sum in exchange for a wife.

– You mean your father sold you? – said Vicente.

– Yes, that's exactly what he did. He sold me. And don't think it was with my free consent. I only accepted because I was afraid for my father. But, if I may say so, I didn't want to marry Mr. Abílio and I would rather be at home. I know he's your father, but he's old, tough and rude, and I'm not used to such men. He is not a gentleman.

Vicente rubbed his eyes, scratched his head and said okay:

– I understand what you are saying.

– I know you do. From what I could see, you and your father aren't very connected, are you?

He grimaced in anger and blurted out:

– I hate him.

– Hate? Why? He may not be a kind or helpful man, but he is your father. Don't you think hate is a very strong feeling?

– No. I really hate him. I hate him for what he is, for the way he treats us, I hate him for what my mother did...

Memories that the wind brings

– What did he do to your mother?

Vicente regretted having touched on that subject and tried to disguise it. He rubbed his eyes, stood up and held out his hand, adding:

– Don't you want to walk with me?

Clarissa rejoiced. If Vincente invited her to walk, it was because he was no longer so angry with her. She took the hand that he held out to her and he walked away with her. She was going to keep asking about his mother, but she thought it was better not to insist. She had already realized that no one liked to talk about it, perhaps because the memories were too painful. However, she felt that there was a certain air of mystery about her death, and curiosity was aroused.

– Why don't you take off your shoes? – asked Vincente, interrupting her thoughts.

– What?

– The shoes, why don't you take them off?

– Oh! I don't know if that would be appropriate.

– Why not? Try the sand. I'm sure you'll like it. Clarissa thought for a few seconds, until she obeyed. She bent down, untied her boots and took them off.

– The socks too – he continued.

– But Vincent, I don't know if it looks good...

– Stop this nonsense, Clarissa. We don't have those things here.

– We don't?

– Well, not here. We are on the beach, far from everyone, what harm can there be?

– I don't know. Your father might not like it.

– I bet he doesn't care. My mother used to do that and... – suddenly, he stopped.

Memories that the wind brings

– So what? – Clarissa asked.

– Nothing. Come on, bet a race.

He shot in front of Clarissa and she, after taking off her socks, threw them to the ground, along with her shoes, and ran after him. The feeling of the thin, cold sand under her feet was indescribable. The wind on her face made her feel light and free, and she extended her arms, running after Vicente. It was faster and she could not catch up with him, stopping suddenly, panting and coughing. She was so exhausted that she didn't even realize where they had ended up. They were at the foot of a pile of stone, not too high, with a nearly ruined fort on top. She seemed amazed, until Vincente, seeing that she would not reach him at all, went to her and told her:

– It is the fort of San Mateo.

– Yes... I know... – she replied, panting – You... your sister said to me...

Realizing how difficult it was to talk, Vincente sat down next to her, took her hand and asked her with concern:

– Do you feel okay?

She shook his hand and after a few minutes, in which she was still breathing, she responded gratefully:

– I'm okay, don't worry. I'm just not used to those careers. Vicente smiled and squeezed her hand even more, leaving Clarissa confused and embarrassed. That boy, though younger, had the power to disturb her, and she did not know how to define what kind of feeling was beginning to emerge within her. She was very startled and blushed. Ashamed, she quickly put her hand away and stood up, saying without looking at him:

– We'd better go back.

Without saying anything, Vincente got up and began to follow her. He too was beginning to experience something he didn't know how to define. Since Clarissa arrived, he had only thought of her as a stepmother who had come to steal his mother's place. But after holding her hand and seeing a shadow of confusion in her eyes, he had doubts about his true feelings. She was beautiful, sweet, and what he admired was sincere and brave. Clarissa was not afraid of facing her father, and this was a great virtue for him.

When they arrived home, Angelina was waiting for them. Since it was Sunday, she had gone to Clarissa's room to see if she didn't want to talk, but she couldn't find her. When she saw her brother approaching her, she felt jealous and asked, pouting:

– Where were you, Clarissa? I looked for you everywhere.

– I went for a walk with your brother.

– Alone?

– How come? – Vincente answered all grumpy. – What's up with that, spoiled girl?

– Nothing... – she answered with a feeling. – I asked for asking.

– Well, now that you know, go run and tell Dad everything. Walk, what are you waiting for? – Angelina, hurt, ran out and locked herself in the room, throwing herself on the bed to cry. Clarissa, not understanding anything, asked in amazement:

– Why did you do that? She's just a kid – . She shrugged her shoulders and responded contemptuously:

– She is a curious fool.

– It's not true. Angelina is a sweet and kind girl, and she is your sister. You shouldn't treat her like that.

Vincente shrugged again and Clarissa went to find Angelina. She was confused by that scene, not knowing what to do, but she needed to tell her that she didn't agree with the boy's attitude. She gently knocked on the door of the girl's bedroom, as she did not respond, pulled the latch and entered. It was not locked, and Clarissa saw Angelina in bed, crying and sobbing, deeply wounded.

– Angelina – she called.

– What do you want?

– Angelina, don't cry. Your brother wasn't speaking well.

– Ah! he said yes. He hates me, just like he hates my father.

– That's not true. He doesn't hate you.

– Yes, He hates. He hates my father because he is the way he is. And he hates me because I can't feel that hate that he wanted me to feel. I told him I'm sorry, but I can't. I know my father is strange and distant, but he is my father and I can't hate him. I know I should, but I can't, I can't.

– Who told you to hate your father? Your brother doesn't know what he's saying. He dislikes what happened to his mother, but it is no one's fault. She killed herself because she wanted to. She made her own choice.

Angelina looked deep into her eyes and cried again. She couldn't hear about the mother who was starting to cry. Sobbing, she said almost in a plea:

– Oh! Clarissa, please don't let that happen again!

– What? What are you afraid of? Come on, talk. I'm your friend, I want to help you.

Angelina was about to respond when her father's suddenly come into and stopped her. He looked at her with an air of recrimination, frowned and, turning to Clarissa, ordered:

– Come on, Clarissa, let Angelina rest.

– Rest? But rest from what? She is sad and scared, don't you see? She needs our help.

– She just needs to be alone for a few moments.

– Mr. Abílio, how can you be so insensitive? Your daughter is a child, she needs love and

Don't you realize what you are doing?

– You don't know anything, Clarissa, and I'd rather you didn't interfere with my children.

– Very good. If so, I'd rather go. I will leave this house as soon as possible.

– Leave? – Angelina was surprised – . Ah! No, Clarissa, please!

– Are you crazy? – added Abílio indignantly. – You're my wife, you can't leave me.

– Wife? I'm more like your maid, or worse, your slave. Who do you think you are to treat me this way?

– I am your husband.

– But you do not own me. When I came here, You said that the house was mine and that I could do whatever I wanted. But now, you keep me away from your daughter. Why?

Abílio didn't answer. He stood there looking at her for a few minutes, and when he spoke, it was as if there was a volcano of fury roaring inside him:

– Do what you want, Clarissa. If you want to leave, I won't stop you. I am not a man to beg anything from anyone, least of all a woman. But don't forget that your honor and your father's are at stake, and I will not hesitate to shake your credit and trust your clients, a credit I helped recover.

He shot out, leaving Clarissa with her face on fire, feeling the blood boil. Angelina, scared, stopped crying without understanding, still asked:

– What did he mean, Clarissa?

Clarissa did not answer. Furious, she went after him and came down the stairs, still barefoot, screaming as she crossed the room:

– Mr. Abílio! – he stopped without turning, and she continued: – you are a mean, cruel and insensitive man, and you think you can buy me off for the rest of your life. Well done. I am bound to you by a duty of honor and by fear of what my family might do. However, I want you to know that, as of today, I no longer intend to talk to you; if you want to talk to me, do it through your children or your lackey.

– It's great for me.

And he left the door, going to take refuge, as always, in Tiago's friendly shoulder.

Again, the wind whipped up the windows, but Clarissa was beginning to get used to it, and that moaning began to sound familiar. Every time I heard that uiuiuiui.... Clarissa would shudder and shiver, but she was no longer afraid. It was a feeling she could not define, but it was not fear.

After the argument she had with Abílio, she was determined never to speak to him again. That man was horrible, and the woman must have killed herself for not being able to bear it, leaving the children at the mercy of her quirks. But she was tired and fell asleep. As soon as she closed her eyes, she smelled a pleasant scent of roses and took a deep breath. Then she opened her eyes and saw old Toña, standing by her bed.

– Shall we go? – invited the former slave, extending her hand gently.

Clarissa's perispirit rose from the bed and began to follow her, until she asked in a moment:

– Where are we going?

– Do not worry. We are going for a walk.

– I don't worry, Grandma Toña. I know that nothing can happen to me next to you. They left and went to the beach, sitting by the sea.

– All right, Toña started, we need to talk.

– About what?

– My daughter, you are being very tough on Abílio.

– Tough? But Grandma Toña, that man is impossible.

Memories that the wind brings

- No, it is not. That is only a mask. Inside, there is a kind and loving man, waiting for you to awaken those qualities in him.

- I'm sorry, Grandma Toña, but I tried. However, he is prideful and mean, and only does what he wants. He thinks he owns the truth.

- Think hard, Clarissa. It is very important that you and he understand each other.

- Why? What does he have to do with me? Until my wedding, I had never seen him before.

- Your mistake, my dear. Abílio and you are old acquaintances. Clarissa looked at her doubtfully and continued:

- Do you want to see?

Clarissa nodded and Toña pointed to the sea. Suddenly, night gave way to daytime, and Clarissa saw a boat in the distance, sailing fast on the sea. At the same moment, she found herself transported to that boat, in which she had been traveling for a few days. At one point, a sailor appeared and said respectfully

- Your Highness, the captain asks you to go to your cabin -. She looked at him with disdain and responded:

- Does he want to see me? Well, let him come to my presence.

Shortly after, the captain appeared and went to stand next to her. She had her back to him, enjoying the sea, and did not turn around when he arrived.

- What do you want? - she asked arrogantly, without looking at him.

- Your Highness, I would like you to forgive me.

- Forgive you? And why should I?

- Because I need you.

She looked at him with amusement and said:

- For what?

– I miss your body, your kisses...

When she turned to him, the captain smiled and Clarissa could recognize Abílio's sullen face in that smile.

– Please, Luisa, come to my cabin later.

– Impossible. My cousin...

– Your cousin is a fool. He doesn't love you as I do.

– However, he treats me with respect and distinction.

– Forgive me again, Your Highness. But your cousin is a nobleman, accustomed to the rules of etiquette. I, however, am only the captain of a caravel. I know nothing about manners. I am a navigator, not a gentleman.

– You shouldn't be so rude. I am a lady, I am noble and I do not like to be badly answered.

The captain, who did not want to prolong that conversation any longer, took her by the hand and, with delicacy and discretion, kissed her, adding with a gallant air:

– I hope to see you soon. Please don't miss it.

That night, when almost everyone was asleep, except for a few men at the helm and the observation posts, he left his cabin and went to knock on the captain's cabin door.

He, knowing who she was, carefully opened the door and lured her in, kissing her furiously and whispering in her ear:

– Oh! Luisa, how I need you, how I want to hug you!

Covered with desire, the captain took her to bed and they loved each other passionately. Luisa, completely intoxicated, thought of nothing. She did not love him, but she had never experienced a more ardent love. She belonged to the Portuguese nobility, and Nicanor, the captain, had become her lover the first day she set foot on that caravel. The trip, which had begun in Calicut, Asia, had already lasted many days, delayed by the ability of Nicanor, who intended, with this, to prolong Luisa's stay at sea and in her bed.

Memories that the wind brings

Nicanor, a skilled and experienced navigator, was the son of a nobleman, but his father had gone bankrupt, leaving him only a few titles and many debts to pay. Thanks to his extraordinary ability as a navigator, he was called to pilot the ship Santa Isabel, which made the crossing between the ports of Calicut and Lisbon, bringing spices and, occasionally, some passengers.

Nicanor had a wife and a daughter. The wife, Agripina, was jealous of her husband, but, even so, Nicanor, upon noticing Luisa's eyes on him, took her as his lover, without revealing that he was married. Although he did not usually cheat on his wife, he occasionally indulged in fleeting adventures without major consequences, whenever his professional commitments took him away from Lisbon.

There was something about this woman that fascinated him, and Nicanor let himself be seduced by her dazzling beauty and her naked gestures. He knew she didn't love him either and it didn't even occur to him that he might find some kind of problem when the time came to break up their romance. Nicanor was intoxicated with Luisa's body, but she didn't want anything to do with her heart. She gave him great pleasure and therefore was in no hurry to return. He knew that when they arrived, Luisa would represent nothing more to him and he thought it would no longer mean anything to her. Then he would be free to run back to his beloved wife.

The vision suddenly faded, and Clarissa found herself back on the beach, in the company of Toña.

– But what does all this mean? – she asked, perplexed.

– It means that you and Abílio already know each other from other lives, but only now have you had a chance to undo old resentments.

– I don't understand.

– As you can see, you and Abílio were lovers in a past life, even though that relationship did not result in any love.

– Yes, but what does this have to do with our current relationship?

– Don't you see? Abílio, then Nicanor, was a man without possessions. You were the rich one.

– ¿And? I can't see any relationship.

– Clarissa, today's roles have been reversed. He has the money... – She scratched her head.

She was already beginning to understand and said discouraged:

– You mean I bought it? – Toña nodded – But how? What have I done? And with what intention, if I didn't love him?

– More or less that. But don't rush to discover these truths. In time, they will gradually emerge as they are needed for your growth and understanding.

– Why are you showing me all this?

– So that I can understand Abílio's position and attitude.

– I do not understand. Nothing justifies what he is doing to me and his children. And who knows what he did to the woman.

– His first wife, Leonor, is also linked to you by sad and painful ties, which in this life she chose to rescue.

– What ties? Who is she? Is she Agripina?

– She herself. That's why I tell you Clarissa, nobody experiences difficult situations at random, and if you have that kind of experience today, it wasn't because chance chose her. It was because you chose it yourself, and if you chose it, it was because you thought it was necessary for your growth, as a way of understanding the incorrectness of certain attitudes you took in the past.

Clarissa was sad. She didn't know what to say. She was still not quite sure what it all meant, but she felt that Toña was right. Something in her heart told her that she had hurt Abilio immensely and now she chose to reconcile with him. Consciously, he did not know these things, but his spirit still retained the memory of that past life, where he had chosen to throw himself into a pit of lust and pride, humiliating and destroying anyone who stood in his way. Suddenly Clarissa remembered the dreams she had had about those black men and, thinking they were related to Toña, she asked:

– Grandma Toña, I've been having strange dreams. I dream of a man asking sorry...

Toña interrupted her with her hand and responded:

– Not now, Clarissa. One thing at a time. To understand these dreams, you must first understand your previous life, in which you were a vain, proud and arrogant woman.

– But these dreams are so real! Do they also remember other lives?

– Actually, yes. There was a time when this man was sold into slavery to white men, without you stopping him.

– Stop him? Me? But how?

– You will soon find out. All I can say is that this man, although he promised to get along with you, could not forget the offense and found a way to repay the evil he believes you did to him. He suffers much from your attitude, but he could not help himself. So he lives in constant conflict because he wanted to forgive you, but unconsciously he took revenge on you.

– Are you talking about my father?

Toña smiled enigmatically, clenched her little chin and said tenderly:

– You are very intelligent, Clarissa. You always were. And you bring in your heart a great kindness, hard- earned through struggle and suffering over the years. Yet he remains a rebellious and reckless spirit, a consequence of his former nobility. But I must remind you of the commitments you have made, and I ask you not to turn away from them. Try to get along with Abílio and you will be able to overcome your difficulties. Help him. By helping him to change, you will contribute to his own growth.

Memories that the wind brings

The next day, when Clarissa woke up, she had few memories of the dream she was having, but she went down to the café with a strange feeling of comfort in her chest.

She only remembered that she had dreamt about Toña, and that she had told her something about having more understanding with Abílio. Looking at him from the other side of the table, Clarissa made a grimace. He is cold and cruel. How to understand him?

CHAPTER 7

It was on a night of the full moon that everything began to happen. Seemingly the moon was stirring the souls to despair, and the south-west wind, which was blowing incessantly, made their lament a never-ending storm. Clarissa, as usual, lay down to sleep. Despite the dream she had with Grandma Toña, she still didn't feel ready to make peace with her husband. So that night in particular, she had retired early. She didn't want to have to listen to Abílio's irritating voice and took refuge in her bedroom.

The dawn was already high and the wind was still blowing: uiuiuiui... breaking the windows with his unbridled fury. Clarissa, already accustomed to that moan, no longer cared, and the noise did not bother her. Little by little, her eyelids began to weigh, and she fell asleep, only to wake up a little later, scared and confused. It seemed that, in the midst of the moaning of the wind, someone was really moaning. She opened her eyes and tried to listen.

Yes, in the midst of the noise of the wind she seemed to distinguish a kind of muffled moan, that was confused with the gale. Listening to her ears, she heard clearly: uiuiuiui...That was very strange. Suddenly, the moaning stopped, and all she heard was the sound of the wind.

At first, it didn't matter, thinking it was just the wind blowing more furiously than usual, crossing a new crack that had been made in a door or window, which gave it that terrifying sound. Gradually, however, Clarissa realized that, behind the uiuiuiui... from the wind, there was even a uiuiuiui... painful, as if someone were in deep agony. Terrified, she curled up under the sheet and waited. Suddenly, she heard footsteps in the corridor and thought that Abílio had stood up to see what it was. The steps seemed to disappear at the end of the corridor, then she heard a dry noise, made as a door closed.

But the sound seemed distant, and she could not clearly define what it was. Suddenly, the moaning stopped, and she realized that only the wind was still howling. What could have happened? She thought of getting up, but she lacked courage. What could that be? Was it some soul or spirit? She didn't know, but something in her heart told her that something extraordinary was happening in that house. Despite her fear, Clarissa thought she would not rest until she found out what it was. If some wandering soul was lost within those walls, it was her duty to help it. The next day, at breakfast, Abílio was not present. She was curious, because he always had meals with the family, but she didn't ask any questions. Angelina, however, upon realizing her curiosity, immediately rectified:

– Dad left early with Tiago.

Clarissa looked at her and said nothing, until she heard Vicente's voice, as grumpy as ever, and asked him:

– Where did he go?

– I don't know. He never says anything when he leaves. After a few brief minutes of silence, in which the three were drinking coffee, each lost in thought, Clarissa asked:

– Did you hear a groan last night?

Angelina and Vicente looked at each other, and it was the girl who spoke:

– Moaning? How so?

– A groan, I don't know. As if someone was crying.

– Well, Clarissa – Vicente mocked – it was probably the wind. Are you still not used to it?

– I'm not sure. There was the sound of the wind, yes, but there was a muffled groan behind it.

– For me, it was the wind...

Memories that the wind brings

– No, it was not. I can already tell the noise from the wind and I'm saying it was something else I heard.

– But what was it?" asked Vicente, trying to appear indifferent.

– One thing, I don't know. As if a person was suffering.

– Person? But what person, Clarissa? It wasn't me. Much less Angelina. Dad then, no way. Who else? Only Tiago is gone.

– And what would Tiago be doing here, at dawn? And even more, moaning?

– Yes. Then it was nobody.

– No. It was someone, I'm sure.

– But who? Was it some ghost? – Vicente mocked.

– That's just it. I think it was a ghost.

– Just kidding! – exclaimed Angelina, startled.

– No, silly, – said Vicente, – she's serious. It was probably Mom's ghost, who came back to pick you up and drag you to the bottom of the sea.

He said that in a thick voice and raised his arms, imitating the movements of a ghost. Angelina, outraged by his disrespect, jumped from the table and expressed:

– Vicente, you are a bad and impossible boy. How can you talk about mom like that? Don't you have any respect?

– Respect... why, she left, right? She finished...

– ¿And? You must respect his memory.

– Memory... but nonsense. You have no more memory. Even that took us far.

– That's not true! You are being cruel.

Angelina was horrified. How could the brother refer to his mother like that? Vincent was about to respond when Clarissa interrupted him:

– Angelina is right, Vincente. We must respect everyone, whether they are alive or dead. Even more so because she was your mother.

Vincente was going to fight a bad fight, but when he saw Clarissa's serious face, he changed his mind. From the day they met on the beach, he had looked at her closely.

A different way. She had a certain control over him that bothered him. And then, she was right. He didn't want to be disrespectful to his mother. He had always loved her and had been very dedicated to it. He swallowed and responded:

– You are right, Clarissa, forgive me. I was only joking.

– You should not. There are certain things we shouldn't play with. And then, if you want to know, I really think it was a spirit or a ghost, as you prefer, that was here last night.

– Now, Clarissa, you can't be serious.

– Why not?

– Because ghosts don't exist. It's all the imagination of ignorant or impressionable people, like Angelina.

He pinched his sister's nose, who patted him on the hand and retaliated:

– I think Clarissa is right. Who said there are no such things as ghosts?

– And who said they exist?

– Well, enough," said Clarissa with authority. This discussion will get us nowhere. I think it's good that you finish your coffee and go. Your father doesn't like to be late.

– But he left, taking the car. And now we have to go on horseback.

– So what happens?

– Nothing.

Memories that the wind brings

After they left, Clarissa was thinking. Something had happened the night before. She wasn't crazy or imaginative. She knew what she had heard and was almost certain that there was a very needy spirit that was there. Perhaps Leonor's spirit, why not? Hadn't she committed suicide? Hadn't her body disappeared into the waves, robbing her of the chance for a decent burial, a grave where she could cry and bring flowers? Her soul might have been restless, needing assistance, but how to help her?

When she finished washing breakfast, Clarissa dried her hands and went upstairs. The big house where Abílio and his family lived was huge. There were five large windows upstairs facing the beach, and five facing the forest cut by the road, in a total of ten rooms, spacious and well ventilated. At one end of the corridor, on the right, was the staircase that led to the first floor and, at the other end, only one wall, completely whitewashed, with no doors or windows.

Only four rooms were used: two in the front and two in the back. Angelina was the first and Clarissa the second, both facing the sea.

Opposite, the rooms of Vicente and Abílio, open to the forest. The other six rooms remained closed. No one went there, and Abílio had told him that he didn't need to do so or clean them, as they were empty. Until then, Clarissa had not been curious about them. Angelina herself had discouraged her, saying nothing was interesting there. Only the last one, which had been her mother's, remained intact, with the same furniture and curtains. The father did not let anyone touch it and asked Clarissa not to go in there.

As Clarissa moved forward, she shuddered. There was, no doubt, something very strange in that house, and she shuddered.

She passed in front of the closed doors, without opening them, until she stopped in front of the door of the room that had belonged to Leonor. A chill ran down her spine and she felt a shudder. She tried the lock. It was blocked. She put her ear to the door and listened. Silence. The place seemed deserted, as it should be. Seeing that the door would not open, Clarissa returned down the hall, experimenting with the others.

They were all unlocked, and she opened them, one by one. Inside each room, there was only a bed, a closet and a dresser, nothing else. The windows, closed, lend an air of mold and dust to the environment. Instinctively, she entered each one and was opening the windows wide. Those rooms needed air. Although no one lived there, they were part of the house, and she made sure they were cleaned and ventilated daily. After all, Luciano was about to arrive, and it was obvious that one of those rooms would have to live.

Back in the room, Clarissa began to think. She hadn't seen or heard anything, but she was sure of what she had heard the night before. It would not be easy to prove her theory, but she was sure there was a suffering spirit there. She wanted to help him, but the fact was that she was also afraid. Last night, she had barely managed to keep her eyes open, shrinking under the sheets. And even today, as she approached Leonor's room, she wanted to escape, fearing that some terrifying vision would materialize in front of her.

But she wanted to find out. What's more, she wanted to help. She thought of asking Vincent for help, but he didn't believe her. And Angelina was just a child and there was nothing she could do. Talking to Abílio was out of the question. Only if... Clarissa applauded with joy.

There was only one person there who could help her, and that person was Tiago. He was a slave and an old man. He should know many things, many secrets and many prayers. Yes, Tiago was definitely the right person to help her. She just needed to convince him. Tiago was a quiet and withdrawn man, and he barely spoke to her. Besides, his loyalty to Abílio was clear. Tiago was one of those men who could give everything for the boss, including his life.

Thinking about it, Clarissa could not help but notice the contradiction in Abílio's behavior. He was a hard and cold man who bordered on cruelty. However, he treated the former slave with respect and distinction, so much so that he remained in his service even after the abolition. The husband still paid him a good salary, besides giving him food and a house to live in. Yes, a very strange relationship. You might even suspect that there was something between them, some secret, that could not be revealed. How many mysteries there were in that house! And Clarissa needed to unravel them. One by one, she would discover all those secrets.

Thinking about it, she waited for Tiago to return. She would talk to him and find out if he knew there were spirits there. If he knew, it was very likely that Abílio knew everything too. He had probably gone to Leonor's room the night before, probably to pray for her soul.

Yes, Abílio must have believed that too, and he probably went to take refuge in the slave religion. Clarissa knew how powerful that religion could be and how comforting, and there, at that end of the world, it seemed to be the only alternative for anyone seeking a little comfort and knowledge of the hidden things. This would explain the enormous affinity between Abílio and Tiago. Certainly, when they went out together, they would go to some *terreiro*, and if that were true, it would be easy to convince her husband to let her help the spirit of the tormented Leonor.

Later, Abílio arrived with Tiago and went straight to his room, without talking to anyone. It was past lunchtime, and Angelina had gone upstairs to do her homework. Vicente, as always, had gone to the beach. It was there that he used to spend his afternoons, walking and looking at the sea. Seeing Abílio go through that, Clarissa went to the kitchen to spy on old Tiago. He walked with his head down, held the oxen that were pulling the cart in his hand, and led them to the stable, a little further back. She took a few minutes and went after him. She waited until he stayed with the animals and called him:

– Good afternoon, Tiago.

The man looked at her suspiciously and answered:

– Good afternoon, siñá. Would you like anything?

– No, nothing special. I was walking, and when I saw you here, I thought of pulling a prose ...

– You'll have to excuse me, but I have a lot of work to do.

– Is it true? What are you going to do now?

– Now? Hum... I'm going to cut wood.

– Now, Tiago, who are you kidding? So I don't know if the warehouse is full of wood?

– Siñá, I don't know what you mean.

– I don't want to get anywhere. I told you, I just want to talk.

– And what does the siñá want to talk about?

She studied him for a moment and when he spoke, it was in the most selfless tone that he managed to impress her voice:

– Tell me, Tiago, what can a girl do here to distract herself?

– What? Listen to me, I don't understand what you mean, but I think it's better to stop this conversation. Mr. Abílio may not like it.

– Why? What's more? What about you? Are you afraid of him?

– Afraid? No, I'm not. Mr. Abílio is a very good man, and I have no reason to be afraid of him.

– Then there is nothing to worry about. And then, I'm not asking anything else. I just want to know what's in it for a girl made here. Any distractions? Church choirs? Recitals?

– I'm sorry, but why don't you ask Mr. Abílio? He can answer that better than I can.

– That's right. But the thing is, Mr. Abílio and I aren't talking.

Tiago looked at her in dismay. He knew about the fight they were having, but he had nothing to do with that. He waited for her to continue, but she changed the subject:

– But tell me, Tiago, where are your people?

– My people? What do you mean, "siñá"? There is no one else but me.

– There isn't? And the other slaves, where are they?

– Slaves? Whose? Mr. Abílio's?

– Uh, uh.

– Mr. Abílio doesn't have any other slaves, no. Besides me, only old Olinda, who has died.

– I understand...

– Why do you want to know?

– Back home, we had many slaves. Not that I approved of slavery, it's not that. But my father did, and I had to respect him. However, I have always enjoyed being among them. I love your language, your customs, your religion. I even know some of your songs...

– Do you?

Tiago was surprised and confused, not knowing what to say. He could never imagine that, a girl so beautiful, so fine, so educated, would like black things. However, that revelation made him feel some sympathy for the girl, and he smiled, listening to Clarissa's little voice, which she said softly:

– Yes it is, Tiago. Grandma Toña taught me many things...

– Grandmother Toña?

– Yes, a former slave. Also, she was very old when she died. She helped raise us. My brothers and I, and also my father, my grandfather and many others in the family.

Memories that the wind brings

- Is this true?

- Yes, it is. Grandma Toña was a very good person, and do you know that sometimes I dream about her? I think it is her spirit that comes to visit me - . Tiago didn't respond, and she continued:

- Do you believe that, Tiago?

- In what, siñá? In the spirits?

- Yes. Do you believe that they will come to visit us?

Tiago scratched his chin and looked at her hesitantly. What was he doing? He was suspicious and confused, but the fact was that he was already enjoying that conversation.

Siñáziña seemed very good and sincere in her words, and that pleased him. With a half- smile on his lips, he responded:

- Yes, I think so. I believe like no one else, in the strength of the spirits.

- Is it true? That's wonderful!

- I'm sorry, but why are you asking me these things?

- Do you know why Tiago? It's that, at home, I used to participate in the rituals of the slaves and I felt very comfortable among them. I would like to hear the sound of the drums, to sing their songs, to dance with them. I even know some songs. Do you want to hear?

- Yes, of course - he answered with curiosity.

She raised her little hands to the sky, waving them, and began to sing:

- *O sinhá vanju, o sinhá vanju e, Ae Bamburusenda, O sinhá vanju e!*[4]

> (4) N.A.: Lady who makes the winds, Lady who makes the winds, Yes, it is Bamburusenda, The lady who makes the winds!

Under Tiago's astonished gaze, she continued to sing and perform that strange ballet. When she finished, she looked at him and asked him

– So, did you like it?

The former slave, completely dazed, ran his hands through the grey hair and babbled:

– Yes, it's very beautiful.

– I think so too. Your religion is really a beauty.

– Siñá Clarissa, what do you really want?

– Nothing, no. I was wondering if you could take me there someday.

– Take you where?

– To the place where they practice their services...

The black man covered his mouth with his hand, suffocating the cry of surprise that he had barely missed. Choosing his words well, he answered:

– Well, I don't think this is a place for the siñá.

– Why not?

– Well, the siñá is white, rich. I don't know if the boss would like it.

– My dear Tiago! Will you convince me now that Mr. Abílio never accompanied you to the place of your services?

Tiago was mortified. What was she doing?

– I don't understand what you want to do.

– I want to know if Mr. Abílio attends to your services.

– I think you should ask him.

– I told you, we are not talking.

– So I'm sorry. I have nothing to do with that and I don't like to talk about the boss' life.

She looked him straight in the eye and continued to speak calmly:

– You know, Tiago, I'm not totally ignorant of spiritual things as you might think. And the fact is that I understand things.

– Things? What things?

– Spirits...

– Your grandmother Toña?

– No. Other spirits...

– I don't know what you're talking about.

– Now, Tiago, you don't have to pretend. I know everything.

– You already know?

– I did listen.

– Heard? What?

– The moans

– But what moaning, madam?

– Moaning inside the house. Like repentance. Tiago stirred restlessly. That conversation was now making him very uncomfortable. Where was she going with that story of spirits and moaning? – Without looking at her, Tiago responded:

– It must have been the wind...

– I'm not sure. It went with the wind, but it wasn't the wind.

– And you think they were spirits?

– Yes.

– That's crazy. There are no spirits inside the house.

– I'm not so sure.

– Siñá Clarissa, what are the spirits doing here?

– Looking for peace.

– Peace? But here? Why?

– Listen to Tiago, I'll be honest with you. I think there are spirits here, yes. Or rather, there is only one particular spirit...

– Same? Whose?

– I don't know for sure. From Mrs. Leonor, who knows?

Tiago was mortified. That was too much. If Mr. Abílio found out, he would be crazy about life. Trying to dissuade her from that madness, he took revenge:

– Look, if I were you, I wouldn't think about those things. The boss might not like it.

– The boss doesn't rule me. He may even think that, but he doesn't! – Clarissa suddenly fell silent. Standing at the kitchen door, Abílio watched them. He had been there for some time. Enough to see her and hear her sing. Without saying anything, he turned his back on them and entered. Like Tiago, he was also perplexed. And more. He was afraid. Abílio was so afraid that he began to cry. If she found out, he was sure she wouldn't understand. And what would become of him from now on?

CHAPTER 8

Abílio was already beginning to regret having married Clarissa. In fact, he regretted having married again. He should have followed Tiago's advice. The black man had warned him that this could happen. But he, tired of the mess in the house and the abandonment of his children, thought it was time to get them a second mother. However, he really should have hired a housekeeper. If she started asking questions, it would be much easier to get rid of her. It would be enough to pay her and fire her. But Clarissa was not a servant. She was his wife, and he couldn't get rid of her the way he gets rid of incompetent employees.

Looking at the servant, Abílio sighed and asked:

– What is she doing?

– I don't know, he said. But I found that conversation about blacks and spirits very strange. And she sang and danced as if she were one of us. Imagine...

– That's right, Tiago. There's something. Is she suspicious?

– It can be... Asking to go to the *terreiro*... See if you can... – Abílio looked at him somberly and answered:

– I didn't think you meant that.

The black man looked back with another, amazed, and exclaimed:

– Did she go crazy? Of that other subject, I don't think she suspects.

Abílio was already beginning to feel insecure. Fear began to invade him, and he hid his face in his hands, shouting with a pleading voice:

– Why did it have to be like this, Tiago, why? But she was suffering, wasn't she? It was her request, wasn't it? What can I do?

Memories that the wind brings

Surprised by the other's reaction, Tiago put his finger to his lips and whispered:

– Shh! It's dangerous to talk like that. anyone can hear

Realizing that he had been exalted, Abílio composed himself, put his hand over his head and agreed:

– That's right. I must be going crazy. But it's just that the guilt is consuming me. Remorse takes me out of my sleep.

– Don't think about it anymore. What is done is done. There is no other choice. You are a married man now, you shouldn't think about such things anymore.

– But how can I forget? How can I forget the only woman I have ever loved?

– Please, Mr. Abílio, be careful. The walls have ears. Let's change the subject

– . Abílio wiped his eyes and looked out the window of Tiago's cabin. The sun was beginning to set on the horizon, and soon the moon would rise over the sea. From where he was, he could not see the beach, but he imagined the glow of the waves in the moonlight. When he spoke again, he was calmer:

– Leonor loved the sea, didn't she?

– Yes, she did.

– Clarissa doesn't like it.

– I think Clarissa is afraid. After all, she went through some bad times.

– It is true.

– In spite of everything, I think you should make peace with Clarissa. It is not right for the husband not to talk to the wife.

– I really wanted to, Tiago, but she doesn't want to. She refuses to talk to me and I have no way of doing it.

– But you have to admit that it's a pretty girl who's the one who's doomed – . Abílio smiled and responded, shaking his head:

– That's for sure. At least I have to agree with that.

– Not only that, no. She is a very determined girl too. Sweet, but determined. I could say. Little Clarissa is a stubborn daughter.

– Really, isn't she?

– She is very good. You can tell how good she is. She has a pure heart. Abílio looked at Tiago with suspicion. Suddenly, he changed his speech and almost defended Clarissa. Without properly understanding, he asked:

– Can I know why you suddenly started praising Clarissa? I just didn't think you liked her.

– I never said that I didn't like Clarissa. At first, just as she arrived, I thought she was a busybody, used to the luxuries of that hacienda. But after she came up with that black religious story, I realized I was wrong. I think she is a very good girl and very smart too.

– Smart, right? Do you think she could end up discovering?

– She doesn't know what happened, and I don't think she can imagine it. But she says she heard spirits. So you have to be careful. She might start digging and discovering everything.

– That can never happen, do you hear me? Never.

– Therefore, it is better to find a way to send Clarissa back. If not, something tells me that she will find out, yes.

Abílio bowed his head and said no more. Just thinking that Clarissa might discover his secret, he was filled with fear. However, he could no longer send her away. He had married her and couldn't get rid of her like a pile of old clothes. He was a decent and honorable man, and he would never commit such an indignity. He had given her his word

How can he now commit such an offense, as if she were really a commodity to be bought and disposed of when it is no longer useful?

No. If she wanted to leave of her own free will, that was different. It would be her will, her choice to win the title of a non-coincident. But if she wanted to stay, the way was to do the possible and the impossible so that she would never discover the truth.

When Abílio returned to the house, he found no one. The last rays of the sun shone on the earth, and he went out on the porch to witness the majestic entrance of the moon. He was walking along the road leading to the beach, trying not to think about anything, when something caught his attention. Sitting on the beach, Clarissa and Vicente were talking, oblivious to everything and everyone, laughing like two close friends. Abílio found it strange, and a terrible feeling began to emerge within him. The son was a rebellious and withdrawn child, but he was young and extremely handsome. Was he in love with Clarissa and she with him?

After all, they were almost the same age.

Not wanting to make himself known, he hid behind an almond tree and began to spy. Clarissa and Vicente spoke animatedly, feeling the freshness of the night breeze on their skin. Clarissa said:

– You know, Vicente, you are a handsome and intelligent boy. Don't you want to go? – He shook the sand with a stick, shook his head and responded:

– If I want to, I want to. But I don't know what I would do far from here.

– Don't you think about going to study in the capital? You could go to the university.

– I have thought about it. But I don't know if that's what I want anymore.

– Why not? Doesn't your father approve?

– Yes. In fact, it's his greatest wish. That's why I don't know if it's mine anymore.

– You and your dad don't really get along, do you?

– I don't want to talk about it anymore.

– Why not? Maybe I can help you.

– Listen, Clarissa, I don't like my dad and that's it. I don't need help and I don't want anyone's help in learning to like him. I like things the way they are.

And then, I don't understand why the interest. Didn't you fight with him too? You're not talking either.

– This is different. Your father slandered me.

– And me too. Me, my sister, my mother... and now you. Do you see that I can only hate him?

– Okay, Vicente, I don't want to fight with you either.

– Great, because I couldn't stand it.

Clarissa felt blood rushing to her cheeks and asked, covered in blush:

– What?

– I couldn't bear to fight with you.

– Why?

– Because I like you so much. Maybe you're the only person I really like. Haven't you noticed yet?

– Vicente, please... you can't be serious.

– I'm more serious than ever. But don't worry. I know you are my father's wife and I mean no disrespect.

She blushed again and babbled:

– I... don't understand... what... what... I mean... You shouldn't talk like that... you're my stepson... and a child.

– I am not a child. And then you said you're not much older than me. How old are you? Nineteen? Twenty?

– Nineteen.

– Because I'm seventeen, almost eighteen. As you can see, we are practically the same age.

– Stop. We shouldn't be saying these things.

– I told you not to worry. I am an honorable man and I would never dare to disrespect my father's wife. However, I cannot hide my feelings.

I like you and there is nothing I can do about it. There is no rule over the heart.

– Stop, Vicente, don't say anything else. This is not right.

– Are you going to tell me that you don't feel the same way about me?

– No... that is... I like you, but like a brother...

– Brother a conversation. Do you think I didn't notice the way you look at me either? – Clarissa was amazed. That Vincente was really bold and pretentious. As he spoke, her indignation grew to the point that she, unable to contain her perplexity, jumped up and exclaimed:

– Stop it, Vincente! Where have you seen such absurdity? I am a married woman. What is worse, I am your father's wife. You are my stepson and you must respect me.

And I want you to know that you are wrong. I feel nothing for you, nothing!

Nothing but brotherly and selfless love. And now that's enough! I won't stand here and listen to these things anymore!

She turned away from him, enraged, and went to the house. She was furious, indignant, angry. She had never heard so much nonsense together! He was so amazed that he didn't even notice the presence of Abílio behind the almond tree, now hidden by the shadows of the night that had just fallen. Even in the darkness, he could see the confusion stamped on Clarissa's face.

From where he was, he had not been able to hear what they were saying, but he could imagine it. Vincente had certainly given her a compromising revelation, and she was outraged and ran away. If that were true, what would become of them? What would he do to help his son? Vincente would come to hate him even more because he would see in him not only the man who had stolen his mother's caresses, but also the man who had prevented him from having the woman he loved. May God help him, because that could not happen. He had already lost his wife. How can we bear to lose our child now?

CHAPTER 9

That night, Abílio could not sleep. He turned from side to side in bed, opened and closed his eyes, covered himself and threw away the sheets. No matter how hard he tried, he couldn't get that scene from the beach out of his mind and he felt great displeasure. He didn't know how to show his feelings, but he loved his children above all else. If Vincente was really in love with Clarissa, what could he do? What if she did it? Abílio would gladly have given up the girl because of the son. But now it seemed impossible. Even if he renounced his wife, could his son be happy with his father's wife in his arms? And what about society? How could he face the evil of others who would never forgive such betrayal?

Perhaps it was only a passing one. She was young, beautiful, intelligent, almost the same age as him. It would not be difficult for a boy to be interested in her. And he, Abílio, was already over forty, no longer a little boy. He recognized that his son looked a lot like him, but he was young. It would be very easy for Clarissa to fall in love with him too.

The more he thought about these things, the more he became restless. Suddenly, he became jealous of the woman. It was a mixture of feelings, a confusion that he didn't know how to define. If, on the one hand, he gave up Clarissa so that his son could have her, on the other hand, the idea of losing her filled him with jealousy. After all, she was his wife, who had married him. Vincente was her son, but he was a man. Was it right to wish him a wife?

And Clarissa refused to talk to him, didn't say a word to him, ignored him. If she stayed away from him, it was natural for her to look for someone to talk to and be distracted. Angelina was a good girl, however, she was very young. But Vicente... No longer supporting that doubt, Abílio stood up in awe. He lit the candle and

Memories that the wind brings

left, heading for Clarissa's room. He opened the door without knocking and entered. She was sleeping and was terrified when she saw him there, standing by her bed, looking at her with a strange glow in his eyes. He put the candle on the table and pulled the sheets off the bed, lying next to her, while she began to stutter:

– Mr. Abílio, you have no right...

– Yes I do, Clarissa. You are my wife, and it is the duty of every wife to surrender to her husband when he wishes.

Abílio lured her to her, trying to kiss her, and lay down on top of her. Clarissa began to fight and, covered with anger, managed to defend herself:

– Even if only what she feels for him are disgust and repugnance?

Abílio let her go, amazed. That was too much. Did Clarissa disgust him? Did she disown him? Why? Why did she want to be in his son's arms? Without saying anything, he got out of bed, recovered, picked up the candle, and left. At the door, he turned to her and spoke, his voice vibrating with emotion:

– I think it was a mistake to marry you, Clarissa, but now there is no remedy. Well done. I say again that you are free to go...

– Free? How can I be free when you threaten me with ruin and dishonor?

– That's not my problem. If you want to go, go. I think I'd even prefer you to go.

– You prefer?

– Yes. I cannot tolerate in my house a woman who does not respect me and who throws offenses of that caliber in my face. Do you want to leave? Let's go. But consider yourself responsible for what you do and the consequences that result.

– Should I understand this as a threat?

– Understand how you want to.

He turned his back on her and left, and Clarissa began to cry. She wanted to run away, to go home, but how? She felt she couldn't leave now. She was connected to Angelina and Vicente, and she couldn't leave them. However, she no longer supported Abílio's rudeness.

Helpless, Clarissa began to think about Toña. How she wished she could be there to help her. The former slave had been like her mother, and she felt lost without her wise counsel. Thinking of her, Clarissa fell asleep. In a few minutes, Toña appeared and partially disconnected her from her body, taking her for a walk along the shore. Clarissa was already getting used to those night walks.

When freed by sleep, she met Grandmother Toña, they went to the beach. It seemed that the sea air cleared her thoughts, helping her to understand what she could not achieve when she woke up.

- Clarissa, - Toña began to say - why did you ignore my advice?

- What advice?

- You know. About Abílio.

- Now, Grandma Toña, that man is hateful. Nobody likes him, not even his children.

- That is not true. The children are just hurt, but there is a lot of love in their hearts for their father.

- Injured? Why?

- You will soon find out.

- I don't know. Mr. Abílio wants me to leave.

- But you are not leaving.

- I confess that I am tempted. If it weren't for the threat of destroying my family...

- That's not why you won't leave.

- Well, it's true that I already joined Angelina and Vicente...

Memories that the wind brings

– This is not the reason either.

– No? And why would it be then?

– Because you know you can't. You know you have a job to do and you can't leave until you finish it.

– Job? But what job? I don't know what you're talking about.

– You do. You need to solve some outstanding problems.

– I don't understand. As much as I try, I don't remember what I could have done to Mr. Abílio that was so serious.

– Do you want to see it?

Clarissa nodded and Toña, approaching her, put her hand on her forehead and began to massage her. Immediately, a blue light began to spread in the darkness, reaching out to the sea, and Clarissa was transported back aboard the Portuguese ship. Her name was no longer Clarissa; it was Luisa.

Leaning over the railing, Luisa watched with pleasure as the boat approached the Lisbon dock. She was nostalgic for her homeland. She had spent a long time traveling, with her cousin and servants, but now it was time to return. She missed the comfort of home, the hustle and bustle of Lisbon, the sumptuous parties and the diversity of loves.

Luisa was a beautiful woman and extremely liberated by the standards of the time. She had dark blond hair, almost the same color as honey, and her eyes were black and shiny. The ladies of the court called her unbridled when she was not around. Her husband, Archduke of Linhares, had been a rich and powerful nobleman who had died some years earlier, leaving her an incalculable fortune and the title of Archduchess. Even before the wedding, Luisa was already a member of the nobility, the daughter of a highly respected count at the Portuguese court.

The marriage, arranged by her parents, had not brought her any joy. The archduke, forty-two years older than her, did not have the fiber she expected from a husband. He was stingy, cowardly, ugly. When she married, Luisa was only seventeen and he was fifty- nine. She rebelled because, at that time, she fell in love with a young baron, named Bertoldo, who was only twenty- seven years old, but whose connection with Luisa did not interest the count, her father. Two years after their marriage, the archduke suffered a heart attack, dying instantly.

During the time the marriage lasted, Louise had barely seen him. He spent long months traveling through Europe, and when he returned, he called her to his room for a night or two and attended his court parties, displaying her beauty like a trophy. But they barely spoke, and it was clear that their relationship was one of formality and appearance, with no common thread between them. So, when he died, Luisa was more than relieved, happy.

She had become a rich and independent woman, still young and beautiful, and was not willing to waste her youth on any other marriage of appearance. She didn't need any more of that. From then on, she could do whatever she wanted.

With all this, it was natural for her to arouse the curiosity and envy of the ladies of society at the time. Luisa, after all, represented a threat. Her free behavior made her take to bed any man she was interested in, whether he was married or single, young or old, rich or poor. Louise liked love and being a lover was her main fun. Her father had even cut off relations with her, forbidding her to go to his house, which ended up taking her away from the rest of the family. But that didn't stop her from having countless friends in court. It was not uncommon for young people to compete for her company, and she was delighted to see the effect she had on them when she entered the halls.

Despite the family's disdain, only one of her many cousins, Carlos Castanheira, had not severed relations with her. In love with the girl from her earliest childhood, there was not a minute left. Carlos was also a nobleman, and his incalculable fortune placed him in the comfortable position of being able to face the fury and intransigence of his uncle without fear. Because of his friendship with Luisa, the family also cut ties with him, and Carlos settled with his cousin, becoming her most faithful lover.

Such dedication could not go unnoticed by Luisa. Carlos was intelligent, cunning, kind and polite. In addition, he was an extremely attractive and friendly man, and was contested by the unmarried girls at court. But Carlos was not interested. He loved Luisa deeply, and the girl loved him, too, in her own way.

She caught him up in her adventures, and he didn't care. He also had his accomplishments and liked the new experiences. As long as Luisa returned to his arms at the end of each adventure, everything was fine. Then, to avoid scandals from her lovers, they were given real rewards, so they left without making any scandals.

But with Captain Nicanor, it had been different. He was handsome, masculine, manly. An unusual man, rude and, at the same time, gentle. He knew how to treat a woman like no one else. He was an excellent lover, ardent and daring; a master in the art of love. This was a delight for the fiery Luisa. As much as Carlos was her accomplice, Nicanor had a wild rage that delighted her, and she gave herself to him with an overwhelming passion, as she had never given herself to anyone else.

Thinking about these things, she leaned over the railing and waved. Many friends, on hearing of her arrival, came to greet her at the dock. She was radiant, greeting them from a distance when she heard Carlos' voice behind her:

– So, Luisa, are you happy with your return?

She looked at her cousin, trying to impress him with some distance, and responded:

– Yes, Carlos. I've been away for almost a year now. It's good to be back home. What about you? Aren't you happy?

Carlos looked deep into her black eyes. He wasn't stupid and realized that there was something different about that Nicanor. In the beginning, Luisa had acted as usual. She jumped into the captain's bed and then returned to him. But in the course of the trip, she began to avoid him and treat him coldly, avoiding his company. It had never happened before, and Carlos could see a different spark in Luisa's eyes when she looked at Nicanor. For the first time in his life, Carlos was afraid of losing her, and his heart contracted. He couldn't get through.

Holding her long, thin hands, Carlos declared, his voice trembling with emotion:

– I, more than anyone else, longed for the arrival.

Pretending not to understand the intention behind those words, Luisa responded with disinterest:

– Is it true? Why? Didn't you like the trip?

– You know why, – he answered, bringing his face closer to hers. Moving away from him, Luisa replied coldly:

– I can't imagine why. It was a very fun trip!

– Make no mistake – said Carlos quickly. – He will never be yours. Louise froze and responded, trying to look natural:

– I don't know what you're talking about.

– You do know it. I'm talking about our captain.

– Stop being jealous, Carlos, please. You know me...

– However, I say again that he will never be yours – . Feeling the anger growing inside her chest, Luisa screamed:

– Who told you? And what do you have with that?

– Nothing. I just don't want you to be disappointed and suffer.

– Well, I appreciate the concern, but I don't need you. I can take care of myself.

– I know you do. I still...

– Don't bother me, Carlos. You are my cousin and my lover. Not my owner – . Furious, Luisa turned her back on him and went to the other side. She no longer wanted to listen to that silly, useless conversation. It was obvious that Nicanor would be hers. She had not the slightest doubt. She felt sorry for Carlos, but she no longer loved him. She loved Nicanor, and he would be hers, one way or another. She was just waiting.

Back in the tumultuous air of the court, Luisa resumed her intense social life.

As soon as she arrived, she ordered a party to be prepared at her castle in Lisbon, to calm the yearning of her friends. All the nobles and nobles of Portugal were invited, including her father, who did not even bother to respond to the invitation.

Luisa always invited him, not out of love, but to confront him. The father, proud and moralistic, rebelled against these invitations, but did not give in to his provocations.

The party was magnificent, and no one wanted to miss the opportunity to attend the castle of the Archduchess of Linhares. Men went because they admired her, liked her beauty, her intelligent conversation, and her free gestures. Women came because they envied her and because they did not want to miss the opportunity to witness one more of her extravagances. Then, when the party ended and they left, they spoke badly of Luisa behind her, calling her libertine and unbridled. Luisa knew about these unpleasant comments, but she didn't care. Those women had their use. It was through them and their gossip that Luisa aroused more and more curiosity and attention from men, and that was what she liked most.

That particular night, Luisa was dazzling, ready to receive Captain Nicanor as her guest of honor. However, the hours passed and he didn't show up, which made her restless and upset. At the end of the day, when she no longer expected him to come, the captain finally appeared, attracted by the arm of the beautiful lady, whose delicate features those present could not help but admire. When she saw her beloved entering the corridors with such beautiful company, Luisa became enraged and went out to meet her like a cannonball: fast and ready to destroy.

As he approached her, she tried to stay calm and pose. After all, she was an archduchess and had not earned the admiration of men and women making scandals of their own. Trying to appear calm, she greeted the newcomers with a cold, penetrating smile:

– Captain Nicanor, what an honor your presence causes me!

– Your Highness – he answered, bowing – it was an honor to receive your invitation. But let me introduce you. This is my wife, Agripina de Sousa.

Agripina, may I present Your Highness, Luisa de Mello Alves, Archduchess of Linhares – . Lightning would not have struck her more violently. On hearing those words, Luisa almost fainted. She felt bad, had a dizzy spell and had to lean on the arm that Nicanor, in a studiously ceremonious way, extended to her.

– Are you feeling well, Your Highness? – she asked, with an air of feigned concern.

– Your Highness," interrupted Agrippina with interest, "would you like me to call someone?

– No, I am well. It was just a slight indisposition, nothing more. Luisa composed herself, smiled artificially and continued: – Welcome to my house, Mrs. Agripina. I hope you enjoy yourself. And now, if you'll excuse me, I need to see how the other guests are doing.

Luisa bent over and came out with lather. So that idiot was married. Why hadn't he told her? And what was he trying to do, take his wife there without even telling her? Did he want to confront her? Or was that how he had found to tell her that it was all over? That coward. He hadn't even had the dignity to tell her personally.

Feeling that she was going to explode, Luisa went up to her room. She needed to think and compose herself. She was a woman of the highest society in Lisbon and had no intention of giving her enemies reason to laugh at her. Not that. She would never be a source of contempt. Rather, she preferred to crush everyone.

Luisa was sitting on the bed, her face sunken in her hands, when she heard footsteps nearby. Looking at the floor, she saw two toes of men's boots and already knew who they belonged to before she even looked at them.

– What do you want? – she asked, without even looking up.

– Luisa, – spoke Carlos tenderly, – "I tried to warn you.

– Warn me of what? That he was married?

– Yes, but you didn't want to listen to me.

Luisa looked at him and sighed, letting the tears run down her face. Carlos, suffering from the penalty, sat down beside her and rested his head on her shoulder, adding full of understanding:

– Don't be sad my love. It will pass.

– Am I sad? Don't be fooled by my tears. I am not a woman to give up easily. If Nicanor thinks he can use me and then discard me, he is very much mistaken. He doesn't know who he's dealing with.

– What do you want to do? Take revenge? Destroy him?

– Destroy him? No. I intend to destroy their marriage.

– This is crazy, Luisa. You will only hurt yourself. He will never leave his wife for you.

– How do you know?

– I wanted to tell you on the boat, but you didn't listen.

The comments among the crew were that the captain is crazy about the woman and would never trade her for another. Although beautiful and rich like you.

Luisa felt the hatred growing inside her and, with her face on fire, she screamed:

– That's what he thinks! I'm not a woman to be rejected or abandoned! What did he do? Did he use me? Well, he is very much mistaken if he thinks I will resign myself to being used and abandoned like a fret. I'm not going. Nicanor will be mine, whatever it takes!

– Don't go crazy, Luisa. What can you do?

– I don't know yet, but I'll find a way. I'm powerful, influential, and he's nobody. I will crush him before he can even beg for my forgiveness.

Distressed, Carlos took her by the shoulders and, looking deep into her eyes, tried to commit himself:

– What's that for, Luisa? Can't you see I love you then? We always got along well, right? Why spoil everything now? Nicanor was just an adventure like so many others. Leave him with the woman and come back to me, as you always did. It was a game, Luisa, it's over – . She looked at him with disdain. When he let her go, she responded coldly:

– Was it a game? It could be... But I'll never be a loser. Never!

– Please, honey, forget about Nicanor. It's over now.

– No, it's not over. Now it's going to start.

– But what about me? How much longer do I have to wait?

She let out a sigh and looked at him with a cold look, adding coldly:

– I think it's time for us to say goodbye.

– What do you mean by that?

– I mean that our romance is over. I don't want you in my life anymore.

– You can't be serious.

– I have never been more serious in my life. I'm tired of you, I don't want you anymore. Please pack your things and go.

– But Luisa and our love?

– Love? – She smiled with disgust. – I'm sorry, Carlos, but it's over. Our love has vanished into the wind. After meeting

Nicanor, I can't love anyone else. I love Nicanor and only him, and he has to be mine.

Carlos was full of hate. He loved Luisa, and that little captain had appeared out of nowhere to try to steal her away. He had to stop him. The captain had to be destroyed. He would do anything to get him out of his way. Luisa could not love him. She had been hurt in her pride by the only man who had dared to get rid of her. It could only be that and, as painful as it was, it would be up to him to show her that truth.

Suddenly, the vision vanished and Clarissa returned to the shore, next to Toña. She was indignant and confused. Why did Grandma Toña show her these things?

- You know, my daughter," answered Toña instantly, "sometimes God allows us to see the things of yesterday so that we can understand today and improve tomorrow.

- I don't know if I understand very well... What was all this about?

- Do you really not understand everything that happened?

- I know I was Luisa and Abílio, Nicanor. But what happened between us doesn't justify what I'm going through today.

- You have compromised yourself for power, for jealousy, for possession. Luisa never loved Nicanor, but she didn't know how to lose him to his wife.

- But he used me!

- You can only use someone who lets himself be used. And then, in a relationship, there are mutual interests, and everyone takes advantage of what is best for them. When the relationship is one of love, the benefit you both get is the most sublime and rewarding. There are no fees, no complaints, no pride, no ownership. Only happiness and pleasure.

But you were connected by physical attraction and sex. There was nothing else that could fill your hearts, and any such relationship tends to run out when the novelties of sex are exhausted. One must be aware of the risks and know how to lose. And you didn't know how to lose the man who was the object of your desires to the woman he really loved.

– But I loved him too!

– You did not love him. If you really loved him, you would have let him go when he decided to stay with his wife. But you were hurt in your pride because losing Nicanor was much more than the loss of your lover, it was, above all, the loss of a power that you believed to be absolute. Only there are no absolute powers, especially over things of the heart. If we cannot rule in our own hearts, much less those that do not belong to us. No one can determine, either yourself or anyone else, who will like it and for how long. She reflected for a few moments, until she became curious:

– But what happened next? What did I do to Nicanor so that he, today, in Abílio's body, would take revenge on me in this way?

– He is not exactly getting back at you. He is trying to overcome the difficulties, but they are still latent in his soul. They are feelings that he cannot define, but that is not lost over the years. It is necessary to modify these feelings, not to despise them.

– Is that why he tries to trample on me? Why can't he, intimately, overcome the damage I did to him?

– You haven't hurt him. He was living by his spiritual maturity at the time, acting in the way he thought was right. Just as he, today, acts in the way he thinks is most appropriate, even though, internally, he strives to change. An effort he has not yet attempted to make.

– But what can I do, grandma Toña? The presence of Mr. Abílio repulses me... Wasn't it you who said that you can't be ruled?

Then I am not to blame for not liking him. How can I try to accept him if all I feel for him is contempt?

– Open your heart and it will be easier. You are closed to your truth and you are blind to anyone else.

– Am I? Mr. Abílio thinks he owns the truth, not me.

– You are so concerned about your suffering that you cannot see that others are suffering around you.

– If you mean Abílio, he suffers because he wants to. No one told me to leave my house.

– If so, you want to suffer too. Why did you ask to be reincarnated with this family?

– But I didn't ask!

– You know what you asked for. And you are suffering from your own stubbornness. But it doesn't have to be that way. No one has to suffer. Just make yourself available for the life that it takes to show you the right path. Do not resist, Clarissa, disarm yourself and surrender to your destiny. It is difficult and exhausting to walk against the force of the wind.

– I don't know if I can do what you are asking. No matter how hard I try, I cannot agree with the tyranny of Abílio.

– You don't have to agree with him. Submission hinders growth and encourages the dominator to remain in the tyranny. Have fun with him, but with love. Express your opinions, your ideas, without fear of contradicting yourself, but do it with respect and love. There is no need to shout or fight, but be energetic when necessary. Be firm, not aggressive. If you manage to do this, you will soon see that Abílio will also disarm and begin to trust you, and you will be surprised what a wonderful man he is.

– Wonderful? I find that hard to believe.

– Well, believe me. Abílio put on a veil and it will be up to you to help him fall.

– I don't know if I can do it.

Memories that the wind brings

– Were you not able to with Vicente?

– With Vicente it was different. He is still a child, very angry and lost...

– Just like his father. But you had patience and determination with Vicente that you don't have with Abílio, right?

– Yes, that's true.

– And did you see how easy it was to win him over?

– Vicente is a needy child. In need of love...

– So is Abílio. The difference is that you easily recognized a friendly spirit in Vincente, whose affinities soon made you break the ice wall he had erected in your midst.

– Vincente, friendly spirit? but who?

– She thought for a moment, and then identified him in her past – was it Carlos?

– That's right. You and Carlos are kindred spirits, and it was easy to get along with him. But your reconciliation must be with Abílio. Don't miss this opportunity, Clarissa, as it will be the only one in this life.

Clarissa lowered her eyes and began to cry. Deep down, she knew Toña was right. She felt that she needed to learn to love Abílio as she had already learned to love Vicente.

But it all seemed so difficult! He was irascible and rude, and she was upset by the fate that her father had sealed for her. How could she overcome the natural dislike she felt for him?

As if listening to his thoughts, Toña took Clarissa's hand and answered simply:

– Pray, Clarissa, pray...

Then she took her back to the physical body and disappeared into thin air.

CHAPTER 10

In the days that followed, Clarissa decided to change her behavior. She wanted to end that fight between her and Abílio. After all, they were married and could live in peace, so why start a war at home? It didn't lead to anything. She didn't agree with the things he was doing, but she didn't have to destroy him like that. She needed to find a way to remedy that situation, overcome her own pride and make the rapprochement a reality. But how?

The opportunity came one sunny and very hot Sunday, when Angelina went to her room early in the morning.

– Ah! Angelina, come in – said Clarissa, seeing her standing at the door.

– I'm coming down.

– Why don't we take a walk today?

– Walking? Where would you like to go?

– We can have a picnic. There are so many beautiful places you don't know... Clarissa looked at herself in the mirror. I was really tired of staying there. Since her arrival, the farthest she had gone was to the beach, near Fort San Mateo.

The city he only knew the day he arrived, and had little or nothing to keep hidden in its streets. She had become tired, traumatized by the impressions of the shipwreck, and had not paid much attention to anything.

– I have a better idea – said Clarissa, after a few minutes, "why don't we go into town?

– The city?

– Yes. I hardly know it. I would like to see the streets, the school, where you and Vicente study, the church. There is a church, isn't there?

– In fact, more than one.

– So, wouldn't you like to be my guide on this tour?

– Hum... if daddy leaves us.

– Yes, he will, I'm sure.

– Are you going to ask him?

– Well, Angelina, I thought maybe you could talk to him.

– I know... you guys are still fighting, right?

– That's right.

Angelina thought for a few seconds, with an index finger on her lips, until she agreed:

– It's okay. I'm going to talk to him.

– Excellent.

– Wait here, I'll be right back.

She ran to her father's room. It was early and he hadn't come down for coffee yet. She knocked on the door slightly, and came to open it himself.

– Angelina! – he exclaimed, surprised that she rarely went to his room.

– Did something happen?

– It happens, nothing happens. But I would like to ask you something.

– What is it?

– You know, Dad, it's just that Clarissa and I have been thinking... we'd like to take a walk around town. That is, if it's okay with you, of course...

Abílio bit his lip and looked at his daughter. He thought Clarissa would return home, but she, for a reason he didn't know, had decided to stay. She was his wife, and he couldn't lock her in the house. He recognized that she never went out and thought it would be a good idea to take her to the city. Who knows, maybe he would pass on some ideas?

– It's all right, my daughter – he said at last. After breakfast, I'll take you. I really have to arrange some things with my friend Maurício, and I can leave you in the square and then pick you. How about it?

– Oh! Daddy, it's perfect! Thank you!

Instinctively, Angelina ran toward her father, threw herself on his neck and kissed him on the cheek, leaving him disconcerted and blushing. The daughter had always been a very sweet girl, but after Leonor left, she ended up moving away from him and rarely kissed him. Or was it he who moved away from her? So the kiss filled him with pleasure, and he clumsily stroked his daughter's head.

After breakfast, Angelina and Clarissa prepared to leave. The girl adorned Angelina's dress and tied a ribbon in her hair, combing it with grace and joviality.

Then he carefully dressed, powdered his face and left. Abílio was already waiting for them in the cart, along with Tiago, who would lead the oxen. Abílio helped his daughter up and, once she was settled, he reached out his hand to help Clarissa. She clumsily took his hand, and for a moment her eyes met.

Abílio felt a chill and Clarissa was moved. What's going on? Why did she feel that emotion for a man she detested?

After climbing the stairs, his eyes fell on the living room window and he saw Vicente, who was looking through the glass. Even from a distance, Clarissa could see a cloud of hate on his face. Paying no attention to the boy, Tiago set the cart in motion, and the oxen began to move. They had not run two meters when Clarissa screamed:

– Wait! Stop!

Memories that the wind brings

Tiago stopped the animals, confused. He thought she had fallen, but she didn't. She and Angelina were fine. As soon as he stopped, Clarissa stood up and cupped her hands around his mouth and called out:

– Vicente! Vicente!

Abílio shuddered. What was she doing? Facing him? She looked at the house again and saw when her son appeared at the front door.

– What happened? – he asked, his voice charged with anger.
– Come here, Vicente, come with us! Let's go for a walk!

The boy was confused, not knowing what to do. His heart, at the moment he heard Clarissa's voice, almost jumped out of his mouth, and he thought he would faint with happiness. But when he saw her in the stroller, together with her sister and father, he was discouraged. He did not want their company, he did not tolerate them.

– Come on, Vicente! – insisted Clarissa.

Abílio thought of telling Tiago to move the cart forward. However, she spoke to her son and he couldn't turn his back on her abruptly. He knew that Vincent hated him, but she did not feel the same way about him. The son did not open up to him, and Abílio did not know how to win his love and trust.

Seeing that he was not making up his mind, Abílio decided to intervene:

– If you want to come with us, Vicente, hurry up.

– Come, Vicente, please – Clarissa continued asking.

– Why do you want him to go? – interrupted Angelina.

– He's a busybody and he'll only get in the way.

– Don't talk like that about your brother, Angelina – interrupted the father.

– It's not right.

She lowered her eyes and whispered:

Memories that the wind brings

– Dad, I'm sorry.

– So, señóziño, how is it? – Tiago asked.

– Are you coming or not?

After a few minutes of reflection, weighing up the pros and cons, Vincent decided to accept. Father and sister be damned. He liked Clarissa and only accepted the invitation for her, to be with her, to enjoy her company, her laughter, her beauty. Without answering, he slammed the door and ran, reaching the wagon in a few seconds. He got on the back and sat down next to Clarissa, smiling at her. Abílio pretended not to notice the enormous sympathy flowing between them and ordered Tiago to leave.

In silence, Tiago moved the cart again and they left. On the way, Clarissa was enchanted by the landscape, taking the opportunity to enjoy all that incomparable beauty. Suddenly, she heard Vicente's voice, asking her:

– Where are we going?

– I don't know, go for a walk. I want to see the city, your school, go to church...

– We'd better go to church first – suggested Angelina.

– Then we can walk around the city.

– Why do you want to go to church, Clarissa?

He looked at the horizon, took a deep breath and responded:

– I would like to pray a little. Thank God for being alive.

Abílio discreetly looked at Tiago out of the corner of his eye. Was she being sincere or just disguised?

– Are you religious? – Vincent asked. Have you always gone to church in your country? – Clarissa threw her head back, enjoying the morning sun, and answered, without opening her eyes – I don't know if I'm religious. I believe in God and his various manifestations. I know that God exists and that he can hear us anywhere: in the church, at home, or in the black earth.

Memories that the wind brings

She ended this prayer by opening her eyes and looking directly into the eyes of Vincent, who responded:

– If so, why do you want to go to church? Why don't you pray at home or ask Tiago to take you...

– Enough, Vicente! – ordered the father – . You said too much.

Vicente remained silent. In fact, he had said too much. His father didn't like people talking about the place Tiago frequented, because he didn't want anyone to know he was going with him. Since his mother left, he had resorted to such beliefs.

They followed the rest of the route in silence, each immersed in his own thoughts. When they arrived in town, Clarissa, Angelina and Vicente jumped up and down, and the girls went directly to the church of Our Lady of the Assumption. They arrived just in time for Mass, and Clarissa attended the service with respect, praying fervently.

He did not believe that temples or images were necessary to connect with God, he recognized that a prepared environment helped a lot, and that the church had a beneficial aura that brought him great peace.

After the mass, they left. Vincent was waiting for them outside, sitting near the bandstand, and got up as soon as he saw them, running to meet them. Flanked by Vicente and Angelina, Clarissa went for a walk in the streets. Streets? In fact, there were very few streets, lit by kerosene lamps, cut through by alleys and streets, where you could see some wooden houses and residential houses. They visited the convent and the church of Our Lady of the Guide, the Third Order of Sao Francisco, and went to the Beach Street, where the city's commerce was concentrated, closed that day, flanked by the Itajuru channel, with green and crystalline waters.

Around noon, they returned to the square, sat down and ate the snack that Clarissa had prepared. They were tired, however,

Memories that the wind brings

happy. They had a lot of fun, and Clarissa had to accept that the city, although small, had its charm. The sky and the sea gave it a natural and fantastic color, and now she was beginning to recognize its beauty. Cabo Frio was, in fact, a majestic place, where nature had been luxurious in its attributes, concentrating the most wonderful things there.

– And then, Clarissa – asked Vicente – what did you think of our city?

– I confess that I am impressed – she answered, without looking away from Angelina, who was running after some puppies, shouting at the girl: – Watch out, Angelina, look at the horses and cars! – Angelina looked at her and smiled.

– Don't worry – she said. – I will be careful.

Angelina returned to the sidewalk, carrying one of the puppies on her lap, and continued to play with it. Seeing the girl safe, Clarissa turned to Vicente and continued:

– The city is still far away, but the natural beauty is incredible.

– However, you will agree with me that the lack of roads makes the city uninteresting to visit.

– Yes, of course. It is difficult for someone to be interested in a place whose only access is by sea and whose crossing can be quite dangerous.

– It is true. Either that, or it's fourteen hours on horseback, through the forest.

– This is impossible. No one in their right mind...

Suddenly, they heard a scream, and Clarissa jumped up, looking for Angelina. The girl had disappeared, as well as the puppy she was playing with. Looking a little further, she saw a small crowd near an ox cart and her heart skipped a beat. Vicente gave her a look that said everything and ran, and Clarissa ran after him. When they arrived, Angelina was lying on the ground in front of the cart, passed out, with a stream of blood running from her forehead. Clarissa paled and almost fainted, and Vicente, more than quickly, knelt beside his sister, placing his ear to her chest.

– She's still breathing – he said with relief.

– It was not my fault – the old man who was driving the cart excused himself – . She jumped in front of me, came running. I didn't have time to dodge...

The man was disconsolate. In fact, Angelina, trying to hold the puppy, had run after him, but the puppy had run away and the girl could not dodge the car in time.

– Angelina! Angelina! – Clarissa called. – Can you hear me? For God's sake, Angelina, say something.

Angelina did not respond. She was unconscious and did not hear anything. Suddenly, they heard a loud voice from the crowd:

– Let me take her! I'm the girl's father, let me through!

When Clarissa saw Abílio approaching, she jumped up and exclaimed, grabbing his hand and bringing him closer to Angelina:

– Oh! Thank God you're here, Mr. Abílio! Help me! We need to get her to a doctor.

– Sir, it was not my fault, – the old man continued to apologize. – It was an accident, it was not my fault. She ran after the dog, I didn't have time...

But Abílio didn't even listen to the old man. Without saying a word, he bent over his daughter and lifted her onto his lap, talking to Tiago, standing right behind him:

– Go get the car.

More than quickly, Tiago went to get the car, and soon they put the little one in the back, resting her head on Clarissa's lap. They rushed in and left.

– Quickly! – ordered Abílio – . To the house of Father Joaquim.

Memories that the wind brings

Tiago cracked the whip on the back of the oxen, which went to Father Joaquim's house. Who would he be? Clarissa was intrigued, but thought it best not to ask questions.

She was focused on the girl and asked God to save her.

– How did it happen? – Abílio asked abruptly.

Vicente looked at Clarissa. He knew there would be a storm there and preferred not to say anything. It wasn't his fault if his sister ended up under a car. Clarissa, however, responded calmly:

– We were talking, while Angelina was playing with the puppy. Suddenly, we heard a scream, and when we looked, she was lying next to the car.

– You noticed, Clarissa. Angelina is a child and you should take care of her. It was irresponsible!

Clarissa bit her lip in anger. She wanted to scream at him, but he held back. Instead, she chose her words well and responded in a calm, yet firm tone:

– You are right, Mr. Abílio, I was distracted. I had already called her attention once and I confess that I thought she was safe on the sidewalk. When I saw her lying on the ground, I felt a deep pain, and if anything happens to her, I will be blamed. – And she began to cry softly. She was so sorry and her tears were so sincere that Abílio felt it. He thought of saying something to comfort her, but he didn't know what. Seeing that Abílio didn't say anything and was sorry for the girl's situation, Tiago moved on:

– There is no need to worry, siña Clarissa, that little Angelina will not die.

Angelina began to moan and move her head, turning it from side to side. Suddenly, she opened her eyes and, seeing Clarissa crying and stroking her hair, she babbled:

– Clarissa... what... what what... what happened? – Shh! my child, don't talk, you've had an accident, but you'll soon be fine. Angelina closed her eyes and fell asleep. Her head hurt and was spinning, and she really didn't feel like talking. Abílio, who had turned around as soon as she began to stutter, turned around, moved forward again and looked sideways at Tiago, who said nothing.

A few minutes later, the cart stopped next to a wooden house, in a place a little farther away from the city, and at that very moment, a very old black man, leaning on a cane and smoking a fragrant pipe, came to meet him.

– What happened? – he asked, looking at the girl, lying on Clarissa's lap.

– Father Joaquim, please help me, he begged Abílio – . My daughter had an accident. It was an ox cart...

– Bring the girl inside.

Abílio picked her up again and went in with her, forgetting Clarissa and Vicente, who followed him in silence. He laid her down on a bed of straw and waited. Just after, Father Joaquim reappeared from the back of the house. He had gone out to pick some herbs. Silently, he examined Angelina's forehead, tested the cut and she groaned in pain. He picked up the herbs and disappeared into the cabin, returning a few minutes later with what appeared to be a cast. Carefully, he put it on Angelina's forehead, who shook off the contact of those cold, wet herbs. When he was finished, he covered it with a sheet and said:

– Don't worry, Mr. Abílio. The girl will be fine. It was just a scare. A little swelling here, a little headache, but soon, soon, it will pass.

Abílio and Clarissa sighed with relief. Even Vincent relaxed.

– Can we take her?

– Yes, I don't see a problem. But don't take the herbs out until tomorrow morning. Let the girl rest for today, and tomorrow will be better. It was nothing serious, believe me. Abílio thanked her emotionally, kissed the old man's hand and left, carrying Angelina.

Memories that the wind brings

Clarissa went after him without saying a word. She had known the slaves well, knowing that this man was a healer. Now he was sure. Abílio even participated in the cult of the blacks and was apparently known in the middle. With that certainty, Clarissa looked at him, who was sitting in the front seat, and thought that, if he believed in the religion of the blacks, he shouldn't be so bad.

There must be something good in him, something he hid, but she would eventually reveal.

Clarissa finished putting Angelina to bed, after serving her delicious vegetable soup with orange juice. The girl fell asleep immediately, was tired and had a little headache, and it didn't take her long to fall asleep. Clarissa went downstairs to meet Abílio. He was sitting on the porch, enjoying the spectacle of the wind, which was raising curls of sand, when she arrived and sat down next to him. Abílio said nothing, waiting for her to say something.

After a few minutes of silence, she began:

– Mr. Abílio, I would like you to excuse me for today's episode. I know I was careless, but I promise it will not be repeated. When I saw Angelina lying under that car, my heart sank, and I felt that if I lost her, I would be losing a daughter.

A strong emotion ran through Abílio's chest, and tears came to his eyes. Without even realizing it, he liked Clarissa's approach, and her voice sounded sweet to his ears. But even if he wanted to, he didn't know how to show his feelings and simply said:

– Don't worry, I know it wasn't your fault. It was an accident, no one could have predicted it. And then, Father Joaquim assured me that it was not serious. Just a slight blow, nothing more.

You don't have to accuse yourself, because even I am not accusing you.

She smiled gratefully and felt as if her heart was opening and reaching out to Abílio's heart, realizing all the anguish in his soul. She put her hand in his and asked:

– What is it that afflicts you so much?

At that moment, Abílio and Clarissa were one step away from sincere reconciliation. Both were overcome by emotion, ready to forgive and forget, ready for love. But Abílio, unaccustomed to those caresses and even attached to the image of Leonor, withdrew his hand abruptly and responded ashamed:

– Don't worry about me, I'm fine. Like you, I was also worried about the accident, but it's over now.

– Is that all? Nothing else?

– No. And I wish you wouldn't ask me so many questions. I am not a man to bow down to the interrogation of any woman.

– Why are you ungrateful! – Clarissa was enraged, blushing with rage. – I come here with the best of intentions, willing to pay you my solidarity and put an end to this disagreement between us, and you treat me as if I were a servant? You know I'm sorry, and from today on, I won't move a straw to try to make peace with you. Keep your bitterness, because it's the one that best suits your permanent state of mind!

She turned furious and headed for the room. Abílio, however, seeing that she had exceeded herself, and not wanting to lose that opportunity, jumped up, ran after her and, pulling her by the hand, made her turn and look at him. Completely dazed, he lowered his eyes and said almost in a whisper:

– Sorry. You're right, I was rude, I'm sorry.

He wanted to take her in his arms and kiss her, but he managed to restrain himself. He could not fail and betray his Leonor. However, the proximity of Clarissa's body, the heat emanating from her body, her soft perfume, all this was making him give in, and Abílio slowly brought his face closer to hers, until he almost touched her lips. At that moment, a gust of wind burst into the room, hitting windows and doors, and knocking over some papers that were on the table. Clarissa, puzzled, began to stutter, bending down to pick up the leaves scattered on the floor:

– Wow.. what... what a strong... wind... It's even scary...

Memories that the wind brings

– It's the southwest. When it hits, it's like this.

Trying to relax the tension of the moment. Clarissa continued that conversation, without the slightest interest:

– Is it the same thing that sank us?

– No. That was the northeast. This is the southwest.

– Northeast, southwest, it's all wind, isn't it?

– Yes.

She finished picking up the papers, placing them back on the table and holding them so they would not fly again. The wind, unaware of what was happening, continued to invade the house, entering the halls, smoothing the furniture, howling through the cracks.

As if under a spell, Abílio was still standing in the same place, seeing Clarissa next to him, her hair in disarray, trying to hold the leaves between her fingers. He was intoxicated and confused, struggling desperately not to feel what he was feeling.

It was not possible. That's why he hadn't married.

– Mr. Abílio! – shouted Clarissa, waking him up to reality.

– Why don't you close the doors and windows? That way it will be impossible...

– What? – made Abílio wonder.

– Windows. Close them or the wind will blow everything away.

– What? Ah! Yes, the windows.

He turned quickly, running to close doors and windows. The wind, trapped outside, seemed to rage, sweeping away the glass in a desperate struggle to get inside. Everything closed, Clarissa dropped the papers and responded, accompanied by the incessant woooooooo... of the wind.

– Thank you. Well, and now, if I may, I will retire. It's late and I'm exhausted. Good night.

Memories that the wind brings

Abílio wanted to stop her and even started moving towards her, but he backed off. He couldn't do that. It wasn't right. Biting his lips and rubbing his hands together nervously, he responded, his voice vibrating with emotion:

– Good night.

After blowing out the candle, Clarissa covered herself and heard the moaning of the wind: uiuiuiui... She was used to it and was no longer afraid. However, she was afraid. An indescribable fear, like never before experienced. She was not afraid of the wind, nor of abandonment, nor of the threat of ruin. She was afraid of Abílio. For a reason she did not know, Abílio had come to populate her thoughts, and she could not sleep, because she was thinking of him. Was she falling in love? She didn't believe it. Perhaps she was impressed by his manners, his firmness, his determination. Clarissa thought he could be a very nice man, if she wanted to. Suddenly, she realized that she was no longer disgusted by him. She even admired him. He was an attractive and masculine man, although his features were furrowed by time and pain. She was thinking like this when, once again, she heard a groan reverberate behind the sound of the wind. He was an uiuiuiui... prolonged, as if someone were inside in deep suffering. Shee listened and listened. The noise seemed to come from down the hall, and she thought of getting up and going there. Should she? It would not be better to stay there, in the comfort of her bed, and not get involved with it. What if it was a tormented spirit? She would faint if she saw one. She closed her eyes and tried to sleep, but that uiuiuiui... feel, mixed with the uiuiuiui... of the wind, left her confused and curious. She needed to overcome her fear and discover what it was all about. She got up in bed and lit the candle on the side table, listening again. The noises were still there, but now they were getting louder. Struggling to overcome the fear, she said to herself aloud:

Memories that the wind brings

– Now, now, Clarissa, stop being afraid and get up. Spirits do not harm anyone. We should fear the living, not the dead.

Armed with courage, she took the candle, got up, opened the door and went out into the hallway, trying to see in the half-light. As soon as she looked down the hall, she stopped in horror, afraid to take another step. She saw. The instant she left, she saw a figure enter the last room, and her blood froze. Thinking quickly, she decided to go there. She walked down the corridor in the dark, feeling the touch of the ground on her feet, while the noise of the wind deafened her ears: uiuiuiui...

But she no longer heard the human moan. When she reached the door of the room that had belonged to Leonor and had seen the figure enter, she stopped and approached her ear to the door, trying to perceive some sound. In fact, it seemed to her that, in the distance, someone was crying. They no longer heard moans, but the agonizing cry of someone. Clarissa put her hand to her mouth and drowned out a scream. That alone could be Leonor's tormented spirit. She was already sure.

Tested the latch. It wasn't locked, and she pushed. The door opened slowly, accompanied by a strong... and she went in. The room was empty

At the same time, the noises stopped. Cautiously, Clarissa placed the candle on the bedside table and studied the room she was in. It was a large room that smelled of mold and darkness. It seemed to be intact long ago; dust was accumulating on the furniture. It had been tastefully furnished. A bed, a small table near the door, some carefully arranged armchairs, a heavy closet leaning against the wall. Near the window, a small green velvet sofa, on which rested a kind of nightgown. She approached and held that garment in his hand. It was made of linen, finished off with rich English embroidery. It could only have belonged to Mrs. Leonor.

Clarissa put the nightgown back on the couch and pulled back the curtains. They were dirty, covered with dust, and she sneezed several times. She let go of them and turned abruptly into the hallway, looking for fresh air. When she turned around, a figure standing in the doorway made her stop and put her hand to her chest, screaming in terror. The figure laughed and approached her:

– Did I scare you?

– Vicente! That's not done. It almost scares me! – Still laughing, she continued:

– I'm sorry, I didn't mean to.

– What are you doing here?

– I ask you, what are you doing here, passing by my mother's room?

She was confused. She didn't want to seem intrusive and didn't want to talk to him about what she had seen and heard. I already knew his opinion about it and wasn't willing to listen to your sarcasm.

– Nothing – she finally said. – I'm not doing anything.

– I know... And you got up in the middle of the night to come here and do nothing? Now, Clarissa, who are you kidding?

– I don't want to fool anyone. And then, I don't think I owe you any satisfaction.

– You're in my mother's room, and that's a good reason to explain to me what you were doing, whether you like it or not.

She did not respond, and he continued: – I know. I bet what the ghosts were like. It was them, wasn't it? You've been seeing ghosts again. Well, Clarissa, frankly.

Why didn't you call me soon? I would have scared them off with a cross. Hahaha.

– I don't see anything funny.

– Not? Go. You are very funny, Clarissa. Hahaha!

– Stop it, Vicente! Why are you treating me like this? You seem to be angry with me. Why? What have I done to you?

Vincent was silent, dazed. Deep down, he was taking out his frustration on her. He had seen her with her father in the living room and was filled with anger. Hearing the wind, he had come down to close the windows, thinking there was no one in the room, and hid at the bottom of the stairs as soon as he saw his father and Clarissa looking at each other in that strange way. She had filled him with envy and resentment, although she did not want to feel those things. Realizing what he was doing, he changed his tone of voice and considered:

– You are right, Clarissa, forgive me. I was only joking.

– This is a joke in very bad taste. I don't like to be changed.

– Well, I'm sorry, I told you. I didn't mean to upset you.

But don't change the subject. I think you're just deflecting the conversation so you don't have to say what you were doing in my mother's room.

– I don't think I need to say anymore. You've already discovered everything, haven't you? – She went through it like a bullet and went back to her room. She wasn't angry, but she was worried about what she had seen and heard. It was a spirit that haunted her, and she needed to help him. Everything told her that the spirit belonged to Doña Leonor, who seemed not to have rested yet. But why? Was it because she committed suicide?

She knew that the suicides were going to a place of great suffering, and perhaps Leonor was trapped in one of these places, suffering and asking for help. Either way, she was willing to help. But what would she do? She would pray. Clarissa would pray that God would have mercy on that soul and send one of his emissaries to seek and comfort her.

Angelina woke up more willingly. Her head still hurt a little, but it was a much lighter pain than the one she had felt the

Memories that the wind brings

day before. When she opened her eyes, the first thing she saw was Clarissa next to her, holding a coffee tray in her hand.

– How are you today? – she asked with a smile. Do you feel better?

She yawned, stretched and touched her forehead, grimacing, and responded:

– I'm better, thanks.

– Excellent. Now, let me help you sit down and have breakfast.

– Thanks Clarissa, I'm hungry.

She started eating and Clarissa admired her. She was such a beautiful and sweet girl! Why did her father treat her that way, almost ignoring her? The day before, she had seen the fear and worry in his eyes, and felt that he must love his daughter. However, Abílio was a hard and cold man, unable to show or express his feelings. Did he really love his children or did he feel trapped by his duty to educate them?

At that moment, there was a soft knock on the door, and Abílio opened it, asking quietly:

– Can I enter?

– Yes you can, Abílio. She is already awake. Abílio came in and sat down on the bed next to her.

– What a scare we had yesterday, eh, miss?

She lowered his eyes and responded with a weak voice:

– Dad, I'm sorry.

– I hope you will be more careful next time.

– Leave it, Dad, it won't happen again.

– Excellent...

Clarissa was amazed. After what the girl had been through, she didn't even ask if she was better, not one word of love or comfort? Nothing, just scolding? Barely holding back her indignation, she looked at him angrily and fired:

– Mr. Abílio, I know you didn't ask, but if you're interested, your daughter is much better off today.

He gave her a scornful look and said coolly:

– I know she is, that's why I didn't ask.

– How can you know?

– Father Joaquim said she would be.

She opened her mouth, dazed. It is true that she believed in the power of slaves and their herbs and potions, but that was too much! Just because Father Joaquim had told her that Angelina would get better was no reason to ignore her. Clarissa thought of striking, but changed her mind. She was interested in Leonor's room and didn't want him to be angry with her.

When the girl finished eating, Clarissa took the tray and left. She was about to go downstairs, but stopped at the top of the stairs and turned around, looking out into the hallway.

Carefully, she placed the tray on the floor, very close to the wall, and went to Leonor's room. When she stopped in front of the door, she hesitated. Was she acting right? She pulled the latch, but the door did not move. It was locked. Who had locked it? Was it Vicente? Or Abílio?

This question led her to another question: who would have opened the door the night before? Certainly, the ghosts did not open doors. They walked through them. But if it were a person, who had opened it? Where had they hidden it? When she entered the room, she saw no one. Was it really a flesh and blood person she had seen? But the door was open, that's what it was. In her opinion, only one person could have opened it, and that person was Abílio. Angelina was hurt and was sleeping soundly. Vincente appeared later and had surprised her from behind. Only Abílio didn't show up. Why? Had he fallen asleep and heard nothing? And why was the door now closed? She needed to know.

Memories that the wind brings

Determined, she turned to the stairs and picked up the tray, going down the steps. There was no one in the room. Vicente had already left for school, and Abílio wasn't there. Where would he be? She turned her face towards the kitchen and practically guessed that she could only be with Tiago. She left through the back door and went to his hut, approaching it very slowly. As she got closer, she heard voices coming from one of the windows. Clarissa bent down and, almost crawling, went to stand directly under the window, listening as loudly as she could. The first voice she recognized was that of Abílio:

– ... I am sure. She can't narrowly discover everything.

– Hum... This is becoming dangerous – responded Tiago, with a voice of extreme concern.

– I know, but what do you want me to do? Oh my God, why did I do that, why?

– There is no point in complaining now. It is done, it is done.

– But Tiago, you don't understand. I had no right to end his life...

– But she asked for it.

– Likewise. I didn't have that right...

– Calm down. Siñá Leonor was suffering, making you and the children suffer. You know that her greatest suffering was this.

– I know, I know...

– And then, they were going to take her away. Nobody wanted that, right?

– No...

– Then she asked you to do what you did. To stop suffering.

– No, Tiago. She didn't stop suffering. She did it so that we wouldn't suffer. And for what? What good did she do?

– Please don't think about it anymore. You have another wife now. It is about her that you must think and you must make sure that you do not discover anything.

Memories that the wind brings

– She will find out. I know she will. Oh my God, what will become of me? What will become of my children if I am arrested?

– Don't even tell me that! You won't be arrested, you didn't do anything.

– But Leonor...

– Siñá Leonor did her will. You did nothing!

Abílio was crying uncontrollably and Clarissa paled, leaving the house as quickly as she could. Terrified, she ran to her room and closed the door, panting and sweating with fear and indignation. This revelation was frightening and cleared up many things. Had Abílio killed his wife? He would have had the courage to end her life, but did he also end her suffering? As far as she could see, it was a request from Leonor herself. And Abílio agreed, he had dealt her the fatal blow. Or what would he have done? Shot her? Poisoned her? Drowned her? Clarissa was horrified. As much as she understood that Leonor had asked Abílio to end her own life, she could not agree with what he had done. A man capable of killing, even out of pity, was capable of anything. She was terrified. What if he decided to eliminate her too?

Trying to stay calm, he tried to reason clearly. No. Certainly, Abílio had killed his wife because she insisted, but he was afflicted by remorse. It was clear that he had repented and was in great pain for what he had done. This was a good sign. At least he wasn't a monster. Clarissa imagined the despair that must have driven him to this extreme act and he was sorry, very sorry. Abílio was a tormented man, and now she could understand why he was acting so coldly. He tried to protect himself and not think. If he thought too much about his beloved wife, for whose death he was directly responsible, he might even go mad.

Thinking about all this, Clarissa concluded that he could not kill her. Abílio was definitely not a cruel and bloodthirsty killer. He had had the courage, she recognized, but he was not a criminal. He had acted out of desperation; his, Leonor's and the children's. The

Memories that the wind brings

children... did they know? Vincent should have known, or at least suspected.

That would only explain the hatred he felt for his father. He had told him several times that he hated him for what he had done to them and to his mother. Yes, Vicente knew that. However, no matter how much he rebelled, he did not feel strong enough to bring him to justice. And should Abílio be punished for the crime he committed? Yes, because he had killed, committed a crime, he should go to jail. But Abílio was no ordinary criminal. He had not killed for greed, revenge or pleasure. He had killed out of love and piety, if that was possible.

In spite of everything, Leonor had not found the peace so waited for. She wandered around the house, tormented and unhappy. She had not been able to separate herself from the material world and was still united with her family. This was not a good thing. She must go on her way. But how to continue on her spiritual journey when her husband and children suffered from her decision? Yes, because Leonor was as responsible as Abílio. If he had killed her, she would have chosen to die. She had committed suicide. It did not matter that it was not by her own hand. Abílio had served her as an instrument, like a knife or a revolver. He had only done what she wanted, but she didn't have the courage to do it. And now, what would she do? Clarissa needed to help. She was already dead, and there was no way she would regret her gesture and come back to life. So all she had to do was to try to help her spirit break free from matter. And that's what she was willing to do.

She waited until lunchtime, when everyone gathered at the table. Angelina, much better, had come down to join the others. In the middle of the meal, looking casual, Clarissa asked:

– Mr. Abílio, why can't I go into Mrs. Leonor's room?

He paled and looked sideways at Vicente, who wasn't moving a muscle, his face buried in the plate of food.

Memories that the wind brings

– Why do you want to go in there? – he snapped. There's nothing for you in that place.

Angelina understood nothing and looked at Clarissa with a searching look. She caressed his small hand and, looking at Abílio, considered:

– Well, Mr. Abílio, I don't see why not.

– Because it's not ready It was my late wife's room, and no one should go in there, do you hear me? No one!

– But why? You still haven't answered me.

– What do you want, girl? – He was clearly angry.

– Me? Nothing.

– So why don't you take care of the house and leave the rest as it is?

– Mr. Abílio – she reflected firmly – I married you and, with that, I became your wife. When I arrived here, you yourself told me that the house now belonged to me too, and that I could do whatever I wanted. However, you denied me access to one of your rooms. Why?

– I already said. Because it belonged to my wife.

– Your wife is me.

He opened his mouth in amazement and responded:

– Where are you going, Clarissa?

– Well, Mr. Abílio, you are now my husband, and I must confess that I am not at all satisfied with your... let's say... fixation... with your deceased wife.

– Fixation? How dare you?

– So, isn't it? You keep the room closed, smelling musty, intact, even with his nightgown on the couch. Why?

– How do you know that

– I went in there the other night when someone, I don't know who, opened the door and forgot to close it.

– It was wrong.

– No, I did not. As you said yourself, I am your wife, owner of this house. What hurts me is knowing that my husband treats me like a stranger, blocking my movements inside the very house that you claim to be mine!

Abílio dropped the spoon, wiped his lips with the napkin and looked at it. That conversation was making him nervous. The children didn't say anything, but he couldn't help answering her. He sighed deeply and responded:

– I don't understand. Clarissa Why is it so important for you to enter the... room of my first wife? What do you want there?

– Do you really want me to say it?

– Yes, I do.

– I intend to pray for his soul.

He stood up indignantly, shouting:

– What? But how? Why? By what right...?

– I don't know why you were so angry. Prayer has never hurt anyone and is not an offense.

Abílio, astonished, didn't know what to say. How could he deny her that? Right there he would be suspicious. After all, she was right. A prayer was not an offense, and he had no reason to disagree. Not knowing what to say, he looked at Vincent, as if seeking help, and the boy answered:

– I don't see any harm in that, Dad.

– Neither do I... – . Angelina also agreed.

Abílio sat down again. He had no excuse for denying what she was asking. Nor could he act as if he were married to Leonor, instead of Clarissa. Leonor had been his wife once, but now she was gone. Regardless of the circumstances, the fact was that he was no longer with them, and his wife was now Clarissa.

Memories that the wind brings

If he were to deny it, she would become increasingly suspicious and discover everything in a short time. He looked at his children for a long time, then at Clarissa, and thoughtful:

– Okay, Clarissa. If that's what you want... I just ask you, at least, don't touch anything.

She smiled, showing all the euphoria and emotion she felt at that moment, and responded:

– Don't worry, Mr. Abílio, I have no intention of changing anything. I'm just going to open the window to get some air, dust and pray. Nothing else.

– Very good. So be it then.

At the end of the meal, Clarissa got up. Feeling victorious. She was sure that, in time, Leonor's tormented soul would be able to leave. She felt a certain fear is clear. But she knew she could count on the help of Grandmother Toña. After all, hadn't she been the one who prepared her for all this? Grandma Toña probably already knew what was in store for her and counted on her to bring some relief to that family. And that was exactly what she was going to do.

CHAPTER 11

Finally, after long years of dating and waiting, Luciano and Jerusa were to be married in the small chapel of the Hacienda de San Jeronimo, where numerous weddings of the Sales de Albuquerque family had already taken place. Both parents were happy, mainly because the haciendas had flourished again, thanks to Abílio's generous Donation. Fortunato, however, felt oppression in his heart. The restructuring of the haciendas had cost him his daughter's happiness, and that was tormenting him day after day. As much as he tried, he could not hide a certain disgust at the thought of Clarissa, alone and lost in a strange land, next to a rude and rude man taking care of children who would probably be hostile to her.

In the letters she wrote, Clarissa never spoke of her life in that distant city and, until then, no one had heard of the shipwreck she had suffered. Everyone did not know about her relationship with Abílio and his children, nor did they even know that the house was apparently haunted. She just said she was fine, asked for news and said goodbye. Nothing more.

As Christmas approached, Flora expected her daughter to come with her son-in-law to attend the wedding and spend the vacations at the hacienda. She had written several letters inviting her, but Clarissa always refused her invitations leaving her mother frustrated and confused. Was she so angry with them that she no longer wanted to visit them? Faced with this distrust, Clarissa was forced to tell her the truth. Her last letter arrived on the day of Luciano's wedding, and Flora opened it and read it avidly:

"*Dear Mother:*

I know that Christmas is coming and that many women would like to gather the whole family there. However, I can't go and I ask you to

Memories that the wind brings

please not insist. If I didn't tell you the reason for my refusal earlier, it was simply not to worry. I don't want you to think that I'm not going because I'm still hurt by what Dad did to me, because I'm not. I'm over that and I've accepted my fate. However, I think the time has come to tell you what happened. The boat we were traveling on was caught in strong winds, and we were almost shipwrecked at the entrance to Cabo Frio Bay. It was a fatal misfortune for many of the crew and travelers, and if it had not been for Mr. Abílio's courage, I would have succumbed as well.

That's why I'm begging you: don't ask me to go there. I couldn't take another ocean crossing. After the shipwreck, I was terrified and horrified by the sea and the boats, and I couldn't do it again. I still remember the fear I felt when I saw myself under the waves, almost suffocating, and my husband's desperation to save us. It was terrible.

Please, Mom, don't worry.

I'm fine now. Tell Luciano and Jerusa that I will be here praying for them and waiting for their arrival.

Greetings to Dad and everyone, from your Clarissa."

When she finished reading the letter, Flora burst into tears and ran to show it to Fortunato. The husband took it carefully, read it and his eyes filled with tears.

He got up from the chair in which he was sitting, went to the window and said in an anguished voice:

– What did I do to my daughter?

– You did what you thought was right," replied the woman, hugging him from behind and trying to comfort him.

– We almost lost her... My God! What would have become of me if she had died? I could never forgive myself.

– This did not happen.

– But it could have happened.

Barely managing to contain her frustration, Flora finally expressed:

Memories that the wind brings

– You should have thought of that before you sent her away – . Fortunato looked at the woman with deep disgust and considered:

– You accuse me, don't you? You don't forgive me

– No, that's it," she said, puzzled. I didn't want to accuse you of anything. You are my husband and it is not for me to discuss your orders.

– But you don't agree with what I did, do you? Come on, tell the truth, please.

– If you really want to know – she said – gathering her courage, I don't agree, no. My children are my greatest treasure, and there is no money in the world to pay for the love I feel for them.

And they should be yours too! You should care about them, especially Clarissa, who is the youngest. You should protect her, not throw her to the beasts!

Fortunato dropped his arms, defeated and even tried to argue:

– It was an act of desperation! You know that we would never have been able to rebuild the hacienda without Mr. Abílio's money,

– There were other solutions. You could have taken the loan.

– But interest, guarantees...

– These were all excuses to justify your attitude.

There were other ways, but you didn't want to do it. Why? Why did you sell our daughter when there were other ways to rebuild your farms?

He looked at her with tears and whispered:

– I don't know. I swear I don't know. Today I agree with you that I could have chosen another solution. But at the time... I don't know... the idea seemed tempting, it was really the salvation of our crops, and it was as if Clarissa had that destiny.

— It was you who sealed its fate the day you sold it to Mr. Abílio.

— You don't know how much I've been tormenting myself about that.

I have always loved Clarissa... but I need to confess something, a terrible thing, a monstrous feeling that I have been trying to fight since I first had it.

He stopped talking, restrained by sobbing, and Flora responded in anguish:

— But what is it, man? What feeling is so horrible as to leave you in that state?

— I don't know... It was like... a pleasure... a penetrating pleasure...

— Pleasure? — she was outraged.

— At first, I vehemently refused the offer. But then, knowing the enormous sum that Mr. Abílio offered me, I was tempted. The price was high, but Clarissa owed me.

— How? How could she owe you something so monstrous?

— I don't know! — he moaned, almost despairing. It was a feeling I still can't define... It was an opportunity I couldn't miss.

— Are you crazy, Fortunato?

— I don't know, Flora, I don't know! God knows how much I regretted it after she left. But it was too late.

— It was not too late to take advantage of the money Mr. Abílio gave you — she responded sourly.

— What else can I do? I had already made the... transaction. There was no turning back. Please, Flora, don't hate me for that.

— I don't hate you. I just don't understand you.

Suddenly, the door to the room opened and Valentina entered, being scolded by her father:

— Valentina! Why don't you knock before you come in?

Memories that the wind brings

– I'm sorry, Dad, but everyone is already waiting. It's time.

Fortunato and Flora looked at each other. It was time for their son's wedding, and they had to leave. Valentina, however, noticing something strange in the air, asked curiously:

– Did something happen? Mom, you were crying! Why?

In silence, Flora extended Clarissa's letter to her. Valentina picked it up and read it calmly. As she read, her countenance changed, but at no time did she show signs of pain or regret. When she finished reading, she commented coldly:

– Good thing nothing serious happened to her, right? Well, that's gone. Let's go. Your son is waiting for you.

– Your sister almost died in a shipwreck – Flora objected. – Doesn't that move you?

– So much drama. The ship sank, so what? It was unfortunate, but Clarissa is fine. There's nothing we can do about it. There's nothing to be done either.

– She went through all this because of me – evaluated Fortunato.

To save me from ruin. To save us all. Including you and your husband.

– Clarissa fulfilled her obligation as a daughter. She did nothing important.

– You could at least acknowledge their sacrifice.

– All right, I recognize it. She sacrificed herself, but so what? You don't have to make her a martyr for that.

Flora was about to object when the door opened again. This time it was Roberto, who came to call them.

– What was it? What happened? – he asked nervously – Luciano is already distressed. He wants to get to the church before the bride.

Without saying anything else, Fortunato left with Flora, soon followed by his daughter and son-in-law. Valentina did not like Clarissa. Since she was born, she felt in her sister a certain danger, a threat, as if at any moment she could take what belonged to her. Why this feeling? Valentina did not know and had never been interested in finding out.

The ceremony was simple, fast and wonderful. Jerusa was beautiful, with a garland of orange blossoms on her head. There were many people present, both from the Oro Viejo hacienda and from other haciendas in the region, as well as some distant relatives from São Paulo and Bahia. The whole house was in an uproar, with the servants running around, adjusting the decoration, decorating cakes and sweets, preparing the rooms to receive some guests.

The next day, Luciano and Jerusa said goodbye. They intended to spend their honeymoon in Rio de Janeiro and then went to Cabo Frio to spend Christmas with Clarissa. If she was afraid to travel by boat, her brother and sister- in- law had no intention of taking away some of the lost joy. However, Flora, knowing of the shipwreck, had tried to divert them from this idea:

– My son – he said – I know you and Jerusa miss Clarissa. We feel it too, but do you think it would be wise to take a chance on this trip?

– Your mother is right," agreed Fortunato – I've been looking into it and found out that there have been several shipwrecks in those waters, always because of the winds.

– Now Dad, so what? I'm not afraid and I'm sure Jerusa isn't either.

– But Luciano, the mother insisted, is dangerous. You can drown...

– We are not going to drown.

– Think carefully, my son. You were married yesterday. Think of your wife.

– Jerusa is not afraid either. We are sure that nothing will happen to us.

No matter how much they tried, Fortunato and Flora could not get them out of that idea, and soon they went to the capital, taking some gifts and souvenirs from everyone.

In Cabo Frio, Clarissa could hardly contain her anxiety about the arrival of Luciano and Jerusa. She had lost her marriage, but she would have their company at Christmas. Helped by Angelina, she arranged a room for them next to her, in front of the beach, so they could enjoy every morning with the multicolored view of the sea. She bought new fabrics for the curtains, put linen sheets and lace bedspreads that she had ordered in the capital, waxed the floor, polished the furniture and put flower pots where possible. All to please the newlyweds.

With so much hustle and bustle, Abílio thought he would forget about going to Leonor's room for a little prayer. But that did not happen and, Clarissa, every day, continued her prayers for the soul of the deceased. She had even asked Angelina to accompany her, but the girl had refused. She had said that the memories of the dear mother were too painful and she had asked Clarissa to forgive her that pain. The woman, touched, did not insist, moved by the stepdaughter's suffering.

Every day at six o'clock Clarissa would enter the rooms of Abílio's late wife and begin to pray for about half an hour. Her prayer was always heartfelt and sincere, spoken aloud. At first, she had been a little afraid. What would happen if the spirit of Mrs. Leonor, attracted by the prayers, decided to appear there? She would die of fear. Even so, she thought she could not give up. It was necessary to advance in her mission. As Leonor had never made herself visible, she began to feel more calm and safe.

Memories that the wind brings

One Sunday morning, Clarissa was walking along the beach in the company of Angelina, picking up shells in the sand.

– Look at this beauty! – said Angelina, showing him a large pink shell.

– It really is a beauty! – agreed Clarissa.

Angelina looked sad and let go:

– My mother loved shells. She made necklaces out of them.

– Is this true? You never told me anything.

– But it is true. Mom created beautiful things with the shells.

– Why don't you show me?

– I don't know if Daddy would let me. He keeps them in a box in Mommy's room.

– Then you can show me.

Angelina looked at the shell in her hand and placed it in the basket she was carrying, bending down to pick up another one, which the wave had just brought. Summer was approaching and it was hot, but the sea, hitting their feet, caused them a pleasant sensation of freshness. Clarissa was delighted, letting herself get wet up to her ankles. Then for a few moments, she asked:

– What did your mother die of, Angelina?

The girl was startled. Clarissa had never asked her about her mother's death, and that had left her confused. She looked away from the girl and stammered:

– Why...? Why do you want to know?

– For nothing. Curiosity.

– I don't think you should get involved with that, Clarissa.

– Why not? What is so mysterious behind Mrs. Leonor's death?

– There's nothing mysterious, but it's just that mom... – ... lowered her voice and stammered hesitantly: – ... committed suicide because of us.

She didn't want us to suffer from her illness.

– Disease?

– Yes. Rheumatism.

– Listen, Angelina, I know that rheumatism causes a lot of pain, but I don't think anyone has committed suicide because of it.

– What do you mean?

– I mean, I don't think your mother killed herself just because she had rheumatism.

– Not? But then... what... what do you think... – . Angelina was extremely confused, not sure what to say.

– I think she killed herself for another reason.

– What reason?

– I'm not sure, but that's what I'd like you to tell me.

– Clarissa, please... – begged Angelina, trying to get away from her. Clarissa, however, took her hand and continued:

– Why don't you tell me? Don't you trust me?

– It is not that. It's just... I can't.

– Can't? Why? What's stopping you?

– Nothing... nobody... Please let me go. I don't want to pick up shells anymore.

– What are you afraid of, Angelina?

– Fear? I'm not afraid of anything.

So why don't you want to stay and talk to me?

– It's because... dad...

– Dad...

– Nothing. anything. Please. Clarissa, let me go. Let me go or it will be worse. Clarissa, surprised, let go and answered:

– Worse why? What or who is stopping you from talking about it? Your father?

Angelina did not respond. She dropped the basket of shells on the floor, sat down on the sand and began to cry. She couldn't take it anymore. That secret was a torment to her little childish heart. Clarissa, realizing her distress, sat down next to her, took her hand and continued:

– Trust me, Angelina. I just want to help you.

– What for? – she responded with skepticism. – There is nothing anyone can do. My mother left. There is no way to bring her back.

– But I can help ease your heart. I feel that you are suffering, your brother is suffering.

There is sadness in his eyes, and Vincente is a very rebellious boy who hates his father. Why? What did your father do?

Angelina sighed and said in a weak voice:

– Nothing. My father did nothing. And I think that's why Vicente is so angry.

– What do you mean he didn't do anything?

He looked at Clarissa seriously and asked:

– If I tell you, do you promise not to say anything to anyone?

– I promise.

– Not even Dad?

– Much less for him.

– Not even Vicente?

– No, believe me

– It's okay. Mom was very sick, yes, but it wasn't rheumatism. She was suffering from... from...

– Of what, Angelina? Speak up soon, for God's sake.

– Leprosy.

Clarissa nodded sympathetically and considered:

– I thought so.

Memories that the wind brings

– Already?

– Yes. A commander, a friend of my father and Mr. Abílio, told him this story. He said that many suspected her of being a leper.

– Oh! Clarissa, you don't know what this disease is. For a long time, Mom managed to stay hidden. But then, with the advance of the disease, we had to flee from Rio de Janeiro.

People became suspicious and afraid, also they did not like coming to our house. Even the children were forbidden to play with us, and my brother suffered a lot of discrimination at school. The principals, suspecting that there was a leper's son among them, demanded that my father take him out of school before he was expelled. I was very young, I almost don't remember.

– Is that why you escaped?

– Yes, Dad had heard about a leper camp, and the doctor recommended that he send Mom there. We came, but Dad didn't want to... He refused to admit her.

We didn't want to either. Until one day... Angelina began to cry, and Clarissa encouraged her:

– One day...

– One day some men appeared. They were from the city and had heard about a leper woman who lived in our house. They said it was dangerous and were here to demand that Dad take her away. My father denied that she was a leper. He said she was suffering from rheumatism and had come for treatment, to sunbathe. My mother never left home. The farthest she went was to the beach across the street. But some people were suspicious and afraid, and wanted her to leave. My father always denied the disease, but many did not believe it. No one had ever seen Mom. Dad was very careful about that.

– But then, why did she kill herself? Angelina hesitated and responded with uncertainty:

– Why did she kill herself...? Why..., because she could no longer bear the pain... suffered rejection and she was afraid that we would be discriminated against again. Then, one morning... she said she was going to sunbathe and... they say she threw herself into the sea. She was never seen again.

– And your father? Where were you that day?

– My father? I don't know. In the bedroom, maybe. Maybe with Tiago. When Dad found out, he was desperate, and so were we.

– How long ago was that, Angelina?

– About three years ago. Since then, we have suffered a lot.

– I can imagine.

– And then you came, and it was like I could find my mother again.

Clarissa embraced her emotionally. She was sure of the girl's feelings for her. Angelina was a sweet and needy girl. She had lost her mother very early, and it was natural for her to miss her. However, did she know of his father's involvement in this case? Not at all. Angelina showed no signs of distrust about what her father had done. Despite this, Clarissa was almost certain that Abílio had killed his wife. At Leonor's request, it was true, but even he killed her.

How great must have been the suffering of that family! Hadn't Abílio acted correctly? After all, the woman was suffering from an incurable disease, which gradually tore her to pieces and caused her enormous suffering. Would she not have done a charitable deed, ending soon that endless torture? No. Abilio had killed, and only the one who had the right to take his life was God, and she was quite sure that Abilio was not God. As understandable and commendable as his intentions were, he didn't have that right.

However, I could understand his desperate gesture. And now, he let himself be corroded by remorse, shedding his tears on Tiago's shoulder. Yes, Tiago had helped him, for sure.

He was his faithful accomplice and friend. Was that why Abílio had turned to the religion of the blacks? Had he found refuge and comfort there for his tormented conscience? It was quite possible. Perhaps he, incredulous of everything and God, had taken the life of his wife without thinking of the consequences, but then, unfortunately, he resorted to the spirituality of the slaves, as a way to relieve and appease his conscience. In any case, Abílio had still involved his children in his madness, and she was sure that Vincent knew the whole truth, and that is why she hated him.

Clarissa looked at Angelina, who was crying as she clung to her, and pressed her even more tightly to her chest. I liked that girl very much and I didn't want her to suffer.

Affectionately, he kissed her fragrant head and spoke tenderly:

– Don't worry about anything, Angelina. I'm here and I'll take care of you.

And she added to Angelina's tears her own tears, asking God to give her strength to help that poor girl.

CHAPTER 12

Upon opening the back door, Abílio came face to face with Clarissa, who was holding the basket of clothes she had just picked up from the clothesline.

– Are you going out? – she asked, trying to give the voice a casual tone.

– Yes, I'm coming. Why? Do you want something?

– Can I know where you are going?

He looked at her threateningly and responded angrily:

– No, you can't. I will resolve some issues that do not concern you.

Thinking that he had intimidated her with his rude tone of voice, Abílio turned his back on her and headed for Tiago, who was already sitting on the ox cart that would take them to the city.

– Is there a problem, sir?

– I hope not.

He sat down next to Tiago and ordered him to move the cart. The other obeyed and slightly whipped the animals, who began to walk calmly.

The car passed by Clarissa and when she was almost in front, the girl ran out and screamed:

– Wait, please wait!

Tiago stopped the oxen and turned around. In a few seconds, Clarissa reached the cart, arriving with a red face.

– Do you want something from the city?

– Yes, I do – answered Clarissa, as she climbed into the back of the car. – I want to go with you.

– You what? – Abílio astonished.

– I said I want to go with you. Why? Any objections?

Trying to control his anger, Abílio bit his lip and crossed his arms. When he spoke, he was shaking, but still tried to be as polite as his indignation would allow:

– I'm sorry, Clarissa, but I don't think you understand. I said I'm going to do some private business. You can't come with me.

– Why not?

– Clarissa – he said angrily – I will try not to be angry with you and take into account the fact that you are still almost a child, stubborn and arrogant. And now, get out of the wagon or I will be forced to take you out by force.

Tiago looked at him in amazement and tried to commit himself:

– Siñá Clarissa, listen. The girl cannot go. She would be bored.

– How do you know, Tiago? Maybe I like it a lot.

– But what do you like, my God? Because if we're not going anywhere for fun...

– I know I don't. And I know where you are going.

– Do you already know?

– I do know. You will see the ritual, won't you? The African cult.

Tiago and Abílio looked at each other in amazement. How could she know? Tiago thought about protesting, but Abílio interrupted him with his hand and added:

– You are right, Clarissa, let's go to Father Joaquim's *terreiro*. But it's a very poor place without comforts. I'm sure you wouldn't like it.

– You are wrong. I really think I would like to visit Father Joaquim's *terreiro*. That's where we took Angelina that day, right?

He shook his head and, struggling desperately not to lose his temper, continued to argue:

– The place is not suitable for young girls. Listen to what I say and go home.

– I am not a child, Mr. Abílio, I am his wife. And then, I'm used to attending the cult of the blacks. In my hacienda, I always witnessed and even participated.

– Your hacienda is a rich and well- kept place, very different from the *terreiros* here.

– Still, I would like to go.

Abílio, already quite irritated, got out of the cart, turned around and lifted Clarissa out of the cart. He put her on his shoulder and left, carrying her to the door of the house while she screamed:

– Let go of me, you rude animal! This is an affront, a disrespect! Who do you think you are to treat me this way?

Carefully, Abílio placed it on the floor and, with his finger

– Listen, Clarissa, you are a spoiled, uneducated child, and if I were your father, I would have beaten you up!

Keeping her eyes angry, she responded calmly:

– It turns out, Mr. Abílio, that you are not my father, but my husband. And if my father never hit me, you wouldn't be the first one to touch my hand.

He did not respond. For a few minutes, he looked at her with a mixture of bewilderment and admiration. Despite her audacity, she had to recognize that she was a woman of fiber and would not be easily dominated. Abílio took a deep breath, turned his back and walked away, hoping she would not follow him.

I was not prepared to continue in that dispute. Clarissa, however, stood at the door, watching him walk away, not making a move. She really didn't want to go. She had done it only to provoke him. Abílio approached the wagon and quickly climbed in, tidying up:

– Let's go.

Tiago set the cart in motion. After leaving the property and taking the dirt road, Tiago turned to Abílio and asked him:

– What did Clarissa say?

– I don't know. She walks funny. First came that story of praying for Leonor. And now this. What are you going to do?

– I don't know, but something tells me to be careful. Siñáziña Clarissa is smart...

– It's funny, that is.

– I still think you should give her back...

– I can't – he answered in a whisper. As much as I want to, I can't give her back.

– Why?

– I already said. I took her out of the house, out of the family. Now I can't get rid of her. It wouldn't be right.

– Is that the only reason?

Abílio looked at him in confusion and began to stutter:

– Yes... yes... this is... No... I don't know... I don't know what I would do without her... The children... that, the children... are used to her. And Angelina...

– Who are you kidding, Mr. Abílio? Me or you?

I was getting more and more confused. Deep down, I didn't know how to respond. As much as his reason told him that he, as an honorable man, could not get rid of Clarissa like an old fret, there was something else that prevented him from sending her back, and he responded in a whisper:

– I don't know what you mean.

– I want to say that you are in love with siñáziña Clarissa.

– What, did you go crazy? Clarissa is a girl...

Memories that the wind brings

– She is already a woman. Your wife.

– But what about Leonor? I can't cheat on my wife.

Tiago stopped the car in the middle of the road and looked at it. I could see all the confusion in his eyes and he felt sorry. Abílio was a good man and was lost in his own consciousness, struggling to face the conflict in his soul. With the usual sincerity, Tiago reflected:

– Mister Abílio, I think it is time for Leonor to leave once and for all.

– What do you mean, Tiago? You've really gone crazy, huh?

– No, I'm not crazy. But listen to what I'm talking about.

Soon, siñá Clarissa will take the place of siñá Leonor in your life and in your heart.

– Not that! Never! I will never betray my Leonor!

Tiago thought it was better not to argue. Only Abílio did not see what was more than clear. They walked the rest of the way in silence, until they reached Father Joaquim's house where, in the backyard, services were held in praise of his Orixás.

Since he lost his wife, Abílio began to devote himself to the African religion. In the midst of all the pain he felt, the cult of slaves emerged as a real table of salvation, bringing to his tormented heart some peace and comfort. He still remembered how it all happened.

It was shortly after the discovery of Leonor's tattered dress. When he saw the woman's clothes on the beach, Abílio thought he would succumb too. It was over and there was no turning back. But that was not fair. Why had he lost his wife in those circumstances? Why did God punish him like that, shooting his wife who cursed the disease, for which there was no cure and from which everyone fled in terror? He was in his room, crying, holding Leonor's irregular dress in his hands when Tiago entered.

Memories that the wind brings

– Go away, Tiago, I don't want to have anything to do with you.

– Abílio pointed out that he has been locked up there for three days. He is not well. The children need you.

– Children need their mothers, but I can't give them that.

– Be strong. You can't live like this.

– Get out, Tiago, let me. I want to die.

– Dying? If you die, all of Leonor's sacrifice will have been in vain. Is that what you want?

He looked at Tiago with tears in his eyes and responded with sobs:

– What do you want me to do? I can't live without my Leonor! I can't!

Increasingly embarrassed, Tiago leaned over to his side, took him by the shoulders and said, looking deeply into his eyes:

– Abílio pointed out that all the pain does not seem to end, but that is not true. It will pass, I know.

Feeling the understanding and friendship in his friend's words, Abílio held on to him and shouted:

– Tiago! Tiago! What can I do to endure this pain?

Please help me! I have my children, I cannot abandon them. But I can't forget them. Please help me! Help me!

Tiago was excited and swallowed dry. I had never seen so much suffering in one man's heart. Squinting to keep from crying, he considered:

– Why don't you come with me to Father Joaquim's yard? He can help you. Abílio wiped his tears with the back of his hands and responded dryly:

– I don't believe in this nonsense.

– It should. The world is full of spirits…

– These are beliefs of ignorant blacks. There are no spirits.

– Still, why don't you come with me? You have nothing to lose. If our meeting doesn't help you, if it doesn't make you feel calmer and safer, at least it will have served to distract you a little.

– I don't want to get involved with these fetishes.

– They are not fetishes, sir. They are the truths of the soul.

– Hum... I don't know, no. The only truth of the soul is that it cannot survive death.

– This is not true. The soul is eternal – Abílio seemed doubtful and insisted: – Come on, he said, what have you got to lose?

Abílio sighed dejectedly. He was right. Although he didn't believe in any of it, what would he have to lose by going there? At least there would be some distraction.

At that time, in addition to Tiago, Abílio had a slave, named Olinda, who helped Leonor with the housework and looked after the children. Although he did not believe in the religion of the blacks, Abílio had always allowed them to be absent to attend these meetings. Only, that day, Olinda stayed home with the children and he went, with Tiago, to Father Joaquim's *terreiro*.

Once there, he sat down on a stool and admired the ritual. The drums began to play and the blacks went to the center of the courtyard, dancing and displaying strange objects. All were former slaves, manifesting the joy of newly won freedom in worship.

Abílio until he found that ritual interesting. It was like a show, but he wasn't interested in learning the basics. He was distracted, thinking about his misfortune, when Tiago appeared, holding an old man's hand, who was leaning on a cane.

– Mister Abílio, I would like you to meet Father Joaquim. He is our caretaker here.

– Abílio looked at him without much interest. He was just an old man like everyone else and had nothing special. He greeted Father Joaquim with a nod and stood up and told Tiago:

Memories that the wind brings

– Let's go. There's nothing else to see here.

He turned his back on both of them and went to where the ox cart, when he heard the firm voice of Father Joaquim:

– He thinks he can escape his conscience, but he can't, no.

He stopped, turned to the old man and asked:

– How so?

– Your consciousness will torment you until the end of your days.

– But what is this? – he shouted. Tiago, what have you been telling that old man?

– Me?! – said Tiago indignant – . I didn't say anything, sir. I even seem to be gossiping.

– So, what do you mean, man?

Father Joaquim looked at him kindly and responded:

– Mister Abílio, if you came to visit my land, why don't you take the time to talk to me?

– I have nothing to say to you.

– But I have.

– I don't see how I can be interested in your conversation.

– What if I talk about your wife?

Abílio looked at Tiago angrily. He was sure he had his tongue between his teeth, which could end up causing him a lot of trouble. Tiago, however, upon realizing what he was thinking, immediately said:

– You're wrong if you think I said anything, senó. I have always been faithful to you, and you know it.

– Whatever you are thinking, Mr. Abílio, said Father Joaquim, Tiago has nothing to do with it. I know what's going on in your heart, but it wasn't Tiago who told me.

– Not?

– Not? – Abílio was incredulous – . So who was he?

– It was the Orixás.

– Well, that was all I needed. Get out of my way to listen to this nonsense.

Father Joaquim approached Abílio and blew something into his ear, without Tiago being able to hear it. He raised his eyebrows, perplexed, and asked in amazement:

– How do you know that? I never said anything to anyone. Not even Tiago.

– Yes Mr. Abílio. The Orixás read in their thoughts and told me about it. But do not worry. I am not here to judge or threaten the master. What the Orixás say is a secret, and no one can reveal it.

– I... I... I don't know what to say – replied Abílio, visibly confused.

– Do not say anything. Sound needs much more to hear than to speak.

– Listening?

– Yes. Come with me.

Father Joaquim took him home, while the drums continued to play at their frenetic pace. The house was more like a hut, however, very clean and pleasant, and Abílio relaxed. Although extremely poor, there was something special about that house that made him feel good about himself. In truth, the spirits had already prepared the environment, depositing vibrations of love and tranquility, and Abílio had captured the beneficial fluids, feeling good and at peace with himself. Father Joaquim pointed to a stool, sitting on another one, right in front of him. Holding his hands firmly, he immediately spoke:

– Mr. Abílio, I don't want you to think that I am some kind of sorcerer or wizard, and that I am here to hurt you. It's nothing like that. When Tiago came to call me to introduce me to the man, I knew nothing about him. During all this time that he frequents my house, he never told me anything about you.

I want you to know that Tiago is a very faithful and dedicated servant.

– I know.

– Yes. When he called me, he just said that he wanted me to meet his boss, and I came, sure enough the boss needed my help.

– Excuse me for being blunt, but how can you, a poor and ignorant man, help me in any way?

– The wisdom of the soul is infinitely superior to the knowledge of the flesh. I am an ignorant man, yes. I cannot read or write, but I understand things that the master does not even imagine could exist.

Abílio noticed a slight change in the tone of Father Joaquim's voice and realized that he was speaking very easily to an ignorant and illiterate black man, but he made no comment on this, continuing his conversation:

– For example...

– For example, spirits.

– I don't believe in this nonsense.

– Not? For the spirits, right now, tell me that your wife...

– I do not want to talk about my wife – he interrupted abruptly, standing up. – I do not give you the right to touch her name, nor will any spirit convince me to pollute your name!

– Take it easy – he said calmly. = No one wants to convince him of anything. Much less about that when the guy talked, which I don't even know what it is.

Abílio stopped short and looked at him in amazement. Suddenly, he began to laugh. Yes, he was facing an ignorant old man, who didn't even understand what he was saying and who probably had nothing useful to say to you. With his laugh, he spoke in a simulated tone:

– I'm sorry, Father Joaquim, I didn't mean to offend you. And now, if you'll excuse me, I'll be home.

Memories that the wind brings

– Have you forgotten what I told you before?

Abílio looked at him perplexed. Actually, the old man had told him something that nobody knew. Only he and Leonor. How had he found out?

– I confess I was intrigued – he answered, changing his tone. How did you know?

– I have already told you. The Orixás told me. This is a great pain that the master has, isn't it? – he did not answer, and Father Joaquim continued: – Because you should not demand so much of yourself.

Whoever cannot swim, does not throw into the sea. And whoever throws himself into the sea runs the risk of drowning. Or else you end up learning alone. It is the law of life.

– I don't understand what you mean.

– No one can try to be more than they are or walk faster than their legs will allow. And no one should feel guilty about it. See sign. You have a very young daughter, don't you?

– Yes, Angelina is only nine years old.

– So? Imagine now if the signer would want you to move as fast as the signer. He can't. She can't take it.

That's why I say: everyone does what they can, and there's nothing wrong with that.

– I still don't understand what you mean.

– He is an intelligent and studied man, but he doesn't understand anything about God, does he?

– No, I don't understand God wouldn't take my Leonor...

He repented the moment he spoke. He did not want to talk about the woman, because he feared that the man would discover the whole truth about what he had done. Father Joaquim, however, with extreme naturalness and love, objected:

– God did not take his Leonor, and we know it, don't we? But the fact is that the Lord lost his wife. That was your choice.

Memories that the wind brings

Yours and hers. But don't complain that it doesn't solve If things happened that way, it was because it was for the best. All the things that happen in our lives are for our own good. We can't see it that way.

Abílio wanted to dispute, but failed. He was no longer in the mood. The old man's words were deep in his soul. He knew what had happened, it was obvious, but Abílio felt he could trust him. That man was an accomplice, not in his crazy gesture, but his feelings. He was an accomplice because he could understand all the pain in his heart.

Unable to contain himself any longer, Abílio kneltnext to Father Joaquim and, with his eyes bathed in tears, opened his heart and told him all the misfortunes he had gone through since the discovery of his wife's illness. Father Joaquim listened to him patiently and when he finished, he put his hand over his head and said:

– Take it easy, sign, all is not lost. Pray and ask God to help the signer, that God will help.

– I don't know how to pray.

– If you know. No one needs to know beautiful words to talk to God. God listens to any prayer.

– I don't think you hear the prayers of a condemned man like me.

– Who condemned the signer? It wasn't God, for sure, because God doesn't condemn anyone. The one who condemned the master was the master himself, who cannot forgive himself for what he did.

– Forgive? how can I forgive myself?

– Being forgiving. Trying to understand that sign and sign Leonor did what they thought was right and best. Later they will learn to do differently.

– Is it? We won't have that opportunity anymore...

Memories that the wind brings

– The spirit is eternal, the choices are infinite. If someone makes a mistake in life, it is to be able to redo it immediately afterwards.

– How? The mistake is made, it's over.

– Nothing ends in life, but is transformed to collaborate with nature. When we die, our bodies turn to dust and go to eat the insects of the earth. But our spirit is released and returns to

the invisible world from which it came, and we have the opportunity to review all our actions, thoughts and words. So, if we find that something is not good, that we didn't do it right, we can ask to return to Earth, when we have the opportunity to do everything differently. No one lives a single life, so we can always redo what was not done well.

– This is all very strange, Father Joaquim. I need time to get used to it.

– Ask God for help, my son.

– God is going to punish me.

– God does not punish anyone. We are the ones who feel punished when we are tormented by the judgment we make of ourselves. There are no punishments in life, but opportunities to learn.

– Do you really think so, Father Joaquim? Do you think you are learning because you were born in a black man's body? Learning what? Suffering?

– It can be. I don't know what I did in other lives to choose to go through this suffering.

But one thing is true: it was me who chose to be a slave because my soul could not believe that it could and deserved to experience something different and less suffered. If I believed that I did not need to suffer in order to grow, I would have chosen another way.

Memories that the wind brings

– This is all very confusing. I'm not sure if I believe in these things.

– You'll believe me, I'm sure. And I will be here waiting for the master. I am sure you will find comfort in my home. You can come whenever you want.

When he left, Abílio felt more comforted. Although he could not or did not want to believe the words of Father Joaquim, the fact was that they caused him much comfort. He stayed a little longer observing the ritual, already looking at it with different eyes, and then returned home. On the way, he went in silence, until Tiago asked:

– I'm sorry if I intrude – he said – but what was it that Father Joaquim said that impressed him so much?

Abílio sighed and lowered his head. He considered himself a worthy man, and that memory, among so many others, enraged him with himself. However, Tiago was his friend, and he knew he could trust him. Even without looking up, he began to tell his story:

– A few months ago, when Leonor started to have these ideas, she started to give me hell almost every day, trying to convince me to do what she wanted. At first, I didn't want to agree. It was crazy and I loved it. But Leonor was out of her mind, upset about the illness and the children. That day, she was acting crazy. She started screaming that she wanted to die and that she would have to end it. I refused, I accused her of being crazy, and she began to beat me, calling me a coward, a monster, an unjust one. I was furious, but I did not respond and tried to stop her blows as best I could. I knew she was sick and I could understand her revolt.

But she didn't give up. Until, at one point, she came at me and started scratching my face, screaming that she hated me and that I was a filthy pig. At that moment, I lost my head and gave her a slight slap. She started crying and I, sorry, ran to her and hugged her, begging for forgiveness. She was out of control and asked me to forgive her too. We cried together and, from that day on, we never mentioned it again. But I swore that I would never touch my wife or anyone else again.

– And did Father Joaquim know this?

– I knew it. He told me that I was ashamed of having lost my mind and slapped my wife.

It devastated me.

– I understand... Well, Mr. Abílio, even so, I hope you liked Father Joaquim.

– I liked it very much. Not only because of what he said, but because of the sage words coming from an illiterate older man. But mainly because of his love and understanding,

And then the place, although poor, is extremely pleasant. I liked the music, the dances, the serene aspect of those people.

It did me a lot of good

– Do you intend to come back then?

– Each time the ritual occurs. I believe that there I will be able to gather the strength to continue living and raising my children.

To this day, Abílio thought about how much he had changed and realized that something inside him was beginning to change again, and he remembered Clarissa. He remembered the day he almost hit her and how much he regretted it, afraid to repeat the nefarious gesture he had made to Leonor years before. But that wasn't all. Was Tiago right and had he fallen in love with the girl? A slight shudder struck him, and he shuddered. He didn't know if she was in love, but he was sure that he didn't want to live without her anymore.

CHAPTER 13

From the door of the room, Clarissa watched Vicente, whose head rose and fell among the white foam of the waves. She lifted his body and then dived, sank and disappeared into the water, only to reappear beyond, after the waves. He seemed to feel immense pleasure in it. The sea was calm and clear, and the waves broke in the distance, going a long way and then dying on the shore.

Clarissa could not see Vicente's face. She could only make out his manly, half- naked body, swimming in the distance, blending into that crystalline green. It seemed that a crystal mine had melted there, so transparent and bright that it was the water.

She was ecstatic. She would have given anything to go swimming with less clothing, but she knew that Abílio would not consent. However, she couldn't settle. What harm could there be in taking a dip? Thinking about it, she made a decision. It was still early, Angelina was sleeping and Abílio had gone out with Tiago to settle some issues. All she had to do was get up, take off her dress and jump in the water. She didn't even need to take everything off.

She would come with her underwear.

Clarissa ran to the edge of the beach, near where Vicente was. Upon seeing her, the boy approached her and drew a smile, greeting her cheerfully:

– Good day. Clarissa

She looked away from her bare chest and tried to look natural:

– Good morning Vicente. What are you doing here early?

– I came to swim. It's so hot!

– It is true...

Memories that the wind brings

- Why don't you come in too?

- Hum... that's what I was thinking.

In silence, she began to undress, and Vincente opened his mouth in amazement.

- What are you doing? - he asked puzzled.

- Taking off my clothes.

- What? But you can't.

- Why not? Aren't you naked?

- But it is different. I am a man. And I'm not naked. I'm wearing long underwear. When she saw that she was starting to unbutton her blouse, she said Are you crazy? What if my dad catches her?

- Don't worry, I won't take everything off.

She took off her blouse, took off her skirt and was left alone with a bra and a combination. She was already much better and lighter. She went to the shore and tested the water. It was cold, but it would be great to cool off from the heat. Little by little, Clarissa entered, feeling that delicious water on her skin. A little more and she came closer to the waves, with Vicente behind her, without saying anything. Suddenly, she stopped. I couldn't go any further. I was afraid of losing my foot and sinking. She couldn't swim and didn't want to drown.

I had been through that experience once; I didn't want to repeat it.

- This is good," he said, turning to his stepson.

The waves were small and broke very close to her, but strong enough to propel her body from one side to the other. She laughed, delighted, and bent over to feel the contact of the water all over her body. Vincente, who was already getting used to her presence, came closer and, seeing her joy, began to laugh and throw water at her, making fountains with his hands.

- Come - called - . Let's go in a little more.

Memories that the wind brings

– No, no, this is good. I don't want to go any further, I'm afraid.

– But there is no danger.

– I don't want to. I know the currents...

Vincente thought it was better not to insist. He knew that she was afraid after the shipwreck, and it was natural.

– So immerse yourself – he encouraged. – Wet your head.

– I don't know if I have the courage.

– Come on, I'll help you.

Holding it in his hands, he immersed himself in the water, until his neck was practically submerged. Little by little, he got off, putting his head in the water. She was already starting to submerge her when she felt the water on her nose and got up terrified. That sensation... she felt that she was sinking and could not breathe. It terrified her and she tried to escape. She remembered the boat, the fall into the water, the liquid mass that covered her head and prevented her from breathing. She began to scream, and Vicente held her firmly by her wrists, trying to hold her back. But she was upset, unable to reason properly, short of breath. All she wanted to do was run away.

– Let me go! – he shouted, struggling, panting – . Arf! Arf! Arf! I want to breathe! Arf! Arf! I can't breathe! Arf! Arf!

– Clarissa, calm down! Are you on the beach?

– No! I'm sinking! Arf! Arf! The waves! Oh! My God!

She fought madly, trying to get rid of him, but the more she fought, the more he held her. Until, being unable to stand any more that agony, Vincente held her against his chest and began to caress her, saying softly in her ear:

– Shh... Calm down, it's all right. I am here. I will always be here. Calm down, don't worry, I'll take care of you...

Little by little she calmed down, until she began to reason. Suddenly, she realized that she was on the beach, not in the boat, leaning on Vicente's manly chest. That contact made her tremble, and she walked away, looking at him in silence. It was then that she realized how beautiful he was, his brown hair, his tanned skin, his eyes so green that they looked like two drops of the sea, his well-formed muscles, which gave him that air of God just coming out of the waves.

Clarissa looked at him in horror at his own thoughts. She turned away from him and began to retreat, her back to the horizon. He extended his hand to hold her, but she retreated all over, her body coming and going with the waves. In that blow, she was approaching Vincente again, until a slightly stronger wave, which burst on her back, threw her against him, and he opened his arms to hold her.

Clarissa entered into that embrace as if it had been made for her, and their faces met, their eyes met, their lips almost touched. She opened her mouth to protest, but Vincente, driven by emotion, pressed his lips against hers, in a fiery and prolonged kiss, to which Clarissa responded without thinking of anything else. Both were ecstatic, until Vincente's hands began to slide over her body, and she was startled. Immediately, she rejected him and slapped him, saying full of indignation:

– How dare you? I am your stepmother...

– But you are not my mother.

He continued to study her, mad to want to embrace her and tell her how much he loved her, but Clarissa, frightened by her own feelings, put her hand on his chest and began to walk away, struggling to overcome the waves that clung to her legs. Soon after, she arrived at the beach. She picked up her clothes and ran without wearing them, hoping to find no one in the way. She turned around the house and went to the backyard. She took water from the well and poured it over her head, rubbing it with the soap next to him. Then, all wet, she ran into the house, through the kitchen, through the living room, up the stairs and into the bedroom, leaving behind her a trail of water on the floor. No one had seen her.

Clarissa was terrified. As much as she hated Abilio, he was her husband, and she was an upright woman. How could she have let herself be carried away by the emotion of the moment and allowed Vicente to kiss her? Vincente... was bold and rude, but there was something about him that moved her. He was her stepson, younger than her, but still... she couldn't resist.

That kiss... Clarissa had loved that kiss, but she couldn't even admit it. It wasn't right. What would she do from then on? How would she proceed so that Abílio didn't realize what was in her heart? What if Vincente started to persecute her? No. He didn't look like the guy who runs after a girl. However, the looks, yes, could be revealing. But Clarissa wouldn't let that happen again. She had married Abilio and would honor his name, not stain it with the worst kind of betrayal. From that moment on, she was determined: she would never be alone with Vicente again and she would not allow him to touch her or insinuate anything. He would make her see that she was captivated by an attack of madness, the fruit of painful memories that made her nose water, and that she was not lucid enough to avoid this infamy. Vincente, in turn, was distressed. Seeing Clarissa leave, he wanted to go after her, but a sense of dignity prevented him from doing so. He was not a scoundrel, waiting for his father to turn his back on him and steal his young wife. He was a decent man and had also let himself be carried away by the moment, touched by Clarissa's suffering and disturbed by the proximity of her body. But it would not be repeated. He was willing to walk away from her and avoid her presence. He would spend so much time away from home, he would run if he had to. He would not throw his name and his family's name in the mud just because he fell in love with his father's wife. He was a distant man and Vincente hated him, but he was his father. He owed her at least some respect. And that, he knew he couldn't deny.

Shortly after, Angelina went down to have breakfast. When she arrived in the living room, she found the table set. Clarissa had already returned and served her a glass of milk and a piece of cake.

– Where is everyone? – he asked.

– Your father left, didn't say where he was going.

– And Vicente?

– I don't know. I think he's on the beach.

Vincente entered shortly after. He was wearing pants that reached his ankles and a white shirt, unbuttoned to his navel. When Clarissa saw him, she shuddered. His hair was still wet and his eyes were glowing when they met hers. He looked at her silently and entered, passing directly by the table without greeting the sister.

– Aren't you coming for coffee, Vicente? – she asked, with her childish voice.

– No, I'm not hungry.

– Where were you, swimming?

– It's none of your business, brat. Get on with your life.

– Wow, that bitterness! – she complained, pouting.

– Leave him, honey – said Clarissa. – Vincente must be bored. Don't call him.

Vincente said nothing and continued on his way, climbing the stairs and locking himself in the room. Clarissa did not want to talk to him, but she needed to call him. It was time to leave or he would be late for school. Reluctantly, she went to knock on his door.

– Vicente! – she called – . It's time. You know your dad doesn't like you being late.

He did not respond. She knew he was inside and that she had heard his call, but she was not willing to insist. She had fulfilled her role.

It was their problem. Staying home and then enduring his father's anger. She rolled over on her heels and began to walk down the stairs. She needed to take Angelina away herself.

As they were leaving the house, Abílio was arriving with Tiago and immediately asked:

– Where is Vicente?

– He's in the room – said Angelina.

– Doesn't he go to school?

– I don't know, Mr. Abílio – clarified Clarissa. – I went to call him, but he didn't answer. Abílio shook his head and said nothing. What was that boy doing?

– Would you like me to take Angelina, sir? – was Tiago's voice, which brought him out of his reverie.

– What? Ah! Yes, Tiago, please.

Angelina got on the ox cart and went with him, while Clarissa returned to the house with Abílio. He went upstairs and she went to tidy up the house. He didn't feel like talking, and didn't seem interested in anything she had to say either.

✱ ✱ ✱

– But what is it, Vicente? – asked Abilio, entering his son's room. – Why did you miss school?

Vincente looked at him with contempt and responded without interest:

– I don't feel good.

– Ah! So? And what do you feel, may I ask?

– I don't know. An uneasiness

– Stop lying, boy, because I know you don't have anything.

When I left, you were heading for the beach. Do you want to convince me that you are sick now?

– I think I got a lot of sunshine.

With great effort, Abílio managed to control his anger. He knew that Vincente was still accusing him of what had happened to his mother and could not conform.

– I know you're lying – answered Abílio. – However, I don't want to argue with you. But don't think it will become a habit, because it won't.

You will complete your studies and then go to Rio de Janeiro to attend a university. Isn't that what you want? – He didn't answer, and Abílio continued: – Anyway, it's the best thing for you.

– What if I don't want to go anymore? – He responded with contempt, only to provoke his father.

I may have changed my mind.

– No, you can't. You'll go to the capital and that's it. You will study and graduate, and live far away from here.

– Why? I like it here.

– This city is not for you. I want a better future for you.

– Who gave you permission to decide things for me? God? Or Mom?

Abílio bit his lip so hard that he tasted the bitter blood. He wanted to slap his son, but he controlled himself. Instead, he lifted him by the neck and, looking at him furiously

– I don't need anyone's permission to rule my children! You go to the capital and that's it. I'm already organizing your college tuition.

Vincent held his gaze and placed his hands over his father's hands, loosening them from his neck. He was surprised. How could the father decide on his life to his liking? He turned his back on him and sat up on the bed, angry, saying:

– Did you enroll me in the university? But in which course?

– In Medicine. Wasn't that what you wanted? To be a doctor?

– I don't know. I haven't decided yet.

– Make up your mind soon. There is still time to change course, if you wish. You can study whatever you want, as long as you study, do you hear me?

Abílio turned on his heels and left, closing the door behind him and enraging Vincent. Why did the father have to be so arrogant and pushy? Who did he think he was to chart his future behind his back? What if he changed his mind and didn't want to go?

But Vincente knew he would. He agreed with his father: it was the best he could do. Even more so now that he had fallen in love with Clarissa. He could not stay and risk losing everything by betraying himself to his father.

* * *

That night, Clarissa went to bed early to sleep. The events of the day had worn her out. Vincente had left her confused and upset, and she had spent the day thinking about what had happened. Abílio came up later. He had been visited by his business manager, who was in charge of his jewelry stores in the capital, and had to take him into town. It was already late, and the man went to the house of an acquaintance, who used to rent him a room every time he had to do business there. Abilio never offered the man an inn, which he thought was strange, but he never said anything. He was generous and paid well, and that was enough to keep him from complaining.

Passing through the door of Clarissa's room, Abílio saw light under the door, a sign that she was still awake. He was going to walk straight through, but changed his mind.

He came to the door, he was about to knock, but he gave up. Clarissa's words still echoed in his mind. She had said she was upset with him, which had hurt him deeply.

He should have gone straight to his room, but he couldn't. It had been some time since he had last loved her and had felt the desire to grow in her body. After all, she was his wife, and he had his rights.

Memories that the wind brings

Though hesitant, he decided to call and waited until she told him to come in.

– Good evening – he said, entering and sitting next to her.

– Ah! Mr. Abílio, it's you. You haven't been here in a long time. Anything you want? – He looked down, embarrassed, and whispered:

– Don't you know?

Without waiting for an answer, he kissed her awkwardly. Surprised, Clarissa wanted to step back, but she didn't dare. He was her husband and had not been looking for her for a long time. Abílio laid her down on the bed and loved her, without her showing any signs of pleasure or satisfaction. She gave herself to him out of obligation, mechanically, without any feeling or emotion. Realizing her indifference, Abílio regretted it.

In Leonor's day, I used to be an ardent man, but with Clarissa it was different.

I was afraid to surprise her and didn't want to allow her to say that I disliked her.

So he acted quickly, just to satisfy his desire, and as soon as he was finished, he got up, smoothed his clothes and finished coldly:

– Thank you, Clarissa. Sleep well.

He left slowly, closing the door in silence. After he left, Clarissa turned to the side and began to cry, thinking of Vicente. How good it would be if she could love him, instead of Abílio!

She was surprised by her own thoughts and reproached herself intimately. How could she think such things?

Vincente was her stepson, and she had already decided that she would never again give him the opportunity to approach her, much less touch her again. With a sigh, she blew out the candle and closed his eyes, trying to sleep.

Memories that the wind brings

It was then that she heard that moan again, coming from the end of the corridor: uiuiuiuiui... She got up on the bed and looked out the window. As there was no wind, that noise had to be something else. She listened and heard again: uiuiuiuiui... the spirit of Mrs. Leonor seemed to have returned.

Clarissa immediately lit the candle again and stood up, going out into the hallway. It was dark and quiet, but she continued to walk to the last room. The closer she got, the clearer the noise became: uiuiuiuiui... That sound was chilling and seemed to come from the walls. It was really a groan, and Clarissa concluded that it could only be from Leonor. When she reached the door of her room, she pushed the latch and entered, kneeling right in the center of the room. With fervor she lifted

She thought of God and began to pray aloud:

– Lord, I am here to intercede for the soul of our dear sister, Leonor. May she, at this moment, receive all the love that...

Suddenly, there was an infernal noise. From the walls of the room, a terrible crash began: boom! boom! She stopped, mortified, frozen with fear. The noise spread, as if it were trying to invade the room, and she was terrified. A gust of wind hit the door, and she almost fainted from fear. Trying to control the panic, she ran towards it and opened it wide, almost falling as she hit Abílio, who had just arrived.

– Mr. Abílio! What are you doing there?

– I ask you, what did you come to do in my ex– wife's room in the middle of the night?

– I heard a noise and...

– A noise?

– Yes. Did you hear it too?

– It was the wind. It started to roll a while ago. And it looks like it's going to rain. I heard the thunder...

– Is it?

Instead of answering, he asked another question:

– Why are you doing that? Why don't you leave Leonor alone? – Disconcerted, she tried to justify herself:

– You will never have peace that way. It is clear that her spirit is tormented and cannot rest. – He looked at her in confusion, and she continued: "You cannot say that you do not believe. I know you attend the black ritual, which is based on the cult of the dead.

– I didn't say I didn't believe it. I just don't see any reason for you to mess with these things.

– I'm not playing with anything. I come here only to pray. And you should be satisfied.

He sighed dejectedly, took his shoulder and spoke in a pleading voice:

– Could you do me a favor?

– A favor...? What is it?

– Could you leave me alone in Leonor's room? Please, I need to be alone with my memories.

– Well, Mr. Abílio, that's what you're asking. I know how much you suffer and I will respect your pain.

– Thank you.

He entered the room and closed the door. What should I do? Would he pray? Clarissa could not contain her curiosity and put her ear to the ground trying to hear something. All he heard was a muffled click and concluded that he must be rummaging through the drawers. Poor Abílio! He could never forgive himself for taking his wife's life. He had ended her suffering, but he couldn't give her the peace she had hoped for.

– Clarissa – called a voice behind her, getting her started.

– Ah! Angelina, what's wrong, honey?

– Could I sleep in your bed?

– Why?

Memories that the wind brings

– I just heard a horrible noise... thunder...

– Are you afraid?

– Uh, uh!

– It's okay then. Don't worry, thunder can't hurt you.

Clarissa went hand in hand with Angelina, went into her room and set her up on her bed. She covered him, lay down beside her and blew out the candle, then she was kissed good night. Thunder rumbled in the distance, and lightning penetrated through the window, causing an unexplainable tension in her heart.

Confused, she looked at Angelina. The girl, feeling safe with Clarissa's proximity, closed her eyes and said sleepily:

– Don't leave me alone, please. I am afraid...

She soon fell asleep, but Clarissa only managed to fall asleep in the early hours of the morning. When she finally fell asleep, Grandmother Toña was by her side, ready to go with her on another of her visits to the spirit world.

This time, Clarissa saw that strange black village again. It looked very familiar, although she had never seen that place before. She was standing near a tree, with Grandma Toña at her side, who told her to calm down. At that moment, a nine or ten years old girl was being dragged by a large man, while, next to her, a woman was crying her eyes out. The woman approached the girl, crying, and said

– Mudima, my daughter, I love you very much. However, I couldn't do anything, because the chief of the tribe sold you to the white man...

The girl was crying desperately, she did not want to leave, until a white man appeared and put a kind of necklace around her neck, pulling her violently. Mudima kicked more and more, and the man, no longer patient, threw her even harder, and she fell to the ground, dragged by her executioner.

In the background, an old man was watching. Looking cold and distant, he leaned on his cane and looked at that scene with a strange glow of satisfaction. He was the chief of the village and had sold Mudima, along with other men, to the white merchant, who had offered him tobacco and liquor in exchange for the valuable cargo.

After the commotion stopped, the old man turned his back and entered his hut, but was stopped by the accusing gaze of Iadalin, Mudima's mother, who, with one finger raised, said without mercy:

– He is an evil man, Tata[5] Igboanan. One day he will still regret it and receive back all the evil he put us through.

(5) N.A.: Tata, father.

Without waiting for an answer, Iadalin left the village without control. She was devastated and needed to think. Dejected, Igboanan went into his hut and pretended to pray – how he liked Iadalin! But she didn't want to be his. He was an old man, he already had two wives, and she, full of youth and life, had married a young tribal warrior and had four children with him, Mudima being her adopted daughter.

Igboanan never resigned himself to the loss of his beloved and was always waiting for the opportunity to take revenge. Until that day, the opportunity arose. When he received a visit from the white man, who asked him for a black girl of nine or ten years old, Igboanan remembered Mudima. She was a slave, the daughter of a brave warrior from a neighboring tribe, whose mother had been a slave after the defeat of that village. When Mudima was born, the mother had not resisted childbirth, and the girl had been raised by Iadalin as if she were her own daughter. But she was only a slave, and slaves had no rights or privileges. So Igboanan sold her to the white man to take revenge on Iadalin, who suffered greatly from the loss of the

Without understanding anything, Clarissa saw those scenes without participating in them, as a simple spectator, feeling a deep pain in her heart. What did all that mean?

Why did Grandma Toña show you these things? She threw an inquisitive look at the other, and Toña, holding her hand, went with her, landing on the beach, in the same place where they always used to talk.

– Grandma Toña, what does all this mean? I don't understand.

– Calm down, my child – replied Toña sweetly.

– Be patient and confident.

– Why did you teach me these things?

– Your brother will arrive soon and many secrets will be revealed.

– Does my brother have any connection with what we just saw?

– If you have one.

– Was what I saw one of my incarnations?

– It was. I am revealing your past lives to you because it is important that you help yourself in the present and help those around you. Even though you don't remember everything when you wake up, the impressions of what you see come back in the form of intuition, and you have been guided very well, making the right decisions, according to what I am trying to show you and teach you.

– But... Who are these people? And where is this place?

– It is a village in Africa, more precisely in Angola, where I was born.

– That's what I thought. And you were there.

– I was.

– You were Mudima, wasn't you?

Memories that the wind brings

– Yes, I was.

– And me? Who was I?

– Don't you know?

– No, I don't know.

– Well, don't think about it now. You still have difficulty accepting yourself in that life, because you don't like what you did and don't want to remember. But it is necessary.

– I don't understand, Grandma Toña. – How will this help me?

– You need to know the truth to free yourself from guilt and pride. Guilt erodes you immensely, because you have not yet been able to forgive yourself. As for pride, life itself is teaching you to tame it and use it in the right dose and at the right time. But now you see, we have to go back.

When dawn broke, Clarissa managed to retain much of what she had dreamed of in her memory. Toña was always by her side, and Clarissa missed her immensely. The former slave had always been her friend and used to protect her from her grandfather's tyranny and her father's rigidity.

The father was not a bad man. He simply had no respect for slaves and really thought the black man's place was in the senzala. Until he mistreated them. He gave them reasonable food and allowed them to celebrate their Orixás on Sundays. On these occasions, Clarissa always managed to attend, and her father did not mind.

He simply did not admit to disobedience or arrogance.

She and her brother detested slavery, and their childhood memories were populated by the countless times they saw poor blacks suffer the injustice of whites. The day Princess Elizabeth signed the Golden Law, her father and grandfather, who were still alive at the time, locked themselves in the house and refused to go to see the stampede.

Memories that the wind brings

Grandma Toña, at that time, did not want to leave, and her father finally allowed her to stay. She was already old, ninety seven years old, freed by the Sexagenarian Law, where she would go. Grandmother Toña lived at the hacienda only a few more days to tell them her life story. Soon after, they found her in her bed, serene, with a half- smile on her lips, as if she were sleeping. Clarissa cried a lot, until, about a year later, she began to dream about her, and it was as if Grandma Toña came to life by her side, as her friend and protector.

CHAPTER 14

Standing at the edge of the Itajuru channel, Clarissa was looking at the boat that had just docked, bringing her brother and sister-in-law, who had just come from Rio de Janeiro, just after the honeymoon. When Clarissa saw Luciano, she could not contain her emotion.

She let go of Abílio's arm and ran towards him, throwing herself into his arms and kissing him on the cheek, on his forehead. He was so happy she couldn't even speak. She also hugged Jerusa and stayed a long time with her cousin and friend, now also her sister-in-law.

– My friend – whispered – you don't know how I missed you!

– Oh, Clarissa – exclaimed Jerusa, barely holding back her tears – how much I missed you too.

Abílio appeared behind her and greeted his brother-in-law:

– How are you, Mr. Luciano?

– Very good, Mr. Abílio. It is a pleasure to see you again.

– The pleasure is all mine, and – turning to Jerusa, he bowed and formally greeted – madam.

She responded to the greeting with a nod, and Abílio indicated the location of the wagon. Tiago, at her side, helped them with their luggage, and the group went home. When they saw that rustic cart pulled by a couple of oxen Jerusa was surprised. She thought they were going by carriage and was amazed at the precarious transportation offered by Abílio. She looked discreetly at Luciano, who gave her an imperceptible sign and said nothing. After sitting in the back of the cart, Abílio sat down next to Tiago,

Memories that the wind brings

as he always did, and they continued on their way. Leaving the hustle and bustle of the port, Abílio commented:

– I apologize for the cart, Mrs. Jerusa, but it is the most practical means of transportation we have here, besides horses and donkeys. But we soon get used to it – . Jerusa blushed when she realized that Abílio had noticed her indignation. She thought of finding an excuse, but didn't know what to say, and Luciano told her to shut up.

The oxcart continued, crossing the sands and the forest. There was not much to see there, and Jerusa thought that Clarissa must be very unhappy there. It was true that the entrance to the bay and the channel that served as a port had enchanted her, but the city seemed a pity. There was no pavement or organization, and the houses were not many.

– How was the trip? – asked Clarissa, trying to break through the visible discomfort affecting her sister-in-law.

– Ah! it was great – answered Luciano – . The weather was good and the winds were favorable.

– How nice. I confess that I was worried and prayed all day yesterday, begging God not to send any northeast or southwest.

– Clarissa was traumatized by the shipwreck – explained Abílio. – And I don't blame her. She went through really difficult times.

– Please, could we talk about something else?

– Of course, my dear – Luciano agreed – . Sorry.

The conversation turned to the city. Luciano and Jerusa wanted to know everything about Cabo Frio, and Clarissa and Abílio tried to clarify them. When they finally arrived, Luciano was crazy for wanting to visit the beach. Unlike his sister, he would not have suffered any tragic experiences on board the ship and would have enjoyed the crossing.

Memories that the wind brings

Jerusa, no. She had been sick the whole trip and had barely managed to keep anything down. But Luciano was ecstatic. He agreed with Clarissa that the place was beautiful.

When he saw the beach, he lost his voice. He had never seen so much beauty together.

- It's really beautiful agreed Jerusa. - How does the sea acquire this color?

- The color varies according to the depth of the water - explained Abílio - . Where the blue is very dark, it is deeper and, as it becomes more superficial, the water also becomes lighter, until it reaches the pale green you are seeing.

- It really is a beauty!

- Let's go in - invited Clarissa - . You must be tired and hungry. If you wish, we can take a walk on the beach.

- We are very hungry - agreed Luciano - . The food on the boat was not the best.

- It's true - said Jerusa. - And you know how Luciano was accustomed by his mother, eating the most delicious delicacies.

- So that you can experience the most varied delights.

- Really? Who's the cook?

- Myself.

- You?

- Yes.

- But... what about the servants?

- There are no servants here - Abílio answered quickly. Clarissa showed them the room she had prepared for them.

Despite being used to the luxuries of the hacienda and the capital, Jerusa was a simple person and didn't bother with unrefined decoration. Luciano, on his part, did not pay attention to such things. All he wanted was a comfortable, soft bed to rest in.

Memories that the wind brings

– Well – said Clarissa, just after Tiago put the luggage on the floor, now I will let you rest – . If you want to take a bath, Tiago will bring you water. Later, I'll come and pick you up for dinner.

– When are we going to meet Mr. Abílio's children?

– At dinner. Now, feel free and rest. Then we'll see you. We have a lot to talk about.

Clarissa left and Tiago went right behind her. Seeing himself alone in the room, Luciano went to the window and looked at the sea. It was beautiful! He turned to Jerusa and asked her:

– So what do you say?

– I do not know well. The place is beautiful, but I don't think it's very civilized.

– Well that's it. From what I could see, it looks more like a village. Anyway, the natural beauty compensates for the lack of urbanization.

– Is it?

– I think so. What about my host?

– Mr. Abílio? I don't know. It is strange. Very formal.

– I think it's their way of being. As far as I know, he is a man punished with life.

– Did the first woman really die from leprosy?

– I don't know. That's what they say. My father told me that she committed suicide. Maybe she couldn't stand this horrible disease.

– How sad! And poor Clarissa, she comes to the end of so much misfortune. It is not fair.

– However, this is now your reality. And she didn't seem so unhappy.

– Do you know that I noticed it too? Does she like Mr. Abílio?

– I don't know. Everything is possible.

Memories that the wind brings

Both were exhausted. The trip had been exhausting and slow, and they, after bathing in the water Tiago had brought them, lay down to rest and ended up sleeping. They woke up with a knock on the door. Luciano was the first to wake up and rubbed his eyes, trying to see in the dark. It was already night and he lit the candle on the side table, pushing Jerusa as she got up. He ran to open the door and Clarissa entered, beautiful and smiling, inviting them to dinner.

- Come. Dinner is ready, and Mr. Abílio's children are already downstairs, eager to meet you.

- I don't understand, Clarissa - said a sleepy Jerusa, - why are you so formal with your husband?

Clarissa stopped and looked at her hesitantly. She had never thought about it and didn't know how to respond.

- Why? - she repeated. - I don't know. I think it's because I don't see him as my husband, but as a commander, to whom I owe respect and obedience.

- What a horror!

- Yes, it's a horror, although it doesn't work much for me -. Jerusa laughed and continued: - You know me and you know my genius. I don't like to be dominated.

- Don't tell me that! - Luciano agreed, in a joke -. I imagine that Mr. Abílio must be having a hard time with you.

- More or less. Well, now hurry up. Everyone is waiting.

When Jerusa met the children of Abílio, she felt a strange premonition. The girl was adorable, but the boy had something strange that he could not define. Looking at him and Clarissa, Jerusa feltdanger in the air. He was extremely handsome, strong, manly and his vivacious look showed his sympathy for Clarissa. She thought he was very dangerous. Clarissa had been forced to marry Mr. Abílio, but she was not unhappy. Did the sister- in- law have an affair with her stepson?

Jerusa looked sideways at Luciano, but she did not notice.

Memories that the wind brings

He was amused by Angelina's naive conversation, and didn't even notice Vicente. The boy, on the other hand, showed no interest in his guests.

He greeted them politely, but did not pay much attention to them.

After the meal, Clarissa and Angelina began to clean the table, taking the dishes to the kitchen. Remembering that Mr. Abílio had told her that there were no employees, Jerusa offered to help and immediately got up and began to pick up the dishes as well. After removing everything, Clarissa took a soup tureen and began to wash dishes and plates. Jerusa was impressed, but said nothing. She didn't want to bother her sister-in-law. Instead, she picked up a cloth on the table and began to dry the dishes, which Angelina kept.

Meanwhile, Abílio sat down, smoking his cigar, keeping Luciano company.

– Your house is very beautiful – he said this, to talk.

– Thank you – replied Abílio, trying to look interested.

– And you were very kind to receive us.

– It was a request from Clarissa, and I couldn't help but respond. I hope that your presence here will make her a little happier.

– Isn't my sister happy?

– This is not what it is about. But I know it's not very nice to have to leave your family to live with a stranger.

No matter how much you get used to it, it's never the same.

– It's true – said Luciano in admiration.

– Clarissa gets along very well with my children, especially with Angelina.

– She is a lovely girl.

– That's right. And she also likes Clarissa a lot.

– It can be seen.

The girls returned to the living room, and Clarissa called them to walk on the beach, enjoying the moonlight. The idea excited Luciano, who asked permission to accompany them. Abílio didn't want to go. He needed to solve the problems, but they could be comfortable. As they were leaving, Abílio pulled Clarissa out by her arm and whispered in her ear:

– Remember: nobody should go to Leonor's room.

Clarissa put her arm away and looked at him coldly, saying dryly:

– Don't worry. Nobody has anything to do there.

And he left the gate, joined his brother, Jerusa and Angelina, and went with them to the beach.

* * *

Christmas was approaching, and Clarissa managed to convince Abílio to organize a party. The children were excited, especially Angelina, who dreamed of receiving a new doll. Since her mother left, she had never received a gift.

Knowing this, Clarissa went to talk to Abílio:

– Doll? – he asked, surprised. – And what does Angelina want with a doll?

– To play with – Clarissa responded impatiently – what else would it be for?

He thought for a few moments and ended up saying that he was right. Before Leonor got sick, there was always a party at her house. But after she left, they never celebrated anything. No Christmas, no birthday, nothing. Maybe it was time to bring some joy home.

– That's right, Clarissa, you convinced me. I am still going to Rio de Janeiro this week to buy some gifts.

– What a good idea!

- Wouldn't you like to go?

A dark cloud passed through her mind, and she opposed it:

- No, Mr. Abílio, thank you. I prefer to stay here. We have guests, and I wouldn't like to leave them alone.

Two days later, Abílio went alone to Rio de Janeiro, leaving the house in Tiago's care. After their departure, Luciano and Jerusa were a little more relieved. In spite of being polite, Mr. Abílio was a strange and distant man, and no matter how much he tried, he could not hide his displeasure.

- How about a walk on the beach? – suggested Luciano, completely seduced by the charms of the sea.

- Now? – Jerusa tried to protest – . The sun is almost up.

- Now, Jerusa, don't be a spoilsport – said Luciano. – We still have time before lunch.

- And we can take our parasols – concluded Clarissa. Jerusa raised her shoulders, defeated and ended up accepting:

- It's okay. Luciano always convinces me.

He kissed her cheek and the three of them went out to the beach. It was a very beautiful day, with some white clouds splashing the blue sky. There was a gentle, refreshing breeze that cooled the heat of the sun's rays, and the three began to walk. Luciano pulled up his pants and took off his shirt, walking on the water and getting wet up to his waist. Further back, Clarissa and Jerusa, protected by umbrellas, continued holding their arms, talking:

- Last night I heard a strange noise – said Jerusa.

- It was the wind – said Clarissa, laughing. – Scary, isn't it?

- Don't tell me that. I buried my face in Luciano's chest and didn't even want to open my eyes – . Clarissa laughed and continued:

Memories that the wind brings

– No wonder. I was going to warn you, but when the wind started, you didn't show up and I didn't want to bother you. I thought you weren't afraid.

– Luciano was not there. But I was terrified. I had never heard a more terrifying noise.

Clarissa was silent for a few minutes. When she spoke again she had a deep, worried voice:

– Jerusa, can I tell you something? You're not going to be afraid or think I'm crazy?

– No, what is it? You can tell me.

– You know that Abílio was a widower, right?

– I know.

– Yes. His first wife died of leprosy...

– So it's true? How awful, Clarissa!

– That's right. But that's not the worst of it. I believe that the spirit of Mrs. Leonor has not yet found peace.

– How do you know?

– I know why I hear things in the house.

– How so? Are they ghosts?

– Sometimes I hear a moan, a scream, as if someone is in a lot of pain.

– Isn't it the noise of the wind?

– It is no different. Behind the howl of the wind, I can clearly distinguish a groan of pain. It is frightening.

– Jesus, Clarissa! Then you scare me.

– Don't be silly. The screams usually come from the second floor, more precisely from the room at the end of the corridor, which was owned by Mrs. Leonor.

– And you think they are her?

– I am sure.

– But why? What does she want?

– I think she is tormented because she committed suicide, so I want to help her.

– Help her? But how?

– I have been going to your room constantly to pray for his soul.

– Are you crazy or what? What if the ghost of Mrs. Leonor appears to you?

– I have thought about it and I confess that I don't know what I would do. I think I would die of fear.

– Clarissa, you are decidedly crazy.

– I know. But I can't help it. I made that commitment and I intend to make it happen. And you know what?

– What?

– Another day. I was praying when I heard a knock on the wall.

– Blows? How so?

– It was a boom, boom, boom of fear. It looked like someone was banging or hitting something on the bedroom wall. I was terrified.

– What was it?

– I don't know. Mr. Abílio appeared, asked me to leave and locked himself in. After that, I didn't hear anything else.

– Strange.

– Yes, very strange.

– What do you think it was?

– I think Mrs. Leonor's spirit must have been enraged by my presence there.

– Well, Clarissa, what did you do?

– Nothing. I left and the next day, there he was again.

– And the noises?

– They stopped. I haven't heard them since that day.

– Was that a long time ago?

– No. It was just before you arrived. – Jerusa squeezed Clarissa's arm and babbled:

– You are right... it is very scary...

– I also believe. But I cannot be intimidated by a spirit that is still confused and tormented. It is my duty as a Christian to help her find peace.

– Are you sure about that?

– I am. Why?

– For nothing. I mean, that sounds so scary to me!

– So far I'm getting used to it. The moans even sound familiar, and those blows, if they happen again, will no longer take me by surprise.

Soon it was time to return, and Luciano joined them. The brother was so happy that even Clarissa was amazed. It seemed that he was at home.

– I feel so good here! – he said. – It's like I've spent my whole life by the sea.

– Is this true? – Clarissa was interested. – I had never noticed your interest.

– It is because we live on a hacienda, far from the beach. And the trips to the capital didn't allow me to see the sea with the freedom I feel here.

– I'm glad you're enjoying it. I was afraid you'd be upset.

– No way! I mean, I speak for myself. I don't know about Jerusa.

– Don't worry, honey, I'm fine. The lack of comfort seemed a little strange to me, but it's over now. And then, just being with Clarissa was worth it.

Memories that the wind brings

Clarissa smiled gratefully at her sister-in-law. She was also very happy with the presence of Luciano and Jerusa, and wished they would never leave. However, she knew that shortly after the New Year they would be leaving for the San Jeronimo Hacienda.

– How is Dad? – she asked, remembering her father.

– Since you came here, he is not the same.

He doesn't say anything, but I know he regrets what he did. He lives whining and sighing in the corners. Mom is the one who can calm him down.

– But what about the hacienda?

– Mr. Abílio paid a good price for you...

– Luciano! – he reproached Jerusa – . Don't talk like that. Can't you see that Clarissa is sad?

– Don't worry, Jerusa, it doesn't bother me anymore.

In fact, that's exactly what happened. Mr. Abílio paid for me and Dad sold me. It was a deal.

– Oh! Clarissa! – added Jerusa, crying. – I'm so sorry!

– You shouldn't. I've already accepted my fate. Today I am married to Mr. Abílio and, faced with the inevitable, I must do everything possible to make my life as pleasant as possible.

– Does he treat you with respect?

– Yes... – she hesitated – . Mr. Abílio is a very strange man, but he tries to do his best. He is temperamental and austere, and doesn't like to be contradicted.

But he is not a bad man,

– If you say so...

– It is true. He is tormented by the death of the woman and does not accept the disease that consumed her. That is why he is so withdrawn and cold. But he is not bad. Just look how Tiago likes it.

Memories that the wind brings

At that moment, they arrived at the house and saw Vicente, who was coming to meet them. Discreetly, Jerusa looked at Clarissa and noticed the air of satisfaction she made when she saw him. Jerusa said nothing. If the sister-in-law were to have an affair with her stepson, that would be worse than a bomb. However, Jerusa knew Clarissa and knew that she was an honest and dignified daughter, and that she could never betray her husband with her own son. However, the feeling that existed between the two was true and almost solid. She had noticed it. Looking discreetly at Luciano, she saw that he noticed something too. She had seen, by his look of disgust, that her husband had noticed the wave of emotion that these two radiated when they met. And if that were true, if they were really in love, the situation, besides being delicate, was dangerous.

Extremely dangerous.

CHAPTER 15

Five o'clock. The sun was setting on the horizon, only a flash of red light extended over the sea. From the window of his room, Luciano enjoyed that spectacle of nature. Nor could he imagine how impressed he would be with that city. It seemed that he was made to live in the sea; it seemed that he had never lived far from the sea.

– Honey – said Jerusa – can't you get enough of looking at the beach?

– No. I confess that I have never seen such great beauty in my life.

You know, Jerusa, if I had been born in Rio de Janeiro, for sure, I would have followed a career in the Navy.

– I'm glad you weren't born. I wouldn't like to see my husband dressed as a sailor.

– Silly!

She approached the window and Luciano kissed her passionately. Then, when they turned towards the beach, they stopped in amazement. Vicente was sitting very close to the water, and the figure of Clarissa was walking towards him. Luciano looked at Jerusa with concern and commented:

– Those two... I don't know, no.

– What do you have?

– I don't know. But they seem to love each other.

– God forbid, Luciano, don't even tell me that!

– It is true, Jerusa. I notice the sparkle in their eyes when they meet.

– Could it be that they are lovers?

Memories that the wind brings

— I don't think so, I know my sister and the way she was raised. As much as she rejects Mr. Abílio, her dignity would not allow her to cheat him, especially with his son.

— I also believe it...

At that moment, a strange noise caught her attention, and Jerusa raised her hand to her lips, stifling a cry of fear.

— Did you hear? — she asked to Luciano.

— What?

— That noise.

— I didn't hear anything.

Jerusa instructed him to wait and listen, but he heard no sound.

— You must have imagined it — concluded Luciano.

Jerusa did not respond. After a few minutes, however, it sounded again: uiuiuiuiui...

— But what is this? — Jerusa was terrified.

This time, Luciano also listened and looked away from the window, looking at the woman seriously. She was about to speak again, but he interrupted her, bringing his finger to her lips:

— Shh!

There was the noise again: uiuiuiuiui... — Luciano looked at her in amazement.

— Is it the wind? — asked Jerusa.

— I don't think so. It's not windy. Look out the window and you'll see.

In fact, there was no wind. There was only a slight breeze from the sea, but it was not enough to shake trees or windows or to generate that whining effect. In fact, there was even someone moaning. Luciano told Jerusa to be quiet and went to the door, opening it very slowly. The sound became louder and seemed to come from the end of the corridor.

Jerusa, terrified, retreated to the back of the room and shrank. She didn't want to go.

But Luciano was willing to find out where that noise was coming from. He ordered the woman to wait for him, closed the door and went to the place where the noise came from.

As he walked, the sound became louder. Jerusa had told him about the conversation he had had with Clarissa, and he was disturbed. Like his sister, he had enough contact with the blacks and their beliefs to know that spirits existed and could communicate with the living. And that groan felt so real! If there were any lost spirits there, he was willing to find them and, who knows, he might even talk to them.

When he arrived in front of Leonor's room, he stopped and put his ear to the door. In fact, the sound seemed to come from inside. He tried the latch and the door gave way. It was not locked. He entered slowly and took a look. Although it was already dark, there was still enough light to realize that no one was there. But the uiuiuiui... was still low, almost in a whisper. It was not constant, but intermittent, and stopped occasionally, then returned. What did that mean? He went to the center of the room and looked around. It was empty. Suddenly, he heard a loud boom from the wall on the other side. He was surprised; he wasn't expecting that, but he didn't leave. Instead, he went to the wall and called:

– Is anyone there? Answer! Who is there? Answer then!

Suddenly, all the noise stopped. He stood still for a few more minutes, but heard nothing else. Certainly, Leonor's spirit, seeing that it had been discovered, hid and became silent, so that he would not discover her. Luciano, however, continued:

– Mrs. Leonor, if you are here, listen to me. We don't want you badly. We just want you to go on your way in peace. Why don't you come and talk to me? I am not afraid.

No sound was heard. But there must be a spirit there, and it seemed very confused. The dead woman needed to find peace, and

Memories that the wind brings

Luciano would not mind talking to her in person. He knew her special sensitivity, something that a Frenchman called mediumship. He was studying spiritist literature without the father's knowledge. In one of his visits to the capital, he acquired some very revealing books and realized the wonderful experiences that tried to demonstrate the existence of spiritist phenomena.

From his earliest childhood, Luciano demonstrated mediumistic gifts. Every time a slave disembodied on the farm, he saw his spirit, which often spoke to him, leaving him truly terrified. In time, he began to observe slaves in their rituals and learned that they worshipped the dead. He learned a lot from grandmother Toña, who talked to him about the Eguns[6]. Even so, he never talked to anyone about their special faculty. He was afraid of the reaction of people, especially his father, who would soon call him crazy and try to have him committed. Only Grandmother Toña and Clarissa knew of his ability.

(6) N.A.: Eguns, souls of the dead.

Now, however, Luciano felt it was time to use his gifts. If a spirit needed help, it would be up to him to give due assistance and clarify the truths of the soul. He would talk to Clarissa and join her in that task, and together they would undertake a kind of session, where they would invoke the spirit of Mrs. Leonor and talk to her.

The spirit was not going to show up, and Luciano decided to leave. He didn't want to force or disrespect it. He went outside and closed the door, turning into the hallway, when he saw Clarissa approaching. It was almost six o'clock and he was preparing for another prayer session. Great, thought Luciano, so he could keep her company and begin his plan.

- What are you doing there? - she asked, watching her brother leave Leonor's room.

- Jerusa and I heard that noise you talked about. - She opened her mouth, surprised, and responded with anguish:

- Why didn't you call me?

Memories that the wind brings

– You were on the beach with Vicente... there was no time.

Sensing the hint in her brother's voice, Clarissa tried to defend herself:

– That's not what you're thinking, Luciano.

– I'm not thinking about anything.

– These, yes, but I want you to know that I only went to the beach because I needed to talk to Vicente about the Christmas party.

– Couldn't wait?

– No, I couldn't. I wanted to ask him to buy me some things tomorrow after school.

– I know... but I don't care. You are an adult and you know very well what you are doing with your life. Just be careful.

– I'm not doing anything, you don't have to worry. Now tell me: why did you come here?

– I told you, I heard a strange noise and came to find out.

– And...?

– And the noise disappeared when I called Mrs. Leonor.

– Did you call Mrs. Leonor?

– Why the scare? You know I'm not afraid.

– Yes, but...

– But nothing. I wanted to talk to her, but she didn't answer me. And what are you doing here? Have you come to your prayer session?

– That's right.

– Can I join you?

– If that's what you want... Maybe you can really help me.

The two were already heading for Leonor's room when a click caught their attention. They turned around at the same time and saw Angelina standing at the door of her room.

Memories that the wind brings

The red eyes said she had cried.

– Angelina! – exclaimed Clarissa. – Did something happen? You are crying! – Angelina came out into the hall and ran to her, throwing herself into his arms and sobbing:

– Oh! Clarissa, I can't take it anymore!

– Can't what else?

– I can no longer bear this anguish!

– What anguish? What are you talking about?

She continued to cry uncontrollably, and Clarissa hugged her, trying to calm her down. Luciano remained still, confused, a strange sensation overwhelming his chest.

There was something wrong, out of place, and he felt it, but he couldn't figure out what it was.

Seeing the sobbing that shook Angelina's chest, Clarissa began to caress her, saying in a soft and calm voice:

– Shh! dear, calm down. Get a grip, it's all right.

– No, it's not! Everything is terrible, everything is wrong! I can't stand it anymore, I can't stand it!

– What is happening? You can tell me. Trust me.

– Oh! Clarissa, help me! Help us!

– To whom? Tell me, Angelina, don't be afraid. What bothered you so much?

– It's mom...

– Angelina!

It was Vincente's voice, which sounded loud from the top of the stairs. The girl was startled and swallowed a sob, lowering her eyes and crying profusely. At once, she turned on her heels and ran back into the room, closing the door.

– You scared her. Vincente – he reproached Clarissa.

– Ah! but what a pity – he mocked – . That was not my intention...

Memories that the wind brings

– Now that's something! – she continued to chide – where have you seen yourself yelling at the girl like that? Why did you do that?

– Angelina talks too much.

– Why? Why would you talk about your mother? What is the problem?

In fact, I don't know why everyone here is so mysterious about the death of Mrs. Leonor...

– I'll give you some advice, Clarissa – said Vicente in a threatening tone – don't stick your nose where it doesn't belong. My mother's death is not your concern.

Clarissa retreated in fear, and Luciano, taking the initiative, looked at the boy seriously and hit back:

– What is it, Vicente? Are you threatening your stepmother?

Vincente looked at him defiantly, until he relaxed and responded:

– Of course not. I like Clarissa a lot, and she knows it. But what I am telling you is for your own good. She shouldn't be messing with these things.

– What things? Didn't your mother die? Didn't she kill herself? What's wrong with talking about her? Instead of answering, Vincente looked at Clarissa again and deliberately added:

– I warn you, Clarissa, not to get involved in these matters anymore. You know how much I like you and I would not like to see you get hurt.

– Injured? – She was stunned – why? Who would hurt me?

– The truth, Clarissa. You may end up discovering something you may never have discovered.

– I don't understand.

– Think about what I told you. So, don't say I didn't warn you.

Memories that the wind brings

Vincente turned and returned in the same way he had come, leaving Clarissa and Luciano astonished, not knowing what to think. Despite the threatening tone that Vincente had used, it was clear that he was not threatening her. It felt more like a warning, a warning that he was playing with something beyond his strength. But what would that be? It could only be related to the father. Only Abílio could instill such terror in the children, to the point of being afraid to even think about the mother.

The more she thought, the more Clarissa became convinced that Abílio had killed his wife. Only now she began to doubt the motives. Was it really out of pity? Or had he used the illness as a justification to commit an atrocious crime and get rid of the woman who had become an obstacle in his life? This hypothesis horrified her, but she began to put things together. Yes, in fact, Abílio got rid of the woman under the pretext of ending her suffering when, in fact, what he really wanted to do was to regain his freedom by getting rid of dead weight in his life. However, his conscience did not allow him to achieve the freedom he so desired.

After Clarissa shared her suspicions with Luciano and Jerusa, the three decided that they would pray for Leonor every day, invoking her, if necessary.

They did not want anyone else to attend, least of all Angelina, because Clarissa feared that Abílio, fearing that she would accidentally incriminate him, would end up sending her to some convent abroad.

Silently, the three of them entered Leonor's room. There was still light, and they moved the small table closer to the center of the room, placing three chairs around it. With the environment prepared, it was necessary to start working. They did not know how to proceed, but Luciano, half familiar with what he was reading, took the initiative and said in a deep and penetrating voice!

Memories that the wind brings

– Lord, at this moment we gather, asking your permission so that we can carry out our task with love and dedication, leading to the heart of our poor sister Leonor a little comfort and peace.

Then Luciano showed Clarissa one of the books he had brought, indicating a page where it read: For suffering souls that ask for prayers. It was a prayer made by suffering spirits, and Clarissa read it with interest and faith. Later, Luciano indicated his prayer: For a suicide, and Clarissa read again, full of feelings, mentally accompanied by others. During all the time the prayers lasted, Luciano thought of Leonor's tormented soul and asked her to manifest herself if she was so desired and allowed. But Leonor did not appear. At the end of the session, Jerusa said a prayer of thanks and closed. It had not taken more than half an hour, which was considered sufficient. They got up, put the table and chairs in place and left, going directly to Clarissa's room. After closing the door, she asked her brother:

– What did you feel, Luciano?

– Nothing – he answered, disappointed. – I felt absolutely nothing.

– But how? – Jerusa was outraged – . Well, if you didn't say so yourself make contact with the spirits, talk to them, feel them?

– It's true – agreed Clarissa. – One would expect you to feel some vibration.

– I didn't feel anything. Just a slight drowsiness, but nothing that would indicate the presence of suffering spirits there.

– What do you think it means?

– Perhaps Mrs. Leonor does not want our company and, therefore, did not heed our call.

– Strange. Why is that?

– I don't know. Maybe she's afraid, maybe she couldn't.

– What should we do? – asked Jerusa. – Surrender?

– Of course not – objected Clarissa. – Anyway, I am sure that the soul of Mrs. Leonor receives the intention of our prayers, even though she is not present.

– That's right – considered Luciano – . The spirit does not need proximity or incarnation to receive the thoughts sent to it. Even very far away, our thoughts reach them and are able to lead them to their full intention that we put into them. That is why it is important to always have good thoughts.

– Luciano is right – agreed Clarissa. – The best thing we can do is to send Mrs. Leonor what we most wish for her: peace. We will always imagine her smiling, serene, calm, walking through flowering forests, and never thrown into dark places and crying. Therefore, we can raise her mental level and bring it to us.

Toña's spirit was there and accompanied the meeting from the beginning. That is why Luciano felt sleepy, but he could not capture the vibration of any suffering spirit.

In the days that followed, the group met, always at the same time, and Clarissa read the prayers. As usual, Luciano felt sleepy, but nothing that could indicate that Leonor was there among them. The noise, however, had diminished. Those moans were almost not heard anymore, and they concluded that she, in spite of fearing his presence, had indeed received his thoughts and was already beginning to feel better. Luciano, intimately, hoped to gradually gain their trust and would come forward to receive personally the fervent prayers offered to him.

Christmas was already very close and, the next day, Abílio would return from Rio de Janeiro, loaded with gifts. He took the opportunity to buy new dresses and dolls for Angelina, elegant suits and hats for Vicente, and even some items for Tiago.

He chose jewelry for Clarissa, souvenirs for his brother- in-law and his wife, the main thing, decorations for Christmas.

On the eve of your arrival. Clarissa could not sleep. Her heart felt tense, as if some misfortune were going to happen. Seeing

Memories that the wind brings

that sleep was not coming, she got out of bed, raised the candle and went downstairs barefoot, sitting on the porch and feeling the cool night breeze caressing her face. She breathed in that salty air and leaned her head back against the railing, closing her eyes briefly. Suddenly, she felt someone touching her and opened her eyes in fear. It was Vincente who sat down next to her in silence. The two remained silent for about half an hour, smelling the scent of the sea that the breeze blew on their faces, until Vincente spoke:

– Dad arrives tomorrow.

– I know. Are we waiting for his return?

– I don't know, maybe.

– I thought you hated him.

He smiled half- heartedly and responded:

– And I hate him.

– So why do you miss him?

– I didn't say I missed him. I just accepted that I was waiting for his return.

– What is the difference?

– I want my father to come and put an end to these antics you've been doing, just for that reason.

Clarissa jumped up, indignant.

– What do you say? – she asked in amazement. – How dare you come here to confront me! Well, we know we're making great progress.

– Ah! Yes. I'm sure my mother will even show up...

– Who knows? It wouldn't be much.

– It is true. Every day, the dead rise from their graves to speak to the living. They go to their homes, eat at their table, even dance with them...

Furious, Clarissa stood up and, pointing her finger at her nose, shouted:

– Listen up, you naughty, arrogant boy! I am your stepmother and you owe me respect! I will not tolerate the sarcasm of a brat like full with anger. The angrier she got, the more beautiful she became. She screamed, but he didn't even hear her. He was fascinated by her presence, her perfume, her voice. Without realizing what he was saying, Vincente let out a whisper:

– I love you...

She stopped in the middle, her finger suspended in the air, right in front of her face. Instinctively, Vicente grabbed her finger and brought it to his lips, and Clarissa blushed, beginning to babble:

– Vicente... but... but... what do you think... what do you think you are... what are you doing... – He didn't answer and continued to hold her hand, and she, without realizing it, squeezed his too, until the emotion overcame her, and a heat began to rise in her neck, reddening her face and bringing tears to her eyes. Only then did she realize what was happening. Quickly, she put her hand away and took it to her mouth, horrified, turning and running like crazy inside the house.

Vincente did not follow her. He only saw her walk away without saying a word. He loved her immensely, even though he knew that love was a forbidden madness. She was his father's wife, and he had to control himself. But it was becoming difficult to contain his feelings. How could he pretend not to love her if he burned with love for her, felt his body burning at the thought of her, spent days trying to see her, at least on the side, for a fraction of a second? How could he deny that he loved her if his thoughts were all for her, from the moment he woke up until the last second before he fell asleep? And how many times had he not dreamed of her, of feeling the freedom of being able to have her all to himself, to love her, to feel her, to touch her without anyone being able to interfere with or condemn him?

Vicente sighed and turned to the beach when he came face to face with Tiago. The old man was standing at the foot of the stairs, looking at him with an air of recrimination.

– Tiago! You scared me! Shouldn't you be sleeping?

– You shouldn't do that.

– Do what?

– Making fun of his father's wife.

– I am not making fun of anyone

– It's no use, señóziño, I saw it.

– You saw too much

– If you want to think like that, I can't do anything.

But I'm a friend of your father's, and I'm a friend of yours, too, and I can't help but warn you.

– Warn what? You're going to tell him, huh?

– You know I'm not a gossip. I know you're a good boy and wouldn't do anything to upset your father. Or would you?

Vincente looked at him seriously and responded, without taking his eyes off his own:

– No, I would not. You know I wouldn't. I'd rather die than have to betray my own father.

– I know, and that's why I'm warning you: your father already realized…

– Are you sure? – he said, overwhelmed by concern and feeling a twinge of remorse in his chest.

– Yes, he didn't say anything, but I know he've noticed the way you look at each other. Just a blind man wouldn't notice.

– If so, then I must leave.

– There is no need to rush.

– I'm not rushing it. I really think it's too late… I can't risk staying and betraying my own father.

Memories that the wind brings

– This does not need to happen. You just need to control your instincts. The signaller is very impulsive and his heart beats like hers. But it can't happen, it can't.

– It will not happen – he repeated, convinced – . I guarantee it.

Vincente left there with a little heart. He didn't like his father, but he couldn't betray him. He was bound by a duty of honor and fidelity that he could not explain.

It was necessary to avoid meeting with Clarissa. I had to control her feelings. One way or another, it was necessary to stop loving her.

CHAPTER 16

Abílio arrived on a trip around six o'clock, entered and left his suitcase on the floor, took off his hat and passed the back of his hand over his forehead. He was tired and wanted to rest. Soon after, Tiago appeared, loaded with packages and asked:

– Where do I put these things, sir?

– You can take them to my office.

Tiago took the packages to the right place and when he returned, Abílio asked:

– Where is everyone?

– Señóziño Vicente is there on the beach, as always. Siñáziña Angelina is in the room.

He shut up and Abílio insisted:

– My wife and the rest?

– They are all there in the bedroom of Leonor...

– What? I told Clarissa I didn't want anyone there.

– Yes, but since you left, they have gathered there to pray for your wife's soul...

Without hearing anything else, Abílio rolled over on his heels and ran upstairs to Leonor's room. He opened the door violently and stopped in amazement. All three had their eyes closed. When they heard the door slam, the three interrupted the prayer and looked at him in fear.

– But what does this mean? – asked Abílio, mumbling.

– Mr. Abílio! – exclaimed Clarissa. – We are praying...

– I remember saying that I didn't want anyone here.

Memories that the wind brings

– Mr. Abílio – interrupted Luciano, – I think it was my fault. I was the one who offered to help my sister with this task. We heard moaning and thought we could help.

Abílio looked at him with disdain. He had nothing against him, but he couldn't let it get in the way of his life. However, he had to restrain himself so as not to arouse suspicion. If it was too difficult, the child would end up being suspicious, and then everything would be ruined. He would be arrested and convicted of the crime he had committed...

– Mr. Luciano – he answered, trying to stay calm, – you are my guest, but you have no right to disrespect my orders. And I gave Clarissa clear orders that no one was to come here.

– Mr. Abilio, you are ungrateful, it's true! – answered Clarissa angrily. – If we were willing to help the tormented soul of Mrs. Leonor, you should be the first to feel grateful. I know you believe in the survival of the spirit. Then why this reluctance to accept our help? What harm is there in gathering together in prayer? We are certainly not disrespecting anyone. On the contrary, we are trying to bring some peace to poor Leonor, whose spirit is still troubled.

– Who told you that? – He returned, confused and horrified. – I am sure that the spirit of my Leonor is very well in the place where she is.

– How do you know? Did you see her by chance? Did you talk to her? Or do you not hear the screams echoing through the walls of this house?

– Things are not always what they seem, Clarissa

– What do you mean? – said Luciano.

– Nothing. I don't want to say anything. And now, please leave. You have no right to be here.

Jerusa, who was trembling with fear of Abílio, got up quickly and pulled her husband by the arm, adding with a trembling voice:

Memories that the wind brings

– Come on, Luciano. Mr. Abílio is right...

He stood up slowly and looked at Clarissa, who nodded and left without saying another word. That man was horrible and could only be committed to Leonor's death.

After the two left and closed the door, Clarissa, barely holding back her anger and indignation, exploded:

– You're hiding something, aren't you?

– What would I have to hide?

– I don't know. Tell me, sir.

– I have nothing to say. I just ask you not to come here anymore. You are disturbing the rest of my Leonor.

– Disturbing? It was just what I was missing.

– I warn you, Clarissa. I allowed you to come because you insisted, but I will not tolerate any invasion or violation of my wife's sanctuary.

– But what is this? What do you love here?

– Don't talk nonsense, I don't love anything. I just don't want them here anymore.

– What are you afraid of, Mr. Abílio?

– I am not afraid of anything.

– Could it be that not? I think so.

– You are wrong. I have nothing to fear.

– I don't think so. You're afraid we'll find out the truth

– What truth would that be?

– The truth about your wife's death.

He paled and took a step back, adding a nervous whisper:

– What are you talking about? Clarissa?

She was confused. She felt she was at a crossroads, but there was no turning back. Full of courage, she looked at him accusingly and shot:

– You killed her, didn't you, Mr. Abílio? She couldn't stand her illness anymore and you killed her!

Abílio thought he was going to faint and had to hold on to the portal to avoid falling. He looked at her with deep disgust and made his voice hoarse and muffled:

– Do you think I killed her?

Already sorry to have made that accusation, Clarissa wanted to back off, but she couldn't see how. She had shot her in the face of her suspicions and now she was in grave danger of having something attempted against her. She had discovered her secret and did not even want to imagine what she would be capable of. Fearful of her reaction, he began to retreat to the window when he heard a sob. Someone was crying, but no one was there. She stopped, dazed, trying to identify where that sound was coming from, but it was coming from nowhere and everywhere. Clarissa looked at Abílio, wondering if he was listening too, but showed no sign of noticing.

With a voice full of pain, he added in an almost desperate tone:

– Get out of here...

She didn't wait a second. It went through him like a bullet, and closed the door as soon as she left. Clarissa came out of the unstable hallway, and Luciano, hearing her footsteps, opened the door to her room and called out to her. She burst into tears and began to vent:

– Oh! Luciano, I think I rushed.

– How so? – asked Jerusa. – What did you do?

– I told Mr. Abílio about my suspicions.

– What? – Luciano answered, barely believing his words – did you accuse him?

– Yes, I accused him of killing his wife.

– My God!

Memories that the wind brings

– And do you know what happened? Suddenly, I heard a sobbing, as if someone were crying. I think the spirit of Mrs. Leonor was there and she heard the whole conversation. She should be even more tormented.

– And now?

– I don't know. I fear for our safety and our lives.

– Do you think he might try something against us? – Jerusa was terrified.

– I don't know. As long as his secret remained hidden, I don't think he was capable of anything. But now that I have discovered it, I may not want any witnesses.

– What do we do? – asked Luciano, more for himself than for the girls.

– We need to get out of here as soon as possible – answered Jerusa, immediately.

– But how? And Angelina? I can't abandon her.

– Mr. Abílio is a criminal, Clarissa! – warned Jerusa.

– Who knows what he did with his first wife, and who knows what he might do with you.

Luciano, somewhat dubious, still reflected:

– We have to be careful with our suspicions and assumptions, so that no one can discover the truth or make a reckless judgment. Above all, we must seek the truth and see that it is revealed and preserved. Did he kill her? Did he confess by chance?

– Well, confess, not confess – considered Clarissa.

But it was written in his eyes, in his anguish.

– Luciano did not respond. He didn't know what to believe. If that were true, they would probably be in serious danger. But if it were a lie, they would be committing a terrible injustice. It was necessary to find out. After a few moments, he said: – I don't think Mr. Abílio is going to try anything against us. What could he do against the three of us? Kill us all at the same time? I don't think so. He is an intelligent man and would not take any thoughtless action.

– Luciano – said Jerusa in horror – are you suggesting that we stay?

– Yes.

Jerusa opened her mouth to answer, but Clarissa interrupted her:

– Perhaps you are right, Luciano. Although I don't believe in Mr. Abílio's innocence, we have to investigate, find out in what circumstances Mrs. Leonor died. Only then will we know what really happened.

– The only problem is that no one is willing to say anything. Tiago is as faithful as a dog.

Vincente, in spite of hating him, seems to maintain a pact of silence with him. And Angelina is still a child and is afraid of her father. What will we do?

– I think we should start with Mrs. Leonor's room. It would be ideal, but, for sure, Mr. Abílio will close it after that.

– That's right. What will we do then?

– I still don't know, thoughtfully considered Luciano, but I will think of something. Something tells me that we will end up discovering the whole truth. One way or another, it will come to us without us having to expose ourselves.

– How?

– I don't know. But that's how I feel.

– You are crazy! – Jerusa reproached him. – This can be extremely dangerous.

– I don't think so – answered Luciano. – Anyway, it's a risk we'll have to take.

– I agree with you, my brother. I could never leave poor Angelina alone. She trusts me as if I were her mother.

Memories that the wind brings

– It is true. And now, let us pray and ask God to help us.

The three knelt and began to pray. At that moment, Toña approached them and embraced them. First Jerusa, then Luciano, and finally Clarissa, pouring particles of white light over them, which invaded them, filling them with peace and trust.

✶ ✶ ✶

At dinner time, only Abílio was not present, and Angelina was surprised by his absence.

– Where is Dad?

– I don't know – answered Clarissa.

– Dad is locked in Mom's room – Vicente said, frowning.

Clarissa looked discreetly at Luciano. How did Vincente know? The brother, seeing the question in her eyes, asked:

– I'm sorry, Vicente, but how do you know that your father is in your mother's room? Did you see him? Did you talk to him?

– I do not. You do.

Clarissa, Luciano and Jerusa exchanged significant looks. It was clear that Vincente knew something. Had his father confided in him?

– Why do you say that, Vicente? – Clarissa answered – Were you listening to us?

– No. And I didn't even have to. I saw when he arrived and I know he went straight to Mom's room, where you were gathered.

I imagine they must have argued, and since he didn't show up, I guess he's still locked up in there.

– Why is that? – said Angelina.

– It's none of your business – responded Vicente angrily.

– That's right. Why are you treating me like this, Vicente? I am as much his daughter as you are and I deserve to know what is happening to my father.

- Now you better shut up.

- Don't talk like that to your sister, Vicente - , Clarissa reproached him. - You know that your father does not approve of that tone of voice.

Vincent did not respond. He didn't have the strength to argue with his stepmother.

- Vincente talks to me like this because he is afraid.

He glared at Angelina, and she recoiled in fear.

- Fear of what? - Luciano wanted to know.

- Fear of nothing. Angelina is a silly girl and very imaginative.

- What are you fantasizing about, Angelina?

He looked at his brother out of the corner of his eye and, noticing his hostile countenance, responded in a very low voice:

- Nothing, Clarissa. It is in my head.

- What kind of things? - added Jerusa, curious.

- Nothing. Nothing important.

- You can tell us - encouraged Clarissa - . You don't need to be afraid.

Vincente continued to look at her with a threatening look and made no attempt to hide his discomfort. Angelina always talked too much. Someday she'd spoil everything.

Fearing what she might say, she stepped forward:

- Angelina is afraid of the dark. She thinks little green creatures are spying on her behind the walls.

And he laughed. The rest, however, did not believe that story. Especially Clarissa, who had lived with the girl for some time. She was not afraid and Clarissa had never heard her tell a story like that. Calmly, she turned to Vicente and considered:

— I think you're fantasizing. Angelina is neither impressionable nor imaginative. It is you who are creating these stories.

Vincente did not respond. He got up from the table and walked up the stairs. He couldn't take it anymore. Silently, he went to his mother's room and called. Nothing, nobody answered. He insisted and called again and again, and until his father answered, he opened the door with irritation, but seeing his son standing there, he could not contain his admiration.

— Vicente! What are you doing here?

— We need to talk.

Vincente entered and closed the door, sitting on the bed that had been his mother's. Abílio pulled out a chair and sat down in front of him, resting his chin on his hands.

— Well — he encouraged — what is it about?

— I think you, better than anyone else, know what this is all about — . He looked at him without saying anything and Vicente continued: — I think Clarissa is very close to discovering the truth.

Abílio let out a deep sigh, shrugged his shoulders and dropped his arms over his body, declaring himself discouraged:

— What do you want me to do?

— I don't know. Maybe it's better to get her out of here.

— I thought about that too, but I think it will be worse.

— Why?

— I don't think she wants to leave. Angelina has become attached to... and you.

Abílio pronounced it with excessive emphasis, which Vicente pretended not to notice. He was worried and fearful of the consequences that might arise if Clarissa discovered the whole truth.

— Dad, you know I didn't approve of what you did, right?

– Yes, I know... But you also know that I had no choice – . Vincente remained silent, and continued: – If I had not done what I did, perhaps they would have taken your mother ...

– Wouldn't that have been better?

– How do you think she would feel, thrown into a leper camp to die, without any service and, worse, without the love of her people?

– But what good did it do? Anyway, we lost her.

– It was her choice. At least now, she has found peace.

– Is it? And the screams? We pretend not to listen, but the truth is we listen too. Are you really at peace?

– Don't condemn me, Vincente, please – I was visibly distressed. What my conscience accuses me of is enough. And now, I still have to put up with Clarissa's suspicions, thinking that I killed your mother.

– She said what?

– She said it.

Vincente shook his head and opposed it:

– We know that this was not the case. You are not a killer.

– I am a criminal, of all kinds. In the eyes of the law, I committed a crime and I must pay for it sooner or later.

– You won't pay, no! No one will know.

– There is no lie that remains hidden for life. Sooner or later, the truth always finds a way to show itself.

Fear was visible in Vincente's eyes, to which he responded with concern:

– What do you want to do?

– What can I do? Anything. Just wait. Give myself to God and wait.

– Do you think that solves it? Do you think God is concerned about us?

Memories that the wind brings

- You shouldn't turn against God, Vincente. He is the one who has supported us until today.

- It's even strange to hear you talk like that. A man like you, austere, relentless.

- I'm not any of those things. I agree that it's a little strict in my orders, but if I do it's to keep our family together. You know how much I care about you. You know that you and Angelina are all I have left in the world. Even if you hate me, I can't deny that I love you...

The emotion hindered Abílio's voice, which was silent in the confusion. He was not used to expose his feelings and was disturbed by the revelation he had made. So much emotion at the end infected Vincente, who, crying, knelt before his father and wrapped his knees, wetting them with sincere tears.

- Dad! Dad! - he cried - Why did this happen to us, why?

- I don't know, my son. It is God's design.

- Here you come with God again. If God was as good as they say, he would never have allowed my mother to get that damn disease!

- You shouldn't think that. I don't know why your mother got sick, but I do know that the illness ended what she started to do to herself. Since we got married, your mother always showed a withdrawn temperament, having difficulty living with friends, servants, relatives.

She found it difficult to relate to others, seemed unable to adapt to the world or people. I really thought I could hurt them.

- Damage them? But how? Mom never hurts anyone.

- I know, but I was afraid to do something that would hurt someone. I don't know where she got these ideas, but the fact is she isolated herself so she wouldn't risk hurting herself or anyone else. Your mother imposed voluntary ostracism.

He didn't feel part of the world, he didn't like to go out, show off, be with people. She felt excluded from everything, marginalized, and when someone tried to get closer to her, she ran away terrified, as if she could contaminate people with some kind of plague. She said, "I am afraid of hurting or harming someone."

- But how, Dad? How could Mom hurt someone?

- I don't know. All I know is that this weirdness started long before I got sick. I knew your mother when I was a child, our families were neighbors and friends. We played together and, in our youth, we soon fell in love. She always trusted me, I was the only one she opened up to. We had a good time together, and she never hurt anyone. Her mother always had a good heart and could never hurt or harm anyone. Not people, not plants, not animals. Anything.

- But then, how do you explain?

- I don't explain. That's why I say they are the mysteries of God. All I know is that his mother, before she became ill, was already marginalized by herself, imposing her distance from society. The illness only embodied an attitude that she had been adopting for a long time. Lepers, unfortunately, are marginalized by society, discriminated against and marginalized by everyone. Just like your mother felt.

- I did not know... Mom always seemed so loving, so dedicated.

- And it was. But that didn't hide the fear she felt at being exposed to living with her peers.

Vincente was crying softly. He shook his father's hand and asked excitedly:

- Why didn't you ever tell me that?

- In the beginning, because you were still a child and would not understand. After you grew up and matured, because you walked away from me, blaming me for what happened to you.

- Ah! Dad, how I wish everything was different.

Memories that the wind brings

- So do I, my son, but today I know that things happen as they should. It is useless to try to impose our will because, many times, what is destined is not what we want. You know, my son, Father Joaquim told me that we choose our destiny, but that we can change it as we become aware of our attitudes. We don't need to suffer.

- Do you want to tell me now that my mother chose to have leprosy?

- Everything happened before she reincarnated, and returned to bodily life. It was her planning, her way of getting rid of her guilt and her past imbalances.

I'm not saying it was the right choice, but it was the one she chose, because she believed it was the best for her. We have to respect it, therefore, respect the choices the spirit makes before incarnating. Rebellion is a lack of respect for the free will of others.

- I don't know if I believe that. Mom was a beautiful and kind woman. What guilt could she bear that would lead her to such a horrible fate?

- Only she can know. And we, as I said, must respect that and avoid any kind of judgment. All is well in the divine nature, and nothing happens except the balance of the universe.

- You say strange things, Dad, but they are so beautiful and wise. How could I hate you for so long?

- You never hated me. Not really.

Vincente continued with wet eyes, feeling that his father was right and that he had never stopped loving him. The father was a wonderful man, hidden under a blanket of rigor and austerity, because he also had his fears, his resentments, his difficulties.

- Daddy, how I love you... - Vicente sobbed, remaining silent because of the emotion.

They embraced each other in tears and stayed there, as if nothing in the world could separate them anymore.

Memories that the wind brings

* * *

That night, Abílio spoke to no one but his son. He left the woman's room and went directly to his room. He didn't feel like talking or seeing anyone much less Clarissa. He lay down on the bed and soon fell asleep. By her side. Clarissa, disconnected from her physical body by sleep, was waiting for her with Toña.

When Abílio saw them, he was startled and rushed back to his body, which shook, and he woke up startled, thinking he had had a strange nightmare.

Seeing him run back into the physical body, Clarissa commented disappointed:

– I think Mr. Abílio doesn't want to join us.

– It is a pity. His soul knows what it will face, and decided not to bring into consciousness what we will see in this hour. Very well, we must respect it. And now come, let us travel...

Toña took Clarissa's hand and took the flight with her, landing on the beach, in the same place where they always talked. It was a beautiful moonlit night and the wind blew a little stronger. Toña pointed upwards and Clarissa looked. Rays of white light fell from the moon and spilled over the waves, silvering them. Suddenly, the surface of the sea seemed to be transformed into a great mirror, and in it Clarissa saw some reflected images, images that would tell her everything she needed to know to face the events of the days to come.

CHAPTER 17

Agrippina was sitting at her private desk, writing a letter to her parents, when she heard a knock on the door and said mechanically:

– Come in. The maid came in and warned her that there was a man there who wanted to talk to her.

– Who?

– I don't know, ma'am, but I said it's important.

– Tell him I'm coming.

Minutes later, Agrippina entered the room where the visitor had been housed. When she came face to face with him, a shadow of recognition passed through her mind, but she couldn't clearly identify where she knew him.

– So, sir ...

– Carlos Castanheira, at your service.

– Mr. Carlos ... where do I know you from?

– From the house of my cousin, Archduchess of Linhares.

– Ah! It is true. Forgive me for not recognizing you, but I have a poor physiognomic memory.

"You don't have to worry, ma'am, it's natural." Agrippina indicated a chair and he sat down.

– Very well, Mr. Carlos, what brings you here?

– Ma'am, I'm sorry for what I'm going to tell you, but I felt it was my duty to warn you.

– Alert me to what?

– From your husband.

He felt as if a fog clouded his vision and replied:

Memories that the wind brings

– What does he have? Has something happened to you?

– Not yet.

– But then what do you want? Please be more explicit.

– Well, Mrs. Agrippina, the mission that brings me here is not the most pleasant, and you need to be strong ...

Agrippina jumped from her chair, put her hand on her chest and exclaimed:

– Something happened! He is dead?

– No, although I think you're about to lose him.

She opened her mouth and sat back down, leaning closer to him and asking:

– Lose him? As well? Is in danger?

– In a way, yes.

– What a danger? Some misfortune, an enemy?

– Not quite.

– Please, Mr. Carlos, be clearer. I'm already getting nervous.

– Well, Mrs. Agripina, I came here with the unfortunate task of alerting you to the case that your husband has had with a certain lady from Lisbon ...

She didn't even let him finish. She jumped out of her chair again and, cheering, began to shout:

– What? How dare you? Get out of here immediately!

Carlos stood up calmly. He expected that reaction and was not surprised. However, before leaving, he turned to her and finished:

– I understand your outrage, ma'am, and I don't blame you. The stab of betrayal is too painful, precisely because it is never expected. But I believe that my mission has been fulfilled and all I can hope for is that I will be strong and courageous to face the harsh reality. Ah ...! and if you need me, you know where to find me.

Memories that the wind brings

He put a piece of parchment on the table, bowed, and left. Agrippina took the scroll, furious, and was about to tear it, but changed her mind. This was absurd. She knew her Nicanor and knew that he could never betray her. However, she kept thinking about some events that had happened at her home in recent weeks.

Nicanor had always been a fiery man, but lately he hardly looked for her anymore, and when he did, he had no interest or enthusiasm. Also, not infrequently they were sometimes when he was gone for two or three days, he came back tired and unwilling. He apologized, saying he was working hard, studying maps, and taking short trips to increase his income, and she believed him. He always came home with money, and she had no reason to suspect him. But now...

Why had that man come to tell her that? For what purpose did you desecrate your husband's name? Was it possible that she was telling the truth?

Agrippina looked at the scroll and felt a chill. She rang the bell, calling for the maid and, after she appeared, ordered her:

– Go call Miguel.

Miguel appeared about five minutes later. He was Nicanor's valet, a dedicated but ambitious and venal man. As soon as he entered, he greeted her and asked:

– Did you send for me, ma'am?

– Yes, I do. I want to ask you something and I want you to be honest with me.

– No, ma'am, what is it?

– Do you know anything about a lover of my husband?

He was surprised and took two steps back. How had she found out? Despite being confused, Miguel managed to maintain his apparent calm and replied:

– I don't know anything, ma'am.

– Are you sure?

– Yes. As far as I know, Mr. Nicanor is very devoted to you.

Agrippina spent some time studying him, not knowing if he spoke the truth. She approached him and, looking deeply into his eyes, considered:

– I know of your loyalty to my husband. However, I am willing to pay for any useful information.

Miguel hesitated. As faithful as he was, he couldn't miss an opportunity like this. If the money was good, it would leave without a trace, and Nicanor would never know the name of his whistleblower. He could see Agrippina's extreme interest and thought he could get a lot of money out of her. Provoke in addition to his curiosity and determination to discover the truth, he replied:

– I'm sorry, Mrs. Agripina, but I don't know anything that might interest you. My boss has always been honest and loyal to you.

She was going to be satisfied. If Miguel said he didn't know anything, it was because he didn't. he was a confidant of Nicanor, but he couldn't be trusted, and he might as well betray him for a good sum. But if she still defended her husband, it was because he was truly innocent, and that accusation was unfounded. With the crumpled scroll that she still held in her hand, she added:

– It's okay. I believe in you. You can go.

Miguel paled. He imagined she would insist, but was easily convinced instead. But he couldn't let the gold run through his fingers like water, and from the doorway he turned to her and announced, with a studied apology in his voice:

– Excuse me, Mrs. Agripina, but I am faithful to my teacher ...

By the way, Miguel left a reluctance in the air, which was enough for Agrippina to withdraw. He knew something, sure, and he just hadn't told her because he said he was faithful to Nicanor. But there was no loyalty that money couldn't buy, and Agrippina was willing to pay a high price for it.

Memories that the wind brings

* * *

When Nicanor got home, Agripina was eagerly waiting for him, but disguised him. He entered cautiously, walked over to her and kissed her cheek. Pretending to be alien, she asked:

– Where were you?

He was surprised by the question, but answered it with apparent ease.

– Working. Why?

– You are welcome.

In silence, Nicanor retired to his rooms. Agrippina generally did not ask him such questions, and he was meditating. Did she suspect something?

If so, he had to be careful. He loved his wife immensely and would suffer greatly if he lost her.

Thinking about it, Nicanor felt angry with Luisa. That damn woman! She had bought him with threats to destroy her marriage and her finances, and he had no choice but to give in to her insistence. She was a fantastic woman, it was true. Warm, fiery ... a true courtesan. But she was a woman to spend a few nights, and not the rest of her life. Luisa seemed to be possessed by an endless fire, which made her want sex more and more. The more he loved her, the more his love asked her. She was insatiable, always ready to give up. And he was forced to respond to her ardor, under the pain of suffering the consequences of his hatred. And then when he got home, he was tired and without the strength or the courage to love his own wife, the only one to whom he gave any real affection.

Until then, Agrippina had not suspected anything. He always apologized, demanded work, and she was convinced. Even more so because Luisa, to compensate her for her services, used to present her with significant amounts, thereby increasing the luxury and comfort of her home. But now ... Agrippina had asked him where he had been with exaggerated disinterest. If she was suspicious, it was necessary to find out and get ahead of her. He would confess his relationship with Luisa and tell her everything as it happened. Maybe that way she would understand and forgive him. Agrippina was very different from other women. Anyone else would rather not find out, or pretend not to know anything, just to keep up appearances, avoiding the rumors of society. But Agrippina was not like that. She was a jealous and possessive woman, and she couldn't hide her feelings. If something bothered her, she soon showed it. She did not know how to pretend or act to please or preserve her husband. If she discovered something, Agripina would be satisfied and could even attempt on Luisa's life. But she couldn't allow that to happen. If she found out, she would forgive her and stay away from any lover. It was a promise and she would keep it, which wouldn't be difficult. At that moment, the door opened and Esmeralda entered. It was her daughter, her joy, her charm. which would not be difficult. At that moment, the door opened and Esmeralda entered. It was her daughter, her joy, her charm. which would not be difficult. At that moment, the door opened and Esmeralda entered. It was her daughter, her joy, her charm.

Esmeralda was a beautiful girl, with white skin, blond hair, almost like Luisa's, clear blue eyes and serene. She was ten years old now and she was the joy of the house.

– "Hi Daddy – she said, throwing herself at his neck. – What did you bring for me today?

– "Um ... let me see, – he replied cryptically, pulling a small package from his cloak pocket, thrown on the couch.

Esmeralda picked up the package and began hastily to open it, ecstatic with its contents. It was a small ivory box, with angels carved around it and lined with sky blue velvet.

– Oh! Dad, it's beautiful! Thank you.

– Not as beautiful as you.

Memories that the wind brings

The girl sat on the sofa and continued turning the box, passing it from hand to hand. Nicanor looked at her and felt an immense tenderness in his heart. She was a priceless treasure, and he could do anything to make her happy. She and the woman were the most precious things in life, and losing them would be a worse punishment than death. Thinking about it, Nicanor kissed Esmeralda on the forehead and called the maid, ordering her to take her and call Miguel. Esmeralda, despite being upset, obeyed and went to put the box in her room. Shortly after, Miguel appeared.

– Yes my lord.

– Sit down, Miguel, I want to talk to you – . Miguel sat down and waited.

– I think my wife suspects something.

He raised his eyebrows and, pretending he knew nothing, replied indignantly:

– Are you sure?

– Of course not. But today she asked me where I was, and that's not natural. She must have known I was working.

– I'm sorry, sir, but don't you think you're not worried about anything?" She may have asked to ask.

– Could even be. But there was something in his voice that sounded strange, artificial, I can't say. Somehow, I feel like she already knows.

Miguel inhaled and released the air very slowly, asking at the end:

– What do you want me to do?

– I want you to pay attention. You are the only person I can trust. If she makes any suspicious movements, anything that indicates she've discovered the truth, I want to be the first to know. I know Agrippina and I know how much she will enrage her. But if I anticipate and tell you everything before anyone else, I am sure you will forgive me. Nothing like the truth to win the trust of a woman like Agrippina. Besides forgiving me, she will feel sorry for me, threatened and humiliated by a powerful woman like Luisa.

Miguel shook his head thoughtfully. It could never happen. He needed to be the first

to tell Agrippina everything, or else he could see his hopes of becoming a rich man lost forever. If Nicanor anticipated it, she would have no reason to give him money, and her opportunity would be wasted. Miguel got up and, trying to give his voice a tone of confidence, said:

– Don't worry, my lord. If I know something, I'll let you know soon. After leaving, Nicanor lay down on his bed and soon fell asleep, unaware that Agrippina opened the door to his rooms and sneaked in, lying next to him. He was so tired that he didn't even notice her, and she stood there with him, thinking about how much she loved him and what she could do to have him with her.

Lying on Luisa's bed, Nicanor watched her get dressed. She had a wonderful body, she was an exuberant woman, but he did not love her.

– I'm going to have to leave you now, – she said. – I need to get out.

– Okay, – Nicanor replied, barely containing his satisfaction.

Nicanor got up and started dressing as well. She was strange. For a few days she seemed different, a little distant, without interest. Before, after they loved each other, they stayed in bed, talking about futility, times when she always reaffirmed her ancestry over him. Nicanor was filled with anger, but said nothing. He knew he was tied to it, and there was nothing he could do. But today, something seemed to have changed. Was it his impression or was Luisa trying to get rid of it? Although curious, he said nothing, finished dressing, picked up his cloak and prepared to leave. When he approached to say goodbye, Luisa stopped him with her hand, looked him in the eyes and declared:

– It was nice meeting you, Nicanor. You are a unique lover. However, as of now, there is nothing between us. It is all finished.

Nicanor opened his mouth, stunned. He didn't know whether to laugh or cry. He would laugh with joy at finally being able to free himself from his yoke. If he cried because she injured his pride and manhood.

Suddenly, he was filled with hatred. It was an insult, and he wanted to strangle her. However, he slowed his momentum. He got what he wanted, didn't he?

Why get your hands dirty with that bitch's blood? Without giving her an answer, Nicanor turned his back on her and left, determined never to set foot in that house again.

When he left, Luisa called for the maid to comb her blond hair. She was tired of Nicanor. He was an excellent lover and made her body tremble, although he did not touch her heart. And then she knew that he didn't love her either, but his wife. When he demanded that he not leave her, threatening him in every way, she gave up, but she was sure he hadn't done it out of love, but out of fear. He loved that idiot Agrippina and had only become her lover out of fear that she would destroy his life and marriage.

He was a rude man, and his conversation was not at all interesting. He only understood navigation and sea routes, and did not know anything about literature, music, arts. She was an extremely cultured woman, with a refined education and refined tastes. On the contrary, he was rude, with a forced and primary education. It had neither refinement nor finesse, and that was already bothering her. How foolish she had been to think she loved him! The fire of passion was extinguished, and she thought of Carlos again. Carlos, yes, he was a man of his own. She remembered that he always told her that they were made for each other, and that it was true. Carlos was made for her. Fine, educated, a true gentleman.

Memories that the wind brings

Luisa called the carriage and headed towards her cousin's house. She missed his smart and funny conversation, and was sorry for treating him so badly.

But he would know how to understand. Carlos loved her and did not reject her. She entered without warning and went straight to her room, entering without knocking, followed by the chamberlain, who was trying to stop her. He was still asleep, with a woman by his side, but Luisa was not moved.

He opened the curtains and the sun hit them in the faces. Carlos woke up scared and put his arm in front of his eyes, to stop the light, and exclaimed:

– Hears! What's going on...?

When he saw Luisa standing in front of the bed, with a wry smile on her lips, Carlos jumped up, exuding happiness. He could hardly believe what he was seeing.

The woman beside him, her face buried in the pillows, continued to sleep, and Carlos had to push her to wake her up. The girl opened her eyes sleepily and, in front of Luisa, shrugged and was about to protest, when Carlos said:

– Very good Miss... – . He no longer remembered her name – ... well, never mind. Get up and get out. I no longer need your services.

The girl, without understanding anything, got out of bed covering herself with the sheet and went after the butler, who led her to another room. When they were at the door, Carlos yelled to the servant:

– Alcino, pay the usual amount and send her home, then he turned to Luisa and said emotionally:

– What a wonderful surprise!

Luisa didn't answer and took him to the bed, lay down next to him and kissed him with all her heart. Then they loved each other like crazy, and Carlos felt extremely happy. It was always like this. Luisa found a lover, but when she got tired, she went back to him.

Memories that the wind brings

She remembered Agrippina and the visit he had made the other day, instantly regretting it. Had she believed it? Did she keep his address? Carlos felt his body freeze and pressed Luisa against his chest. Although she did not reveal the name of her husband's lover, he was afraid that she would decide to investigate. From what he had heard, Agrippina was an extremely jealous woman, and if she found out the truth, she could ruin his plans with Luisa. But now that it was all over, maybe she didn't care. Perhaps she hadn't even heard him and destroyed that piece of parchment. From the way she had treated him, it seemed as if she hadn't believed him, and the conversation should have had no other consequence.

But how wrong was Carlos! Agrippina, increasingly suspicious, thought it was time to look for Miguel again. Taking advantage of her husband's absence, she called for him.

– Where is Nicanor?

– He left, ma'am.

– Excellent. That way we can talk more freely – he waited for her to begin, and she began the topic: – Very good. I know you know something about my husband and I want you to tell me everything.

– I don't know anything, ma'am – he ventured.

She looked at him disdainfully and spilled a handful of gold coins on the table, and Miguel's eyes gleamed greedily. That was a fortune!

– You really don't know? – Agrippina insisted.

He licked his lips and, without taking his eyes off the coins, replied:

– Well, Mrs. Agripina, I do not want you to think that I am a scoundrel and a traitor ...

– I don't think anything, just tell me what you know.

– What exactly do you want to know?

– I want to know if my husband has a lover and what her name is – . He sighed, suspending, and responded theatrically:

– Mrs. Agripina, you shouldn't ask these questions. But as you really want to know, your husband does have a mistress, yes.

She put his hand to his mouth, trying to stifle the cry she had almost lost, and continued:

– Who? Tell me her name, come on!

Miguel raised his greedy eyes to her and answered without hesitation:

– Your Highness, Mrs. Luisa, Archduchess of Linhares.

That was a tremendous shock to Agrippina. She could never imagine her husband cheating on her with a lady of the highest nobility in Lisbon. She thought of a courtesan or even a distinguished married lady, but not someone of such high lineage. She was powerful, and destroying her would be the most difficult task. With tears in her eyes, she said to Miguel, trembling with hatred:

– Take your money and go!

Miguel quickly collected the coins. He needed to leave as soon as possible or Nicanor would kill him. With that money, you could start your life far away. He would go to Spain. He had relatives there who would not hesitate to welcome him. Even more so now, that he had become a rich man. Without looking back, he closed the door to Agrippina's rooms, who collapsed in the chair, sobbing incessantly.

CHAPTER 18

Nicanor entered the house with enthusiasm, and Esmeralda ran to meet him, throwing herself at his neck and kissing him repeatedly. Behind her, Agrippina was looking at him with a sour look. He was still not sure what to do, but in any case the daughter had to not suspect anything. She was a very sweet girl, and Agrippina adored her. He needed to prevent her from suffering.

After father and daughter finished their effusive greetings, Agrippina took the girl by the hand, kissed her on the cheeks and, stroking her hair, said:

– Now go play with Ana, will you? Mom and Dad need to have a conversation.

The girl kissed her mother and left with the nanny, and Nicanor, curious, gave her an inquisitive look.

– Something happened?

– You, better than anyone, can tell me.

But not here. I don't want anyone else to hear our conversation.

She left, and Nicanor went after her, curious. In his heart, he already knew what it was about and was afraid. What if she left him and took her daughter? After being accommodated, Nicanor asked:

– Okay, here we are. What happened?

– We have always been faithful and honest with each other, right? – He didn't like it at all, but he agreed, – That's why I'm going straight to the point.

I heard you were involved with a certain court lady ...

Memories that the wind brings

Nicanor didn't give her time to finish. Throwing himself to his feet, he grabbed his legs and began to cry.

Excited, Agrippina almost stroked him, but stopped. Could not soften – . Crying, he asked:

– How did you know? Who told you?

– Then it's true ... and I thought there might still be some mistake – . Little by little, Nicanor calmed down. He wiped his eyes and, on his knees, pleaded:

– Agrippina, by God, in the name of the happiness of our daughter, forgive me.

She was amazed. She thought he was going to deny it, claiming to be the victim of some intrigue or gossip of some envy. But instead, he acknowledged his guilt before she finished accusing him. Trying to maintain self- control, she continued:

– Do you confess that you have another woman?

Please let me explain what happened – he begged. Later, if you don't want more to see me, I'll leave without even asking.

He looked at her, waiting for an answer, and she agreed:

– Very good. Ahead.

Nicanor took a deep breath and began:

– I met this lady on my last trip to Calicut ...

– Who? tell me your name

– It does not matter.

– Yes it does. I know who it is, but I'd like to hear it from you.

Fighting to contain his shame and embarrassment, Nicanor spoke in a low voice, almost in a

– The Archduchess of Linhares – she shuddered, but said nothing, and he continued: – As whisper:

It said, I met Luisa on my last trip to Calicut.

Memories that the wind brings

She and her cousin, Mr. Carlos Castanheira, were my passengers. Throughout the crossing, she was looking at me provocatively, hinting at me with incomparable boldness. When we got to Lisbon, the situation got even worse.

The Archduchess is an influential and powerful person, her husband had ties to the court and she threatened me if I did not accept her as her lover. At first, I wanted to resist. I said that I loved my wife and that an affair between us would be impossible. But she was not satisfied. Using all her influence, she threatened to ruin us, and I ended up giving in, fearing what she might do.

– And what could she do, Nicanor?

– Ruin me. With his influence, she said that she would arrange for my release from my position as captain. You know, the ship doesn't belong to me, and what would us be if I lost my position? Where would you find another ship? All my life, all I learned was how to navigate. What would we live on without a boat? She asked the king to grant me a license and proceeded to give me money so that I could continue to support my family without arousing suspicion. She threatened to tell you everything, and she was scared. How could you bear living without you and Esmeralda?

Trying to contain her jealousy and resentment, Agrippina muttered:

– Do you still see each other?

– No. A few days ago, without explanation, she finished everything and fired me. Believe me, Agrippina, please! I never loved the Archduchess. I only agreed to get involved with her out of fear of losing you and Esmeralda. You have to believe it!

Agrippina did not know what to say. Her husband seemed sincere to her, and she was well aware of the Archduchess's fame. It was very possible that she had bought him. He, for some time, always showed up at home with money, much more than he would earn in his career as a captain. And then, seeing her husband there, lying on the ground at her feet, overwhelmed and humiliated, crying like a helpless child, she had no doubts. Nicanor told the truth. He had been an innocent victim of that debauchery.

It was necessary to take revenge on her, but how? Agrippina recognized her power and needed to act with caution. She leaned next to Nicanor and hugged him, whispering in his ear:

– Don't worry, I believe you. But that viper will pay us.

Nicanor reduced it with emotion. I couldn't bear to lose it. And then, he had even told the truth. Or almost everything. He had only omitted the fact that he and Luisa became lovers even on the ship, and that she had made no effort to conquer him. But what to do? He was already at sea for a few days, away from home and his wife, the body that longs for the ardor of a woman. Nicanor was a man and saw no harm in amusing himself with worldlings. They were simply women of easy life, with whom he did not have a lasting or loving relationship. In general, he saw them only once, every time he was away from Agrippina, and then got rid of them. But with Luisa it was different. She was a lady, more than that, an archduchess, and he couldn't get rid of her as if she were a prostitute. And then she fell in love and didn't want to let him go. What other way could it but conform and accept its impositions? But now he was free. Despite the hatred he felt for Luisa, Nicanor thought it best to forget her.

I can request a transfer to any other port, – he suggested hopefully. We can continue with our life away from the court and the evil of Luisa.

No, – Agrippina said sharply. – Where would we go? You already know the most prosperous port in Portugal and Lisbon.

And then I like the court. It wouldn't be fair that we have to get away from here because of that ordinary.

Nicanor did not insist. He would do what he wanted, as long as he did not abandon him.

Memories that the wind brings

The next day Nicanor stepped forward to resume his post as captain, and two weeks later he embarked on a new voyage to Calicut. Seeing herself alone, Agrippina thought about starting to act. She remembered the parchment that Mr. Carlos Castanheira had hit him and went looking for him. She had crushed, but had not thrown it away. She had to remove it from the fireplace, but she caught it before the fire consumed him.

In possession of Carlos's address, Agripina called the carriage and ordered the driver to take it there. Carlos had left and was told that he could meet him at the home of his cousin, the Archduchess of Linhares, where he was spending a season without a scheduled return date.

The information did not surprise Agrippina. Carlos could only be Luisa's lover and a spiteful lover, which justified her attitude. When she left him for Nicanor, Carlos had to swallow his anger and jealousy, but decided to take revenge by denouncing his lovers. Only now, after their breakup, had Luisa probably gone back to Carlos, which was a shame. Agrippina thought she could count on Carlos's favors to devise a plan of revenge against the archduchess, but that now seemed impossible. If they were truly lovers, Carlos would never help her do anything against Luisa.

Agrippina returned home dejected. What would you do to get revenge on that woman? Upon entering, she was immediately greeted by her daughter, who received her with the usual affection.

Esmeralda was a pure and sweet girl, and her love made Agripina forget her problems for a few moments.

– Would you like to go for a walk? – She asked to Esmeralda. – It is a beautiful morning.

– Oh! Mom, I would love to.

Agrippina ordered the maid to fix her daughter. She needed to get out, breathe fresh air, distract herself.

Nothing better than a walk in the open air to relax from ideas. They rode a small carriage until Agrippina ordered the

Memories that the wind brings

driver to stop. They would walk. She got out of the car in the company of her daughter and her mistress, and they began to walk side by side. Esmeralda was satisfied, running after the birds, always with the maid following her.

– Esmeralda, be careful! – yelled the mother.

But Esmeralda didn't listen to her. She was running and jumping, and she didn't even know how she was walking. Until, inadvertently, she ran into a passing man and collapsed to the ground. Agrippina ran to her, but the girl had not been injured.

Just a few scratches on his elbow, which he had leaned on when he fell. The man she had encountered, at a certain age, crouched beside her, seemed to be examining her.

– "Okay," – he told Agrippina. – Nothing happened.

– Esmeralda, my daughter, I should see where you are. The knight could have been injured or hurt.

– Oh! no, ma'am, '– said the man. – I owe you an apology. I was distracted...

– You're very kind, but I know it was Esmeralda's fault ...

– No way. And, if I can, I'd like to walk you home.

– Thank you very much, but that won't be necessary. Our carriage is back there. He followed the direction his finger was pointing and saw the carriage stopped a little lower.

– Even so, madam, I insist that you let me accompany you.

Agrippina did not argue further. The man was just trying to be nice, and she didn't want to appear rude. He extended his arm towards her, and they were walking towards the carriage. On the way, they spoke:

– Allow me to introduce myself, ma'am. I am the Marquis of Avis, a physician, at your service.

"Nice to meet you, Marquis," – she said with a smile. – My name is Agripina Vasconcelos, and this is my daughter Esmeralda.

– It is a pleasure to meet such a beautiful girl.

Memories that the wind brings

"Thank you," – Esmeralda replied, embarrassed.

They reached the carriage and were saying goodbye when the Marquis added:

– Wouldn't you like to go to my house for lunch?

– Oh! no, – Agrippina rejected. – We don't want to disturb you.

– It will not be a bother, and my wife would be very happy to receive your visit. And then, it will be a way to make up for the little incident just recently.

– Thank you very much for your invitation, but we cannot.

– Why not? Why do we hardly know each other? Now, Agrippina, but what is that?

I'm already an old man and my wife won't mind. On the contrary, I am sure it will perk up.

Agrippina thought for a few minutes. That Marquis could be useful. He was a nobleman and should know all the nobility in Lisboa. And who knows he would also know the Archduchess of Linhares? That thought encouraged her, and she finally agreed:

– If so, that's fine. I accept your invitation

From there they set out for the Marquis's residence, which was just two streets below. It was a beautiful castle, and they were received with honor and courtesy. The Marchioness of Avis was a very polite and kind woman, and she soon fell in love with Esmeralda. She had lost her daughter, many years ago, when she was still a child, and she never got pregnant again. So when she saw Esmeralda, her heart was tender and she was delighted with the girl. In addition, she was cheerful, intelligent and educated, and the Marchioness felt very comfortable in her company.

During lunch, Agrippina was waiting for the opportunity to present the subject on the Archduchess, to see if they knew her. The Marquis, unprepared, asked:

– And your husband, lady, what does he do?

Memories that the wind brings

- My husband is the Captain of the ship Santa Isabel.

- A captain? It must be very interesting

- Yes it is. Currently, he travels from Lisbon to Calicut, bringing spices and some passengers. You are traveling right now.

- You must feel very lonely, right? - Asked the Marchioness, penalized.

- Sometimes. But I'm used to it now.

- And when will he return?

- In a month, I think.

The Marquis looked at his wife, who nodded and continued:

- You know, Mrs. Agripina, in a month and a half, more or less, we will celebrate our fifty- year wedding anniversary.

- It is true? That's wonderful!

- "Yes, it is," - added the Marchioness. - When we got married, I was eighteen and he was twenty- three. We would have been very happy if it hadn't been for the loss of our little girl.

The Marquise's eyes filled with tears and Agrippina spoke with regret:

- So sorry.

- This is past and we have to live in the present, right?

- Hey! Yes.

– Well, as my wife said, we will soon be married for fifty years and we plan to have a beautiful party in our castle in the country.

– A party?

– It will be a week full of parties. During the day, hunting. At night, the dance. We would like you to be present.

Agrippina looked at them in amazement. She didn't know what to say. That invitation was an honor, and she couldn't refuse. But she was embarrassed and replied shyly:

– An invitation like this is an honor, especially from such illustrious people. However, I don't know if my husband will agree.

– Now, please convince him. We would be very happy with your presence, especially with the presence of little Esmeralda.

Esmeralda smirked and turned to her mother, almost pleading:

– Oh! Please mommy, come on! Accept. Please say yes!

– I don't know, little girl ...

– "Come on, Mrs. Agripina," – the Marchioness insisted. – I'm sure you will have a lot of fun. All the nobility of Lisbon will be present.

That news was wonderful. All the nobility of Lisbon included the Archduchess of Linhares. Agrippina knew of Luisa's reputation. However, there was no nobleman or hidalgo at court who did not invite her to parties. But she needed to be sure. Trying to contain her nervousness, she asked point blank:

– Will the Archduchess of Linhares be present?

– Mrs. Luisa? Why do you ask?

– Well, I met her at a party at her house, as soon as she returned to Lisbon. She crossed in my husband's boat.

– But what a coincidence! – Asked the Marchioness.

– We were at that party too. Too bad they didn't introduce us.

– Yes, it is a pity.

– But also, there were so many people ... – . lamented the Marquis.

– Is the Archduchess your friend? – Asked the Marchioness.

– Not quite. The archduchess was so kind inviting us to her party …

– Well, don't worry. Mrs, Luisa is an ardent lover of hunting and never fails to attend a party. It will certainly be present.

Agrippina said goodbye to Avis, elated. It had been an extraordinary coincidence! Her plan was beginning to work. Soon she would have that ordinary one in her hands, and then yes, she could finish her revenge.

CHAPTER 19

Sitting in his cabin on the ship Santa Isabel, Nicanor was thinking. How did Agrippina find out about her relationship with Luisa? The romance was secret, they did not share it with anyone. They did not attend society together, they did not show themselves in public, they did not go to common places. Someone had told him. But who? Was it Carlos? Or Miguel? The two of them were the only ones who knew the whole story. Or was it an old lover of Luisa who discovered them by chance and decided to take revenge? As far as he knew, he had no enemies, but Luisa ...

Nicanor, however, was almost certain that Miguel was responsible. From the day Agrippina revealed to him that she knew the whole truth, the servant had disappeared, along with his wife's jewels. She had told him that Miguel had stolen and fled, but had not allowed him to go after him.

It was all very strange. How could Miguel have had the opportunity to enter Agripina's rooms to rob her without her noticing? And why didn't Agrippina want him to find the thief?

These questions annoyed him more and more. Basically, Nicanor believed that his wife had given Miguel the jewels in exchange for information, and the servant, driven by greed, had told him the truth. But what would have caused Agrippina's mistrust? It no longer mattered. The only thing that mattered was the fact that he had gotten rid of Luisa, and Agrippina had forgiven him.

Soon the ship docked in the port of Lisbon, and Nicanor, after fulfilling the duties that the post requires, immediately set out. He missed his wife and daughter, and longed to hold them in his arms. When he got home, Agrippina was waiting for him, wringing her hands nervously. The day of the feast of the Marquis and

Memories that the wind brings

Marchioness of Avis was near, and he feared that Nicanor would not arrive on time.

Knowing about the situation, Nicanor did not want to accept the invitation. After all, it was a couple they barely knew and perhaps they were only invited out of courtesy, but Agrippina insisted on going. It didn't matter what the invitation was about, it was the invitation itself. Nicanor did not feel in a position to deny Agrippina anything and ended up accepting, without even imagining that he could find Luisa among the other guests.

Two days later, the three of them went to the castle of the Marquis. They were received with great distinction and accommodated in comfortable and luxurious rooms. Agrippina and Nicanor occupied a room, and Esmeralda was placed in the next room. Once installed, they went down to see the property. The castle was huge and very well maintained, and Esmeralda soon felt free to run and join the other children. The Marchioness informed them that there was no danger and that they could leave the girl at ease, since there were pages in abundance, with orders not to neglect the children.

Seeing their daughter leave excited with other children, Agripina and Nicanor went for a walk through the gardens, carefree. They returned around lunchtime, which would be served on the terrace, and were surprised by the scene they saw. Seated at a table, was the Archduchess of Linhares, holding nothing more and nothing less than little Esmeralda, who seemed delighted with something she was saying to her.

Nicanor thought he was going to faint. His first reaction was to try to escape. He turned to the woman and immediately apologized:

– Sorry honey, I could never imagine such a thing. Let's get Esmeralda and get out of here as soon as possible.

– "Don't be in such a hurry," – said Agrippina, with a strange glint in her eyes.

– How not? What happened to you? We can't stay here.

– We can and will stay.

– Why? I do not understand. Do you want to feel humiliated?

– Who said I would feel humiliated? – Before Nicanor's astonished look, she called: – And now come. Let's find where to sit.

Remembering that Agrippina had said that she would like to meet the Archduchess again, the Marchioness of Avis placed her beside her, and Luisa was surprised to see them approach.

She opened her mouth, startled, and was about to speak when Agrippina, pretending to know nothing, took a step forward:

– Your Highness, what a pleasure to see you. Do you remember me? – The other pretended to remove the memory, and she added: – I am Agrippina,

Captain Nicanor's wife, on whose ship you returned of Calicut. I was at your house once. I don't know, do you remember?

Somewhat puzzled, Luisa studied the woman in front of her. She remembered her very well, but what was she doing there? Trying to sound disinterested, she replied:

– I vaguely remember …

– Mrs, Luisa – Esmeralda called – this is my mother and that is my father.

Luisa almost dropped the girl on the ground. So that lovely girl was Nicanor's daughter? What a piece fate was playing on her! Despite her free and uninhibited genius, Luisa had always dreamed of being a mother, but fate had never honored her with motherhood. When she saw Esmeralda running between the tables in the company of other girls, her heart sank and she called her to her side, offering her a glass of soda. They started talking, and Esmeralda told her that her parents were walking around the property, but Luisa didn't even remember asking their names. And now ... It was necessary to remain calm and natural, and she said:

– Really, honey?

At that, the Marchioness arrived, with a satisfied smile on her face, saying with joy:

– I see you've already met.

Seeing Luisa's inquisitive air, Agrippina immediately tried to say:

– Forgive me for the audacity, Your Highness, but I told the Marchioness that I met her at a party at her house, and she ended up putting me by your side. Does it bother you?

– Of course not. Why would it bother?

From a distance, Carlos looked at them suspiciously. He could never hope to see the captain there, especially with his wife. Agrippina could not suspect anything. When she had gone home, she had not told him the name of her husband's lover and she could not guess. That certainly was just a coincidence. Gathering up his courage, Carlos went to his place. He had been accommodated with Luisa and would not give up her company. Even more so with that captain there.

Seeing Carlos approach, Agripina glanced at him. He noticed her look, but didn't say anything. He acted as if he did not know her, he sat next to Luisa and ate the whole time they were there, Carlos waited for Agripina to approach him and ask him something, but she did nothing, and he concluded that she no longer did. He remembered or did not believe the story he had told her. Better this way. I didn't want to have to worry about him. The concern for Nicanor was enough.

Luisa was no longer interested in Nicanor. On the contrary, she wanted him out of sight. With the exception of Carlos, Luisa disliked her former lovers very much. They were excellent when they served her, but once the relationship ended, their presence annoyed her. And now, she was forced to tolerate the company of Nicanor and that horrible woman.

After lunch, Luisa tried to keep her distance from Nicanor and Agripina. She just couldn't get away from Esmeralda. The girl was wonderful. So sweet, beautiful, polite.

It was a real gem. Luisa thought that Nicanor was going to take her daughter away from her company, but that did not happen, perhaps so as not to attract Agrippina's attention.

During the dance, Luisa remained distant, only dancing with Carlos, and Nicanor only had eyes for Agripina. Every night, after the guests went to their rooms, Carlos went to Luisa's room, and the two loved each other intensely. She was a widow and it was not good to be seen sharing the same bed.

Therefore, Carlos arrived after everyone had already gone to sleep and left before waking up.

The next day and the next day, everything happened the same way. In the morning, they went hunting. Then they would have lunch, take a nap, have dinner, go down to the dance, and retire.

Carlos continued going to Luisa's room, without anyone noticing. Little by little, Luisa began to relax.

Agrippina seemed to suspect nothing and, with the exception of lunchtime, when they had been summoned, they hardly spoke. And Nicanor didn't even exchange glances with her.

Only Esmeralda enchanted her. She enjoyed the girl's company. She took her for a walk, told her stories, gave her gifts.

Nicanor did not approve of this friendship, but Agripina did not seem to mind.

"Not for attention – she said. – If we deprive her of the Archduchess's company, everyone will be suspicious.

Nicanor was silent. Maybe she was right. Their friendship was natural, and there was no reason to stop it. If he began to push

Luisa's daughter away, people would think that there was some rivalry between them, and that would lead them to suspect that he was another of her lovers, used and then fired like any servant.

It was Saturday, the day before leaving for Lisbon. This was the last day Agrippina would have to take revenge. The party had been wonderful and the dance was over.

Later than usual. By the time everyone left, it was after two in the morning, and a heavy rain fell on the field, with lightning and thunder spreading across the sky.

In her room, Esmeralda was shaking. He was terrified of storms, he couldn't stand the thunder. She woke up scared, and the light coming from the window, as a result of the rays that pierced the sky, prevented her from falling asleep again. She thought about going to her parents' room, but gave up. They could be doing those things and, in the clearing, they would scold her. Esmeralda remembered that once, during a storm like that, she had surprised them while they loved each other. She didn't understand what was happening between them, but she still remembered the scolding she had taken for entering her room at that hour. Fearing more reprimands, she stopped looking for them.

What to do? Fear kept her from sleeping, and she was still at risk of wetting the bed. She always urinate when she was scared. She couldn't control herself.

Suddenly, lightning struck very close to the castle, and the noise of the thunder that accompanied it shook the walls.

Esmeralda was in agony. She couldn't stay there anymore.

Completely terrified, she quickly got out of bed and ran out the door, into the hall, which received the flickering light of the beam that went through her.

Stained glass at the end of the gallery. Barefoot and cold, she ran to Luisa's room and opened the door wide.

Memories that the wind brings

She had just gone to bed to wait for Carlos' visit and she thought it was him, arriving. Seeing Esmeralda standing in the bedroom door, pale as wax, crying, Luisa was startled. He got up and hugged her, carrying her to his bed. It was freezing cold and Luisa tucked it under the covers.

– What happened, Esmeralda? – She asked fondly. – Oh! Mrs, Luisa, I'm scared! Please let me stay here! Don't send me to my room, please!

– What are you scared of? Storm?

Esmeralda moved her head saying yes and hid it in the pillows.

– It is awful! Chilling!

Luisa smiled and stroked the girl's hair.

– And where are your parents?

– They ... they ... don't want me to interrupt them ... – . She stopped, afraid to say something she shouldn't have said.

– It's okay – Luisa said, hugging her lovingly.

– You can stay here.

– I can? – Esmeralda repeated, wiping her eyes.

– Of course. Do not worry. It's just lightning and thunder. They can't hurt you. Feeling safe, Esmeralda settled into Luisa's bed and soon fell asleep. Shortly after, Carlos, as he always did, entered Luisa's rooms for their usual night of love. As soon as he was out the door, Luisa put a finger to her lips and indicated no noise. Seeing the girl sleeping there, he looked questioningly at Luisa. Slowly, she adjusted the girl and got up. She took Carlos's hand and left, saying in a very low voice:

– It's Esmeralda. She's scared, but I managed to make her fall asleep. Come on, let's go to your room today. Carlos did not contest. His body burning with desire, he went with her to his rooms and closed the door, throwing himself on the bed and kissing her eagerly. Nothing else mattered at the time. Carlos only thought about Luisa, and Luisa only thought about Carlos.

Around three thirty, the door to Agripina's room slowly opened. The storm was beginning to abate and thunder erupted in the distance. Nicanor, in his bed, was sleeping soundly, and did not even realize that the woman had left. Agrippina looked from side to side, seeing if someone was there, but no one was there.

They were all asleep. The night was busy and the wine was consumed beyond normal. No one would wake up, especially with a storm like that.

In silence, Agrippina went to Luisa's room, carrying in her hand the silver dagger she had brought with her, a gift from Nicanor on one of his many trips to Calicut. She slowly pushed open the door, which gave easily. She tiptoed in and walked over to the bed. There the rival slept – she thought – , the woman who had almost fallen from grace in his life, increasing his pride. Her hatred was such that she did not even realize that the body lying there was not that of an adult, but that of a child and, worse still, that of her own daughter. Agrippina only saw the long blonde hair spread out on the pillow, and that was enough to believe it was Luisa.

She stepped closer and raised his dagger, surprised by a bolt that had struck closer. For a few seconds, she still hesitated. She was not a murderer but hatred and jealousy had driven her to that extreme. That woman was a scoundrel. How many houses had she already broken with her unbridled lust? By killing her she would be freeing the world from another courtesan, who only served to destroy the hearts and homes of innocent women like her.

Thinking about it, she filled herself with courage and, with the inherent violence of the reckless and irascible, she struck the first blow, hearing a muffled moan, which only increased his desire for revenge. In her hand she felt the weak resistance of flesh, which soon gave way to the fury of the sword. After the first stab, the rest became easier, and Agrippina continued to deliver successive blows on what she thought to be her greatest enemy, unaware that she had stabbed her own daughter.

Seeing that the body that lay there inert, the blood spread on the whiteness of the sheets, Agrippina was satisfied and ready to leave. She was already at the door when a morbid desire to see the dead woman's face made her turn around. She wanted to see Luisa's bloodless face, her glazed and expressionless gaze, her perfect body cut by the stabbing. I'd take a look and leave before someone woke up.

She approached the bed again, on tiptoe. At that moment, by a strange coincidence, the rays began to fall on the castle, their blue light penetrating through the barely drawn curtains. Agrippina put her hand on the dead woman's body, took a deep breath and pulled it out, turning it at the exact moment when another beam, descending from the sky with dizzying fury, Luisa's bed lit up. It was enough that Agrippina could see, instead of his rival, the innocent and lifeless face of his daughter, looking at her with dull eyes, on her face an encourageable expression of surprise and pain.

Agrippina backed away in terror, leaning against the wall and hiding her face in her hands. Instantly, she started screaming like crazy, attracting the attention of everyone in the castle. Realizing that the screams were coming from the Archduchess's room, everyone ran towards it, and Luisa herself was the first to arrive, fearing that some misfortune had befallen little Esmeralda. Nicanor arrived shortly after. Seeing that horrible scene, he began to cry convulsively, throwing himself on the body of his daughter and calling her name:

– Esmeralda! Emeralda! Talk to me, girl! It's dad to! Talk with me please! – The Marquis, compassionate and shocked, approached him and, putting his hand on his shoulder, said with deep regret:

– She is dead, my son.

— Dead? No, she is not dead. Can not be. sHe is only ten years old. What harm did she do in the world to be dead? Come on girl, wake up, talk to daddy. It's daddy. Awake. Esmeralda, please wake up ...

They all regretted saying something. In the light of the chandeliers, Esmeralda's face grew paler and paler, showing her deathly lividity. Women were crying, and even Luisa, normally insensitive to the pain of others, could not hold back the tears. The commotion was so great that no one noticed that, leaning against the opposite wall, Agrippina was looking at that scene with a glassy look, as if she did not know what was happening. It was only when they heard a thud that they glanced their way, just in time to see her body lying on the ground, holding the dagger in her hand, still stained with her daughter's blood.

The justice of men sentenced Agrippina to life in a distant sanitarium. If her insanity hadn't been so obvious, she would have been executed. But Nicanor, who had always served the Crown with fidelity and dedication, managed to free her from the death penalty, on the condition that she be locked up in an asylum forever.

Nicanor was devastated. Life for him no longer had meaning. However, he still loved his wife and felt responsible for all of that. The romance between him and Luisa was made public, and it was clear to everyone that Agrippina had killed her daughter, thinking of killing the Archduchess. The more he thought about it, the more Nicanor felt guilty, sure that thanks to him the woman had become a murderer. He blamed himself for his daughter's death, judging that Agrippina was only a victim of his betrayal.

Agrippina, on the other hand, went mad the same moment she saw Esmeralda's lifeless face. Since then, it was considered the most abominable creature and even ordered the execution itself.

Memories that the wind brings

She had committed the most heinous crimes and did not deserve any forgiveness. She deserved public contempt, execution, and exile. When Agrippina learned of her sentence, she sighed in relief. She would be locked up forever in a place where she would only have to live with her guilt and pain.

Over time, Agripina's health deteriorated. Unable to shake off the guilt, she gradually closed herself off, judging herself unworthy even of the pity of others. Little by little, her body began to change and her back bent, as if it wanted to bury itself in her own chest, suffocating the pain that tortured her. It didn't take long and the sharp curve in his back turned into a hideous hunchback, giving him an air of a grotesque caricature. Agrippina could no longer bear life and began to no longer accept the treatment offered by the nurses at the institution where she was hospitalized. Soon she began to reject food and water, and her already fragile body could not resist a simple flu.

Agrippina disincarnated, carrying with her a deep feeling of guilt, which accompanied her for centuries,

With Agrippina's death, Nicanor was annihilated. He no longer had any reason to live. He had lost the only people in the world that he had truly loved. Surrendered to deep despondency, he was overcome by heartbreak. He left the ship he had served on for so many years and locked himself inside. The employees were fired and anyone was refused. Not infrequently, he was seen wandering the streets aimlessly, as if lost in his own world of suffering.

Money, which was not much, soon ran out, and Nicanor was forced to sell his belongings to survive. He was a coward, he did not have the courage to end his life and he spent his days waiting for death to remember him and go looking for him, without having to deal the fatal blow to himself.

Once, wandering the streets when a gentleman caught his eye. Tall, well dressed, with gray hair, he got out of a carriage and entered a big and beautiful house, more like a mansion, where did he know this man from? Pulling on the memory, he ended up remembering. It was Miguel, his former chamberlain. What was the scoundrel doing there? The image of Miguel brought back all the memories of his tragedy, and it was full of hatred. Certainly, it was he who told Agrippina everything.

Despite being dirty and smelly, Nicanor went to knock on the palace door. He was greeted by the servants, who would not let him in, and began to shout:

– Let me go! Get out of my sight, crow! I am Captain Nicanor and I demand that you let me speak to Miguel.

You were really Miguel, who, upon hearing those words, came immediately. When he came face to face with the former lord standing there, clutched by the servants, puffing and delirious like mad, he felt a pang in his heart. He had just arrived from the trip and knew nothing of what had happened. What would have happened to leave mr. Nicanor in that state? Was there a tragedy? Although he knew nothing about the sad denouement of Esmeralda and Agripina, he felt that a misfortune had befallen that family, and the remorse that had been suffocating him for so many years suddenly touched his heart.

Miguel ordered the servants to release him, and Nicanor entered, looking at him suspiciously. The mansion was just a luxury, and Nicanor was filled with hatred. Falling on top of the other, he grabbed him by the collar, screaming:

– You scoundrel! Monster! You will pay me for everything you made me suffer!

Immediately, Nicanor was grabbed from behind and thrown to the ground, subdued by the mistresses

– Do you want us to call the guards? – asked one of them.

"That won't be necessary," – Miguel replied, feeling compassionate. – I let it go. He won't hurt me.

Although upset, the servants released Nicanor, who stood up and glared at him with bloodshot eyes.

Memories that the wind brings

– Screw you!

Before Nicanor grabbed him again, Miguel replied calmly:

– Why don't you sit down and listen to what I have to say?

Nicanor stopped. Although suspicious, he clenched his fists and sat up. Now he would know the true identity of his whistleblower. Seeing him seated and calmer, Miguel sat in front of him and asked:

– You promise you won't hurt me? – Nicanor agreed – . I can trust in you? With a vibrant voice of hatred, he replied:

– Yes. You have my word.

Miguel ordered the servants to leave, looked into Nicanor's eyes and began to say:

– First of all, I want you to know that I appreciate you very much and that I never wanted to hurt you.

– Stop beating around the bush and get straight to the point. I want to know the truth. Did you

tell Agrippina about my affair with Luisa?

Despite regretting it, Miguel feared Nicanor's reaction when he learned the truth. Although he did not know the end of that story, he could see that he was not at all happy. By the state of Nicanor, he was practically destitute.

By the time it had all happened, Agrippina had sold all her jewels and given her a considerable sum, thereby starting a new life. Using intelligence, he tripled the capital and became a rich man. He had spent almost all that time in Spain, far away from home, from the rumors of Lisbon, until longing for his homeland made him return home. He had just arrived, bought that mansion and settled in. Despite his possessions, he had not married and did not want to end his days alone, away from his compatriots.

Miguel looked at Nicanor trying to think of a compelling story to tell. A story that would relieve him, at least partially, of the guilt he carried. His conscience was enough to accuse him. Nor did he need Nicanor's anger. The day Agrippina bought it, she had learned the origin of that revelation, and based on her words they said her version:

— One afternoon, a gentleman, a certain Mr. Carlos Castanheira, approached Mrs. Agripina, who told him that he was taking important news — when Nicanor heard that name, he felt a chill that Miguel did not notice, and continued — , who knew that you were meeting a certain lady in society, whose name I preferred not to reveal.

— That scoundrel! I imagine!

Miguel made a gesture to him to calm down and resumed the word:

— When he left, Mrs. Agripina came to me. She was your trusted servant, and it was not credible that she did not know anything. I said no, that you were faithful and had no other woman. But Mr. Carlos had left him the address, and his wife, not satisfied with my answer, went to look for him and ended up telling him about Mrs. Luisa. In return, she must keep the identity of her informant a secret.

— Miserable!

Nicanor got up immediately, being controlled by Miguel, who made him sit down again.

— After that, she called for me. She said that she already knew the woman's name and was forbidden to reveal the name of Mr. Carlos. I assured her that she would not say anything, but that, if you suspected of me, I would be obliged to tell you everything, which she did not accept. After a few days, she appeared with a lot of money. She had sold all her jewelry, and what she presented to me was it more than enough to get me far from here She had no way out OR I accepted it, or was I was in danger of being murdered. If it weren't for you, for mr. Carlos, who would become angry. So I decided to accept. It was my life that was at stake and I was in no condition to negotiate. Heartbroken, I took the money and disappeared.

After the narration was over, Miguel glanced at Nicanor out of the corner of his eye to see the effect his words had had on him. Nicanor had believed without hesitation. His eyes blazed with hatred and Miguel was relieved. Nicanor got up hastily and headed for the door.

– Wait! – Miguel yelled.

Miguel left and returned a few minutes later, bringing a small bag and placing it in Nicanor's hand. He closed his hand and left, heading straight home. Only when it arrived did he look at its contents. The bag was full of gold coins, which Nicanor threw away. It wasn't the money that interested him. What he wanted was revenge.

Nicanor washed, put on his best clothes, and sat in the living room to wait.

At dusk, he went to the weapons closet and took out a harquebus. He filled it with gunpowder, inserted the bullet, and placed it around his waist, under the silk cover. Then he went to Luisa's house. He knew that she and Carlos had married shortly after Esmeralda's murder, and it would be even better if she witnessed her husband's death, just as he was forced to watch his wife die little by little. He knocked on the door and waited. When the servant came to answer, Nicanor greeted him and said, in a confident and authoritative manner:

– Tell Mr. Carlos Castanheira that Captain Nicanor is here and ask to speak with him. Tell him it's urgent.

Carlos and Luisa did not understand the reason for that visit. They had not heard from him in many years, and his presence there had astonished them. The visitor was ordered to enter, and when Nicanor appeared at the door, Carlos approached and asked him with a certain cordiality:

– Captain Nicanor! What and surprise! How can I help you?

Memories that the wind brings

Without answering, Nicanor drew his weapon, took aim, and fired. Carlos felt a sharp pain in his heart and placed his hands on his chest, which immediately became stained with blood, and fell. Was dead. Luisa, terrified, let out a cry of terror and ran towards him, screaming wildly:

– Assassin! Assassin!

Nicanor dropped the arquebus, turned to the door, and left. Moments later he was arrested at his home. Taken to trial, he was sentenced to death, but he didn't care.

He had avenged his wife and daughter, and now he could go to meet them.

Luisa, in turn, thought that she would die with Carlos. She was no longer a child, and the fire of youth was behind. But she was a strong woman and she finally recovered. To drive away her ghosts, she set out on new journeys. Nothing better than other airs to forget your pain. She had heard of the lands of Brazil, which the Crown was trying to colonize, distributing lands to nobles, hidalgos and royal officials, and his spirit of adventure began to make her restless. Day after day, Luisa only thought about coming to Brazil. But how to undertake such a journey? If, on the one hand, adventure excited her, on the other hand, she did not like to share a land with savages and exiles. And afterwards, there was still a great difficulty: she was a woman, and the Crown did not usually honor women.

However, the colonization process intensified more and more, and several Portuguese left to try their luck in the new land. Although part of the highest nobility of Portugal, Luisa intended to leave as well. She was already tired of that life and those people, and she had made her decision. She didn't care that she was a woman. She had money and it wouldn't be difficult for her to handle it.

She sold all his belongings and left, taking a large sum of gold with him.

Memories that the wind brings

On the day of her departure, she boarded the ship that would take her to Brazil and her cabin. She didn't want to get involved with the crew or the other passengers.

Later, when the ship had already set sail, Luisa heard a knock on the door. It was the captain, coming to greet her, followed by a man, still young, who entered and bowed. Seeing him, Luisa let out a cry, and he stopped, horrified. Both of them could hardly believe their eyes. Luisa was facing the first love of her life, at that time a young baron, whom she had not married due to her father's prohibition.

The young man, named Bertoldo, disillusioned with the loss of his beloved, never married and entered maritime life, becoming a renowned captain in the service of the Crown. After many years dedicated to the Navy, Bertoldo decided it was time to retire and, in exchange for the services rendered, he received land in Brazil, where he moved with his widowed sister. Luisa and Bertoldo got married as soon as they arrived in Brazil. She got along with Ines, her sister, but she hated slaves. Brazil began importing them from Africa, and Bertoldo acquired some to help him cultivate the land. Luisa hated her company. They were considered inferior beings, creatures without a soul and without feelings. Also, they spoke that horrible language, which was impossible to understand.

Over time, Luisa began to tire of Brazil. It was a land of savages, without the luxury and pomp of Lisbon.

The adventure was over, and all that was left now were endless days, hidden in the mill, with no parties or distractions. Irritation was a constant in her life, and Luisa began to dismiss her dissatisfaction with the slaves.

She humiliated them for whatever reason and inflicted severe punishments on them, as a way to compensate for the troubles he was going through in the new land.

Ines used to be more condescending, but Bertoldo, seeing Luisa's irritation, almost equaled her in mistreatment. He spoke to the slaves only by yelling and hitting them for whatever reason. He didn't mind separating families, nor did he feel remorse when he had to sacrifice a disobedient or runaway Negro.

The longing for the court began to weaken the body of Luisa, who blamed Brazil and the slaves for her misfortune, and she began to get sick and weak. Following the advice of Ines, Bertoldo took her back to Portugal, hoping that she, feeling the air of the Court, would restore his energies. Her body, however, was already weakened.

Due to the many excesses and abuses that he had practiced, allied to the age that was approaching, she did not resist the crossing, and Luisa died at sea, cursing life, slaves and Brazil.

CHAPTER 20

When Clarissa found herself back on the beach, she looked at Toña with a deep sadness in her eyes, trying to understand the reason for all that.

- The past sometimes helps us understand the pain of the present, Toña kindly clarified.

- Does everything mean that I am suffering from something I did in the past? Am I paying for my woes? - Clarissa asked scared.

- Come on, Clarissa, you're not even suffering that much. The difficulties you go through are more the result of pride than pain. And you are not paying for anything, nor do you understand your actions as evil. You are just trying to balance the balance of your life, so that the acts of the past and the consequences of the present create harmony for the future. No one acts alone, and the lives of all of you are intertwined, as human nature is to interact with others.

Without coexistence with others, experiences would fall into a void, because nobody learns by giving and receiving only from themselves and for themselves.

- And what does all this have to do with Mr. Abílio? He may have been related to me in the past, but what he did to Mrs. Leonor has nothing to do with me.

- What did he do to Leonor?

- He committed a terrible act, killed his wife to get rid of shame ...

- Who told you that?

- Don't you think it's clear?

- I can't find anything. And you shouldn't find it either. The truth is not always what it seems.

– You mean it wasn't Mr. Abílio who killed his wife? But then who was he?

– I don't know, and if I did, I couldn't tell you.

When we accuse someone, we are actually trying to hide our own faults. Judgment is something that must be left to the depths of consciousness, and your only witness will be divinity. We have no right to judge or try to adjust the attitude of others to our personal concept of right or wrong.

– I'm sorry, Grandma Toña, but I don't think murder is a personal concept. Everyone knows it's wrong.

– I'm not saying it's correct. I'm just trying to make you see that you are closed in your truth that Abílio killed his wife. What if it didn't? What if she committed suicide? Killing is neither right nor right, because no one has the right to take charge of the lives of others. But, have you ever stopped to think that Abílio could have acted wrong because he believed that what he was doing was right?

– But you said yourself that killing is not right!

– I didn't say it's correct. I said he thought it was right. Whatever he did, he did it because he thought it was right.

He did not act maliciously or selfishly. He acted out of love and pity.

– Very strange that way of loving and being pious. I hope he never loves me or feels sorry for me.

– You are very strict in your concepts and you are still very proud. You should stop to look inside yourself.

Toña's words made Clarissa reflect on her life and the difficulties she had experienced since her arrival in Cabo Frio. Accustomed to always being served, she was suddenly forced to cook, take care of the house and a child, and even had to put up with the rudeness of a cold and rude husband. Pride had touched her and she had to review it to continue living.

— "I know I'm proud – she agreed, in a tone between shameful and arrogant. – But life has taught me a lot, and living with Mr. Abílio and his sons ended up bending my pride. Although I don't want to, I am forced to lean into some situations, mainly because I don't want to see Angelina suffer.

— This is very good for you. You are learning the lesson that you came to learn.

— But at what price, right? Mr. Abílio is a cruel, hard and incomprehensible man.

— Do you really believe that? Or does your pride not let you see the human being behind the ice mask?

— I do not know... –. she replied, now confused. – There was even a time when I doubted his cruelty, due to your implication with Tiago. I thought a man that knows the value of friendship shouldn't be so bad.

— Why did you change your mind?

— I don't know. For his actions, his words, his intransigence ... His behavior is intolerable.

— And yours? Doesn't the way you act cause you some kind of reaction? .

— It's not my fault if he feels remorse for killing his wife. And I don't think it's fair to take it out on me.

— Maybe Abílio is just reacting to the way you treated him and continues to treat him.

— He bought me.

— And you? Didn't you buy it in another life too? Wasn't that how Luisa acted when wanted something? Or have you already forgotten everything you saw?

— So, what do you want? Revenge? So where is divine justice? The offended acquire the right to take revenge on their debtors until their thirst is quenched?

– There are no offended or debtors. What there are are growing spirits that interact and collide Abílio. The body dies, but the spirit remains and the soul retains unresolved feelings. If feelings are not well balanced, the spirit also causes unbalance in life, and all around you suffer the consequences of that. It is necessary, at some point, to readjust the balance. This is not revenge. It is growth.

Once again, Clarissa saw the crystal truth behind Toña's words and lowered her eyes, embarrassed by her stubbornness.

– You're right, Grandma Toña, as always. Excuse me. In fact, I was trying to defend myself by accusing Mr. Abílio. This is not fair.

– You also helped things take the course they did. I don't know the fault of any of that, I just understand. Luisa was a powerful and arrogant Archduchess, she used to have what she wanted and when she wanted it. Nicanor remained a weak spirit, lacking the courage to assume his attitudes. And Agrippina was carried away by jealousy and pride as well. There is no malice. Behaviors change as the spirit is purified through successive existences, because only with reincarnation do you understand and transform your actions, feelings and thoughts. That is all part of growth. We are created knowing nothing, and it is through incarnation and reincarnation that we learn and conquer the true values of the spirit.

– "You speak very wise words, Grandmother Toña = Clarissa observed in admiration. She doesn't even look like the old slave I met at the hacienda.

– So you can see what the incarnation does to us, one day I was a slave, but I was not always like that. I have lived other lives of luxury, arrogance and pleasure, like you.

But I learned, just as you are learning, and I will have much more to learn in the future.

Clarissa reflected for a few seconds, until she responded with interest:

– And Agrippina? I think it was she who suffered the most from her attitude, indulging in overwhelming guilt.

– Agrippina could never forgive herself for killing her daughter and ended up escaping to live with others. It was a very strong guilt, which contaminated her entire soul, so to speak, and continued to torture her in the invisible world and again in this one. That was what generated the predisposition to the disease that Leonor was a victim.

Agrippina placed herself on the edge of the world, trying to isolate herself from her companions, just as leprosy did with Leonor and all those who contract it. Certain people bring with them extreme difficulty adapting to the world and getting involved with those who inhabit it. This characteristic ends up manifesting itself through illness, which embodies the difficulty of the spirit, making these people discriminated against and feared. They isolate themselves and, with the manifested leprosy, this isolation acquires external proportions, since they are eliminated from social life due to the impossibility of living with humanity, generated by the fear of contagion.

Clarissa was excited, feeling responsible for what had happened to Agrippina's child.

– I really liked Esmeralda! – She started to cry.

– I could be proud, arrogant and many other things, but no one can deny that I really liked the girl. Only God knows how much I suffered from his death.

– I know. And that's why she chose to be born with you, so that you could guide her through life, just as mothers do with their children.

– You mean Esmeralda is ... is ... Angelina?

– Yes. Esmeralda and Angelina, a being who has reached an enormous understanding of life and its maturation processes, and who has agreed to reincarnate between you and Abílio to encourage them to reconcile.

– Reconciliation? With Abílio? I think this is impossible.

– Nothing is impossible. There are difficult and easy things, but only what is really not wanted is impossible.

– Let's admit it's possible. How do you expect us to do that? Mr. Abílio is inaccessible ...

– No means no. He is as human as you, he has the same needs, dreams and desires. They are both proud and don't like to give up, but they have a lot of love in their hearts.

They just need to show that love, so they can transform hatred and resentment into friendship and understanding.

What is missing is someone to take the first step.

– And does that someone have to be me?

– That can be you.

– I don't know, Grandma Toña. I know you grew a lot spiritually, but who knows how many lives it took for that. And I don't think I can make so many changes in one existence.

– You just won't be successful if you miss the chance. Whenever you want, everything is achieved. Take Miguel, for example ...

– Miguel?

– Yes, Miguel, the servant. Out of ambition and pride, he betrayed his boss's trust and helped spark a series of unfortunate events. It was for no other reason that Miguel requested a new opportunity to serve his lord, this time as a slave, to learn the value of loyalty and humility, and to let go of ambition.

– Is Tiago Miguel?

With a mischievous smile, she confirmed:

– Everything is perfect in nature, right? The perfection of God and of life can be felt in all his creatures, who already carry in them the seed of good and discernment, if only they feed it with love and courage. And now come on, my girl, it's

time to go back.

– Just one more question, grandmother Toña: why did Mr. Abílio chose to be Vicente's father?

– Abílio, at that moment Nicanor, came to give Carlos back what he had stolen from him before, which was life. Then he chose to be his father to give him life and transform the hatred of the rival into the sublime love of the father. Well that's enough.

The day will soon dawn, and you must return to the body. Tomorrow, when you wake up, even if you don't remember much, you will keep impressions of what happened, which will help you to persist in your determinations.

Then Clarissa returned to the body and soon woke up. She didn't really remember anything, but she felt good and determined, as if a strange force had dominated her during the night.

CHAPTER 21

Christmas was near, but the atmosphere in Abílio's house was not the calmest. Clarissa was always anxious, as if waiting for something to happen. Luciano was suspicious and Jerusa was scared. Angelina, on the other hand, did not notice the mood of the others or pretend anything. Only Abílio and Vicente looked different. It was as if complicity had been established between them, and the two lived exchanging glances and whispers.

– Did you notice the gestures of Mr. Abílio and Vicente? Asked Jerusa, as soon as she was alone with Clarissa.

– I realized, yes. What happened?

– I don't know. Before they seemed to hate each other, but now …

– Now they seem like great friends. Do they share any secrets?

– Maybe. If Mr. Abílio actually killed his wife, Vicente may know about it. This would explain the hatred he feels for his father. Or felt, I don't know. They look very close now.

– In any case, it is natural that Vicente, feeling the threat around his father, tries to protect him. After all, family ties are very strong.

– Is that so? Or did Mr. Abílio also threaten his son?

– I don't know, Jerusa, but I feel something much deeper than we imagine.

– How is that?

– I can't say. It is as if there is a mystery in the air. Something that we cannot imagine.

– What could it be?

Memories that the wind brings

- I don't know, but I plan to find out soon.

Looking out the living room window, they saw Vicente, who was running along the beach and jumping into the water from time to time. That vision filled Clarissa with tenderness and desire. Why couldn't he get it out of my head?

- He messes with you, doesn't he? - Jerusa asked, sure of her sister-in-law's feelings for the son.

- Huh? What? What did you say?

- You don't have to try to fool me. I know how you feel about Vicente. Clarissa looked at her in horror and replied indignantly:

- What do you mean by that?

- I will not tell anyone, but I advise you to take care of yourself. Your interest in him is visible.

Feeling the blush covering her cheeks, Clarissa hid her face in her hands and said, full of shame:

- Oh! Jerusa, what can I do? I feel ashamed, I don't want to feel that. But I can't help it!

- Are you in love with him?

- I don't know

- You already ... - Jerusa did not have the courage to finish the question, but Clarissa, horrified, responded more than quickly:

- By God, no! We've never done anything that we could really be ashamed of Jerusa sighed in relief and replied:

- Goodness... - . She took a deep breath and, after a few seconds, concluded: - He is a beautiful boy, and your interest in him is perfectly understandable.

- Vicente is just a rebellious and naughty boy. But he's just a kid.

- For real? So why were you interested in him? Don't tell me it was just because Mr. Abílio is old and rude.

– No ... no ... And if you really want to know, I don't even think Mr. Abílio is so old ...

– Actually, he isn't. He is an attractive man, and Vicente looks a lot like him. Is that why you fell in love with the boy?

Clarissa blushed and said confused:

– Jerusa, please don't talk like that. I don't even know if I'm really in love ...

– Shh! Silence! Look! He comes closer.

In fact, Vicente was arriving, all wet, his hair dripping in disarray, his brown skin tanned with the sun, his eyes as green as an expanse of the sea.

Seeing him, Clarissa caught her breath and felt like running to him and hugging him. At great cost, she managed to contain the momentum.

When he entered, Abílio also came out of the kitchen and, seeing him standing there in the middle of the room, dressed only in pants, bare- chested, he soon realized the effect he was having on Clarissa. With a touch of jealousy, he immediately tried to scold him:

– What are these suits, Vicente? Respect the ladies!

With an ironic look, Vicente looked at the girls, lingering in Clarissa's eyes, and said respectfully:

– You're right, dad. I'm going to change – . He leaned over and passed them quickly, up the stairs, soon followed by his father. The two gaped at each other. Clarissa then, who never saw Vicente treat her father with such deference, could hardly believe what she had heard. Something was really happening, and she didn't know what it was.

After Vicente entered the room, Abílio stopped in front of the door, undecided. He knew that he and Clarissa weren't exactly in love, but delighted with each other's figure. The mutual interest was visible, and it tormented him. Clarissa was his wife and Vicente was his son. What do I have to do? Separate from her and set her free, so that she can live a dark and misunderstood love with him? Even if they were separated, could Clarissa and Vicente live happily before the accusing eyes of an implacably hypocritical and conservative society? They would probably have to go. But where would they go? What would they live on? They were both still young, and Vicente was about to enter college. Would you be willing to give up your future in the name of an illicit and dark love? They could never marry. Would they be able to live on the fringes of society, facing the comments and excuses of others, who would do anything to avoid living with them? On the other hand, he couldn't cover them there. It would not be nice. Clarissa was his wife, and it would be difficult for him to witness her love too. Now that he was beginning to love her ... Abílio felt that his heart was already opening to his wife and he thought that he still had the opportunity to be happy with her. But Clarissa didn't love him, and he couldn't make her love him. Feeling anguish overwhelm his chest, he turned desperate. I couldn't share that with my son. It was not fair.

He hurried down the stairs and out the back door. He needed to talk to someone, and the only one who could understand him was Tiago. The old man received him with the usual tenderness. Abílio was bitter, sad, incredulous in life, and it was necessary to make him regain his confidence. After calming him down, Tiago suggested:

– Come on man. Let's go to Father Joaquim's house. It must have some good advice to give you.

In silence, Abílio allowed himself to be carried away. He was on the verge of despair and did not know how to act. Suddenly, the whole world seemed to collapse on your head, and you had to do something.

When he was involved in the fraternal embrace of Father Joaquim Abílio, he began to cry. Why did so many misfortunes happen in your life? What had he done to deserve that punishment?

Memories that the wind brings

He had lost his first wife, Clarissa and their son were in love. Angelina was a sad and needy girl. Where and what was wrong? Father Joaquim caressed him tenderly and tried to console him:

- Don't despair, my son. All is well in the nature of God

- Sometimes it's hard to believe, Father Joaquim.

- So? You should not. Think that God always works for the best.

- I do not know what to think. I feel frustrated, sad, devastated. I want to give up, but I can't. What can I do to bring some happiness to my home?

- Love, my son, but true and clear love.

Don't hide your feelings out of fear, pride, or shame. Get rid of the guilt and stop feeling sorry for yourself.

Abílio was paralyzed.

- Pain?! - he responded in amazement - . Who said I feel sorry for myself?

- And you don't feel it? The other shook his head. - So why do you think you are a poor unfortunate man, for whom nothing in life works?

- It's unfair, Father Joaquim. I was punished for life, I did not choose that.

- You're kidding yourself. Everything that is happening has already been expected and programmed by you and those who share your life with you.

Abílio continued crying and lamented:

- My son ... fell in love with my wife. What can I do?

- Do nothing. Let destiny act according to the choices and needs of each one. You are a tormented man, who has much to blame, both in this life and in the next. It is time to get rid of all that and reconcile with yourself.

Do what the heart tells you that everything will be fine.

– My heart deceived me.

– The heart never deceives us. We are the ones who try to deceive him, but only what we achieve is to deceive ourselves. Fear not, my son. Life takes many turns, but it always stops where it has to.

After talking with Father Joaquim, Abílio returned home a little calmer. Despite the former slave's total ignorance, he had the gift of saying wise and joyful words, and life no longer seemed so bad.

*** * ***

In the company of her brother, her sister-in-law and Angelina, Clarissa was returning from a walk on the beach. When they got home, Jerusa and Luciano asked to leave.

They were tired and wanted to rest from the heat. Clarissa sat with Angelina on the porch. Soon the breeze would start to blow and the air would become soft and pleasant. They sat together, and Clarissa wrapped her arms around Angelina, resting her head on her shoulder, staying there for a few minutes.

– Clarissa …

– Hmm …?

– I can trust in you?

– Of course you can. Why? You want to tell me something? – Angelina hesitated for a few moments, but ended up answering:

– Yes…

– What is it? Come on, Angelina, you know you can trust me. Is it about your mother? – The girl was startled and looked up, scared, asking anguished:

– How do you know?

– I don't know, but I can imagine. Come on, Angelina, tell me what you know. You need not fear. – Angelina looked at her without saying anything. Her chest felt heavy, she couldn't bear to keep that secret any longer. Yet she had

promised ... She had promised her father, her brother, and herself. If she revealed the truth, she knew what could happen. Her father would probably be arrested, and she didn't want that. She had committed a crime, and crimes were punishable by jail.

Angelina clung to Clarissa and began to cry. She didn't know what else to do. She was distraught, tormented, she wanted to get rid of that dire secret. But how? She had promised never to speak. What if the father was arrested?

Thinking about it, Angelina regretted it. She loved Clarissa and trusted her, but she knew she didn't like her father.

What happens if she report him? The fear of seeing her father behind bars made her stand up in terror. She glanced at Clarissa, who was still trying to hold on to her, and raced off in anguish, heading for her room. Clarissa got to her feet hastily and was about to run after her when she felt a hand grab her wrist. She turned abruptly, thinking it was Abílio, but what was her surprise when she found herself face to face with Tiago, who was hugging her tightly.

– Tiago! Let me go! What do you think you're doing?

– The siñá'll excuse me, but I won't let you go, no. Just let me go if you promise you won't run after little Angelina.

– I do not promise anything! You are not my owner or Angelina's. Let go of me right now! I'm commanding!

Tiago ended up releasing her. After all, he had held her in a moment of desperation. She was coming from the back of the house and had overheard part of the conversation. He was sure that the girl was about to tell her the truth and he couldn't allow it. Her lord's life was in danger, and she would do anything to protect him. Still, Clarissa was a determined and stubborn child, and it would be hard to lose her. Trying a softer and more conciliatory tone, Tiago considered:

Memories that the wind brings

– Siñá Clarissa, why don't you leave things as they are? Clarissa looked at him deeply and replied:

– What things? What are you talking about? What happened here that I can't know? Why so much secrecy?

Tiago looked back at him in deep disgust. When he spoke again, there was so much anguish in his voice that Clarissa was almost convinced:

– Don't you feel sorry for Abilio's pain? Don't you see how much he suffers from all this? He is a good man, and all he did was think about the happiness of the family, mainly Siñá Leonor.

– Happiness? Nobody does what they did in the name of happiness.

– How do you know, huh? Siñá doesn't know anything. You think you know everything, but you know nothing. Mr. Abílio is a good man ...

– I won't discuss this with you. It is clear that you are faithful to him as a watchdog and will do everything you can to protect him.

And now, excuse me. My problem is not with you.

She turned her back on him abruptly and went home. The sun had just set on the horizon, and the gloom of the night crept into every corner of the house. In silence, Clarissa went to Angelina's room. He liked the girl and he didn't want her to feel pressured or to walk away from her. She knocked softly on the door and entered. Angelina was sitting on the bed, flipping through a storybook, and barely looked at her. Sitting next to her, Clarissa began to count:

– Don't be sad or angry with me, Angelina. I didn't want to force you to say what you doen't want to say. I like you and I am your friend, and I want you to know that you can always count on me ...

She didn't even have to finish the sentence. Angelina dropped the book and hugged her, crying convulsively. In that moment, Clarissa realized how fragile she was. Angelina was just a girl, punished by tragedy, unable to live the joy of girls her age. She had no friends, she wasn't distracted, she wasn't going anywhere.

She was a lonely and needy child, and Clarissa felt a lump in her throat, an immense urge to cry with her.

Silently, she let the tears run down her face and stroked her hair, rocking her gently, until Angelina's tears gradually subsided.

– Sorry, Clarissa …

– You don't have to apologize. You did nothing.

– I can't say, I can't!

– Okay, Angelina, don't get excited. You don't have to tell me anything.

Angelina said nothing more. She clung to her more and more, remaining silent. She did not want to speak. All she wanted to do was stay there, in her friendly and welcoming embrace.

CHAPTER 22

From the day Clarissa threw that murder charge in his face, Abílio became even colder and more elusive. He avoided the company of his wife and, at times when forced to be with her, he tried to say little, although he could not hide a certain air of anguish and disappointment.

Meals began to take place in near silence, each absorbed in his own thoughts, not having much to say.

Since there weren't many distractions, and no one was very excited to speak, they all left early, and that night was no different.

The wind, which was already very strong, suddenly began to blow more intensely, and soon, a heavy rain fell on the earth. It was a storm, with lightning bolts and terrifying, and thunder broke very close, shaking the walls.

Clarissa was almost asleep when she felt someone shaking her. She opened her eyes slowly and saw Angelina standing next to her, trembling.

– Can I stay with you, Clarissa? – she complained – . I'm scared.

It was always like this when it thundered: Angelina was terrified of storms, lightning, and thunder. The moan of the wind didn't scare her, but those flashes and shocks terrified her. Hugging Clarissa, Angelina soon fell asleep, and Clarissa also closed her eyes again, sleeping afterward. Outside began the diminishing thunder. Only the wind did not breathe and continued her funeral groan: uiuiuiui ...

Around three in the morning, a strange noise was heard, like footsteps in the corridor, around the house. Along with footsteps, a sound of crying, voices wailing and groaning, muffled screams ... silence. In his room, Luciano woke up and looked at the woman, who was sleeping soundly, and decided to investigate. He quietly got out of bed, lit a candle, and went out into the hall. As soon as he closed the bedroom door, a strong gust of wind blew out the candle, but he continued anyway, the view was already used to seeing in the dark. He felt the walls, soundlessly, and reached the stairs, descending slowly.

In the living room, he forced his eyes further, trying to identify the scattered shadows on the floor and walls. He saw nothing, but felt a gust of wind brush against his skin and he realized that the front door was open. With extreme care, he went there and was amazed. In the distance, two figures struggled in the water, rising and falling in the waves. What did that mean? From where he was, he couldn't see whose they were, although he was sure there were two people in the sea.

Were they drowning? Perhaps it would be better to run to help, but something inside Luciano immobilized him, froze his legs and prevented them from moving.

As if hypnotized, he just watched, until one of the figures, dominating the other, lifted him onto her lap and came out of the water with him, heading towards the house. Heart jumping, Luciano turned around and ran, dropping a glass jar that was on a buffet. The noise of the glass on the floor assured him that the vial had broken, but Luciano did not stop, fearing that he would be discovered and accused of spying.

Quickly, he managed to return to the room without being seen and quickly opened the door. Hearing the click of the latch, Jerusa opened her eyes and asked sleepily:

– Luciano? It's you?

– Shh! – he exclaimed under her breath. – Shut up do not say anything!

She fell silent and he lay down on the bed next to her. Not understanding anything, Jerusa still asked:

Memories that the wind brings

– What happened?

– Nothing. Just lie down and pretend to sleep.

The urgency in Luciano's voice made Jerusa tremble, and she turned to the side, closed her eyes, and pretended to be asleep. Under the covers, she felt the nervousness of her husband, who did not move a single muscle. They were both paralyzed for a few minutes, until the bedroom door slid open slowly, and Jerusa narrowed her eyes, afraid to even look. However, the visitor did not dare to enter and left shortly after, causing Luciano and Jerusa to breathe a sigh of relief.

The girl was terrified and approached her husband, without the courage to ask him what had happened. She was so scared that she pressed herself tightly against his chest, until she fell asleep, she only woke up the next day, when the sun was already penetrating the window.

As soon as dawn broke, Luciano told Jerusa what had happened the night before and almost fainted.

Despite the conjectures, neither of them could imagine what had actually happened. When they arrived for breakfast, the fragments of the jar had already been removed, and Luciano tried to look away, not attract attention. Trying to look natural, he pulled out the chair for Harea to sit on and sat next to him, pouring himself a cup of coffee.

– Did you have a good night, Mr. Luciano? – Vicente asked.

He was surprised and looked at Jerusa discreetly. Even Clarissa found that question strange, but didn't say anything, and Luciano replied:

– I am fine, how are you?

– Not so good, sorry.

– Why? – He replied, now interested. – Did something happened?

Memories that the wind brings

Everyone's eyes were fixed on both of them. No one dared to say anything, and Vicente continued:

– What happened, if anything, is not your problem, is it? And I really think you shouldn't be spying.

– What? – Luciano said with his face on fire.

– "Vicente – Clarissa interrupted, – what is this?

– Your brother knows what I'm talking about, Clarissa – Vicente answered, looking at the other with They all looked at Luciano, waiting for an answer, and he said, apologizing:

– I ... I heard a noise last night. I thought you were a thief and went down to check.

– Did you really think? – Vicente continued, with a certain fury in his eyes – . Or did you not think it was some lost soul?

Vicente's mocking air caused immense irritation to Luciano, who retaliated accusingly:

– You're right, Vicente. I heard a noise and went downstairs to find out, but all I saw were two figures on the beach.

– Strange, don't you think?

Clarissa looked at Vicente with a question in her eyes. The boy raised the glass to his lips and looked at the interlocutor, shooting him with his eyes without blinking. Suddenly, Abílio came forward and said:

– Forget it, sir. Luciano. I don't think I'm really interested in knowing. They all looked at him questioningly, but it was Vicente who spoke:

– Let me tell Mr. Luciano what happened, dad, or he will think he saw two demons fighting on the beach.

Abílio smiled at his son and objected:

– I don't think it's convenient. Mr. Luciano has nothing to do with our problems.

Memories that the wind brings

– As well? – Clarissa interrupted. – I don't understand ... – Abílio glanced at his son, who continued:

– But I must tell you, my father. Otherwise who knows what Mr. Luciano. Well done. Last night, my father, like so many times, went out to the beach at midnight and I followed him. It was raining a lot, and I thought it was unwise to go out in such weather. And thank God I followed him, because a higher wave almost does not take him to the bottom of the sea ... .

There was something very strange about the look that father and son exchanged, and Vicente then fell silent, looking at the others in a studied way. That story made no sense, and Luciano replied indignantly:

– Excuse me, sir. Abílio, but do you really want us to believe that you left at night, in the middle of the storm, just to swim?

– I don't want to make you believe anything, sir. Luciano – objected Abílio, in a cold tone – . And for me, I wouldn't even give you any explanation. However, my son insists on telling you what happened.

– So it is. Believe if you want. The fact is that my father, a lively man, deeply knowledgeable about these seas, is carried away by a wave that is a little stronger and more complete. The luck, I repeat, was that it was there.

I listened when he left and followed him, reaching him just in time to avoid a tragedy.

– Interesting and fantastic story.

– Why? You do not believe?

Luciano, incredulous, answered calmly:

– Not.

– You know, sir. Luciano, the soul of a man can contain torments much greater than what you imagine ... and very different from what you suppose.

Vicente ended that sentence by looking at him threateningly, and Luciano was about to object, when Clarissa took a step forward:

– What do you mean, Vicente?

– Nothing. I do not want to say anything.

The atmosphere was visibly tense. It was clear that Vicente, from one moment to another, decided to call on his father's defense for himself, and the boy was perhaps a much more dangerous threat than Abílio. While he was mature and thoughtful, Vicente was young and rebellious, very capable of cruel and thoughtless attitudes.

Before Clarissa could say anything, Angelina's small voice was heard, thin and fragile as a scream:

– Oh! Stop, please stop! I can not take it anymore!

– Angelina! – Vicente censured.

– Not! Not! – continued the girl – . I can not stand it anymore. The truth! Clarissa must know the truth.

– Shut up, Angelina! – Vicente yelled, standing up and slapping her in the face.

The girl raised her hand to her cheeks and began to cry profusely, suddenly standing up and looking at her brother with burning eyes. Everyone was too shocked with that attitude of saying something, even Abílio, who stood still, showing no reaction. The girl, hurt in her pride and feelings, shot:

– I hate you, Vicente! You are a monster, and mom would never have left us if it weren't for you! Completely out of control, Angelina ran out the door, heading for the beach, and Clarissa would have followed her if Abílio hadn't stopped her.

– Clarissa stop! – ordered categorically – . Nobody leaves here. Angelina is my daughter and it is with me that she will understand.

She stepped out purposefully, her footsteps sinking into the sand, stepping firmly in her daughter's footprints.

When she returned home, Angelina was calmer and more in control. It came from the father's hand, who squeezed it, trying to get her to safety. Everyone in the room was still present, eagerly awaiting your return. As soon as they entered, Vicente ran towards her and, taking her hands in his, raised them to his lips and spoke with a heartfelt voice:

– Sorry, Angelina, I didn't mean ...

The girl, touched, wrapped her fingers around him and said softly:

– Okay, Vicente, it's over.

However, the scene was moving, and no one could move, everyone held their breath and had wet eyes. There was a silent complicity between them that left Clarissa confused and upset at being excluded from their secret. They soon left, leaving Clarissa, Luciano, and Jerusa uncomfortable, feeling that they were nothing more than strangers in that house.

– "I think we'd better go – Luciano said. – And you should come with us, Clarissa.

– I can't go, Luciano, not now. We are already so close to the truth!

– But what truth? – Jerusa objected, unable to wait to return. – Why did Mr. Abílio kill his wife?

– Yes .

– What does it matter now? If he really did kill her, what difference does it make to us?

– A lot. This proves that he is a murderer.

– And? What are you going to do?

– "Clarissa is right, – Luciano agreed, after a brief reflection. – If Mr. Abílio is really a murderer, so she may be in great danger.

– "That's why you should come with us, – Jerusa declared.

– As for me, I didn't spend another minute in this house. I was leaving today.

– "I told you I can't go, – Clarissa insisted. – I will not abandon Angelina.

– Angelina is not your daughter and, apparently, she is an accomplice of her father's atrocities. Can't you see you can't save her?

– You're wrong, Jerusa. Angelina is just a scared girl. It is my duty to help her.

– "Honestly, Clarissa, – " Luciano reflected, – "the only one I'm worried about is you.

– What about Mrs. Leonor? Have you forgotten our commitment?

– Our engagement ended the day that Mr. Abílio kicked us out of that room.

– Is that what you think, Luciano? Are you going to give up helping her now too? Soon you, who raise flags and weapons in defense of the truth? So who says you are so spiritual?

– This has nothing to do with spirituality. It has to do with security. Mr. Abílio is a dangerous man ...

– I'm very surprised that you say that, brother. Didn't he even suggest he was innocent the other day?

– That was the other day. But now I don't know. And if you want me to tell you, I don't even care to know. Innocent or guilty is not our problem. Let's get out of here, and let him stay with his ghosts.

– Even if I wanted to, I couldn't go – Clarissa answered, feeling a chill and lowering her voice – Not on a boat.

– Are you so afraid of boats?

– I have it. You don't know what I went through.

– "We understand – " said Jerusa. But we will help you overcome this fear. Everything will be alright now, you will see.

– I already said I won't, but if you want, you can go. And you don't even have to wait until Christmas. You can go now.

– "Don't be ungrateful, Clarissa, – Jerusa said. – We are just trying to help.

– That's not the help I need. What I need are brave people who fight with me to discover the truth – . Luciano remained impassive, and Clarissa appealed: – Are you with me, Luciano? Why did you flinch? Did you surrender making truth and justice prevail?

– I don't know, – he replied, discouraged. – Something inside me tells me that we are not going to like what we are going to discover.

– Whatever it is, we have to find out. There is no greater crime than taking someone's life, and there is nothing in the world that can overcome the truth.

– Can't the truth be crueler than we think? Is death really the most horrible way? Is there not a more cruel fate in the world than the loss of the physical body?

– As well? What do you mean by that? I do not understand.

– I don't understand very well either. All I know is that something inside me tells me that, behind this story, there is something much more painful than it seems.

– Isn't that another reason to stay?

Luciano was in doubt. The sister was right, but he was experiencing immense internal conflict. If, on the one hand, his soul and his heart asked to stay, on the other, his mind was telling him to go away and not get involved in it anymore. It wasn't her problem.

– "Luciano, please," Jerusa begged, fearful that he would change his mind.

The doubt was immense. He wanted to do the will of Jerusa, but it was his duty to help his sister. He looked from one to the other, trying to find the correct answer to his questions, oscillating between going and staying. Until it was decided. He had to do what he thought was right, not what he was asked to do. He looked back at his wife and sister and finally concluded:

– All right, Clarissa. We will stay until after Christmas. If everything remains the same there, we will leave, with or without you. This right?

– Oh! Luciano, thank you! I knew I could count with you!

The next day, Clarissa had her face against the window, thinking about the latest episodes of that mystery, when Angelina came in and put her hand on her shoulder, frightening her immensely.

– Sorry, Clarissa. I called, but you didn't answer.

– I'm glad you came, Angelina. I am very happy to see you here.

– I hope you are not angry

– Get mad? Why would it be?

– Because of what happened yesterday.

Clarissa shook her head and hugged her, speaking in a sweet voice:

– I wasn't mad, just worried.

– With what?

– With you ... I don't want you to hurt yourself.

– I'm not hurt, Clarissa. It already happened.

Memories that the wind brings

There was sincerity in Angelina's eyes, and Clarissa shook her hand and asked in a sweet voice

– Why did Vicente do that? What are you scared of?

Angelina pulled away, trying to escape, but Clarissa stopped her. Why not open up to me? I want to help you. Don't you trust me?

Angelina's throat seemed to choke. She wanted to tell the truth, but she was also afraid. Fear of the consequences, of what might happen if she spoke. She coughed nervously, smoothed the hem of her dress and began to speak very softly:

– My father did something horrible ...

– What? What did he do?

– I can not tell. All I can tell you is that he committed a crime and now he's afraid of having to pay ...

– What crime What, more precisely, are you talking about? It's about your mother, right? Tell me, don't be afraid. Your father killed your mother, didn't he? You can say.

Scared by Clarissa's direct and insensitive accusations, Angelina broke free of her and ran for the door, finishing before leaving:

– Don't hate my father, Clarissa. He was always a good man
...

The bedroom door closed slowly after she left, and Clarissa remained thoughtful. It was clear that the girl knew everything that had happened, but was afraid to speak. Fear that her father would try something against her, but that he will have to answer for his crime. Regardless, Angelina loved her father very much and didn't want to see him behind bars, which was understandable. Did he have the right to take his father away from the girl, having also lost her mother?

CHAPTER 23

Looking vague and distracted, Clarissa paced the beach. She was distraught, not knowing what to do, and went out for a walk. It was still early, and everyone was asleep. There were so many things to solve! She had long mastered the idea that she needed to find out how and why Abílio killed his wife, but only then did she begin to wonder what she would do when she found out.

Would she have the courage to report him? For what? To prevent him from spending time with his children, whom he loved in her own way? And what about Angelina who was afraid of losing him? And Vicente? Clarissa liked Vicente a lot, she couldn't hide anymore. If she had met him before, although she was a little older, she was sure that she would fall in love with him. Or wasn't she already in love? She shook her head, as if trying to chase away that thought, when an even more terrifying one occurred to her: If Abílio was arrested, the way would be cleared so they could assume their love.

She could stay there, taking care of Angelina, and Vicente would become her lover. Lover? But what was she saying? She was an honest, decent and dignified woman. How could she be left with such petty and monstrous ideas?

Horrified by her own thoughts, Clarissa stopped, ashamed of herself. Had it been too much sun? It was still early, but the heat of that time might have affected her judgment. The sea was a serene, crystalline blue, very welcoming, and he thought of cooling off. She was afraid of the water, but wanted to try and took her shoes off. The chill of the water made her feel good, and she shifted a bit more, lifting her skirt just above her knees.

Memories that the wind brings

The floor sagged as she entered, and she dropped the dress over her body, amused by the balloon it made around her. Dressed in the dress, she went in a little further, until the water reached her waist, and leaned her torso forward, lowering her head and pulling her hair over her head. They soon touched the water, and she poured them over the sea, until her nose and mouth approached the water as well.

More than quickly, she lifted her body, splashing water everywhere, thinking she was going to suffocate. But nothing happened. The sea was calm and the water was far from her nose. Trying to overcome that fear, Clarissa closed her eyes and lowered her head again, letting her hair hang over her face, until they spread through the water. Soon, Clarissa's hair was submerged and the water touched her scalp.

She started and jumped back, but didn't lift her head from the water. Rather, it sank her down again, and the coolness of the water seeped through her pores. It felt wonderful! Despite her fear and uneven breathing, Clarissa shook her head, tossed her hair in the water, and slowly opened her eyes, startled at the inverted view of a man standing behind her. She straightened quickly, hair falling over her face and around her shoulders, water dripping onto her heaving chest.

– Vicente! – scream – . What are you doing there? You almost scares me!

In fact, it was the boy who was behind her, holding a rod in one hand and, in the other, two fish tied firmly to a line.

– "Hi, Clarissa, I'm asking you, " he said mockingly. What are you doing here in the water, with clothes and everything?

– "I went for a walk," she replied sourly. And you? I thought you were still sleeping.

– I was fishing.

– Where? I did not see you.

– There, behind the rocks.

Clarissa followed the direction of his finger with her eyes. Then she looked at him again and said coldly:

– Well done. Go back to your fishing trip.

She started to get out of the water, passing him. Barely containing the disturbance that the boy's presence caused her, Vicente held her vigorously by the arm, causing her to turn her face in his direction.

– What are you doing? – she screamed – . Let me go! – He released her and looked hurt.

– Why are you treating me like this, Clarissa? – He asked, wounded. – What did I do to you?

– "Nothing to me," she replied. – But I don't like how you treat your sister.

– I already apologized.

– It's enough?

– Angelina thinks so.

– Angelina is just a girl and does not see anything wrong with anything.

– What are you looking at? Do you see evil in me? In my father?

– What happened to you, Vicente? – She said, changing her voice. – I thought you were my friend but now...

– Now...

– I do not know what to say. You seem to see me as your enemy.

He approached her and met her with his deep green eyes. For a moment, Clarissa forgot what they were talking about, and the urge brought her face closer to his, and their lips touched. But this time it was Vicente who rejected her, pushing her with a certain savagery in his eyes:

– No!

Memories that the wind brings

She also took a step back, nervously concerned with her hair, and considered:

– I think we shouldn't talk to each other anymore.

– How is that?

– It's better for both of us not to talk anymore. Despite everything I feel for your father, you are my stepson and it is not right to get carried away by emotions.

– What emotions? What are you talking about?

– Nothing. And now, excuse me, I have to go back. It's almost coffee time. Although he wanted to let her go, Vicente couldn't help himself and grabbed her arm again, holding her close to his chest.

– What emotions are these? – he insisted angrily – . What are you trying to tell me?

– I told you, it's nothing. And now, let me go! – She screamed, fighting. – You are hurting me! But her spirit was weak and her desire was immense. Vicente was not willing to let her go.

He wanted to, but couldn't. No matter how hard he tried, he didn't come out of his head. He loved her and He knew his love was forbidden, but he couldn't help it. It was too strong a feeling to control, and he was no longer able to hide it within himself. Yet he had his father. She was his father's wife, and he loved and respected him too much to be involved in this sordid betrayal. He would rather die than have to betray his father.

With the contact of Clarissa's trembling body against his, Vicente felt that desire was softening him and he began to allow himself to be overcome by emotion. She, in turn, had long ceased fighting. She was afraid of her feelings, but she couldn't resist either. She seemed so fragile to Vicente, trapped by his arms, watching him with wet eyes, her lips parted in a silent sigh. She did not resist. On impulse, he pressed his lips to hers and kissed her passionately, holding her hotly.

Memories that the wind brings

He laid her down on the sand and began to stroke her. Clarissa, without resistance, gave up, until suddenly he pulled away from her and stood up suddenly, moaning with regret:

– I can not! I can not! I love you Clarissa, but I can't! I'm sorry ... – Vicente picked up the rod and the fish that lay on the ground and ran, leaving Clarissa lying on the sand, her chest rising and falling, her eyes closed, imploring forgiveness from herself. He ran home and went to the well to wash herself, dropping the fish in the kitchen. The father was in the living room, reading a newspaper, and tried to be inconspicuous.

– Vicente! – he heard his father call. – Is it you, my son?

He stopped in the middle and, without turning around, replied:

– Yes, daddy, it's me.

– Where were you?

– Fishing.

He realized that something had happened, and Abílio dropped the newspaper and approached his son, just as Clarissa was arriving, all wet and dirty with sand.

Abílio looked from one to the other and immediately understood. For a few minutes, an awkward silence slipped between them, and the three of them stood still and confused, looking at each other without saying anything. At one point, tears clouded Abílio's eyes, who approached Vicente and hugged him almost in despair.

– Something happened? – Clarissa asked, fearing that Abílio had seen them on the beach.

– "No, Clarissa, " Abílio answered, not letting go of his son. Go wash up and pour the coffee, please.

Clarissa did not answer and did what they told her. As soon as she left, Abílio released Vicente and, staring at his family, said sadly:

Memories that the wind brings

– You? love her, don't you?

Instead of answering. Vicente began to cry and threw himself at his father's feet, pleading with anguish:

– Forgive me, father, forgive me!

– "You don't have to ask me for forgiveness, Abílio managed to say, despite the tears that drowned his voice. No one is to blame for loving.

– But she is your wife!

– I can resign, if you want.

– What? How?

– I can go and join your mother. Soon…

– Do not say that! Never repeat it again, my father, never again!

– Calm down, Vicente. You don't have to get out of control.

– There was nothing between us, I swear! There never was, never!

– Take it easy, my son! I believe in you.

A little calmer, Vicente wiped away his tears and faced his father.

– You love her too, don't you?

He bit his lip, fighting to keep the tears from spilling out, and shaking his head, he murmured:

– I don't know. I swear I don't know.

Later that night, Clarissa found herself next to Grandma Toña, but this time there was no more beach. Not that beach, but another, far from her homeland.

Memories that the wind brings

– What does that mean? – Asked Toña, surprised by this sudden change.

– This is the last stage of your life that you should review before the events that will happen.

After that, there will no longer be a need to evoke the past.

– What do you mean, Grandma Toña? I'm not understanding.

– But you'll understand. For that, you must accept your past.

– Accept what?

– You will see.

In silence, Toña took Clarissa's hand and led her to a black village. Like spectators of a dream, the two entered the village and began to follow everything that happened there.

CHAPTER 24

Igboanan finished tasting his lunch, licked his fingers, and discreetly looked at the handcuffs. Dalomba, the oldest, began to collect the stews, and Dallá, young and rebellious, at a signal from the first, began to help her, humming a song and looking in disguise through the ajar curtain, which served as the entrance door to the cabin.

Feigning innocence, Igboanan asked:

– Are you waiting for someone?

She turned around, surprised, and quickly replied:

– No, Igboanan, I'm not expecting anyone.

She did not answer. She knew she was looking for someone with her eyes and she knew who, but she had to feign ignorance. She had long ago discovered her affair with Kandjimbo, a slave who served in her house, but she couldn't let it show. It was necessary to deal with the boy without Dallá noticing. She did not want to expose herself to embarrassment, and everything had to be done with the greatest possible caution.

After the meal, Igboanan got up and prepared to leave. He needed to talk to the priest as quickly as possible, ask him for help in that difficult case. Suddenly, he heard a noise in the village. Everyone was talking at the same time and running, and Igboanan came to the door to see what was going on. In the midst of the crowd of his people, a white man came slowly, a sharp whip in hand, bringing with him another black man, who smiled and greeted his people. He felt a strange sensation and went out to the center of the square, waiting for the others to come closer. When they arrived, the white man bowed and, at their signal, the black began to speak. Despite the other's strong accent, Igboanan understood perfectly:

– Hail, Tata, we arrived in peace.

– What do you want here? – Igboanan asked outright, sensing imminent danger in the white man's presence.

The black man discreetly looked at the white man, who gave him another signal, and continued:

– We came in peace, oh! Tata Y we brought gifts.

The black dropped a large bag on the ground, which he had tied behind his back, and carefully opened it, taking out some objects and showing Igboanan, who picked them up and asked:

– What is this?

– Brandy and smoke. I know they are of great value in your town ...

Igboanan sniffed the tobacco and brandy and grimaced, looking at them questioningly. The white man, who until then had been silent, whispered something in his ear, the black man, who agreed and stepped forward, extended his hands to Igboanan.

– "My master asks you to let us show you, " said the black.

Igboanan handed the items to the white man, who opened the bottle and took a sip, offering it. I held her or awkwardly and imitated the other's gesture, tasting the brandy. He made a new face, spat the liquid on the floor, and wiped his mouth with the backs of his hands. Then he raised the bottle right in front of his eyes, studying its contents, shook his head and said, clicking his tongue:

– Good brandy ...

– After that, he smelled a sweet smell of tobacco and looked again. The white man, after improvising a kind of straw cigarette, took a drag and offered it to Igboanan. He took the cigarette, smelled it too, and again repeated the white man's gesture, breathing in the smoke. That smoke was much stronger than what they used to use in their pipes, and he coughed repeatedly, feeling the tears welling up from his eyes. After coughing, he rocked his head again, cleared his throat and said:

– Good...

The white man spoke to the interpreter in a strange language, which no one knew there, and the black repeated:

– My teacher wants to offer you these gifts ... – . Igboanan looked at him suspiciously, and He continued – ... in exchange for some favors from you.

Shaking his head, increasingly suspicious, Igboanan asked:

– What favors? I'm doing no one any favors, especially whites. I know what they did to other villages.

Although the white man did not fully understand what Igboanan had said, he knew she didn't want to accept his offer and glared at the black man. The interpreter, more than quickly tried to explain:

– No, Tata, my teacher is different. He did not come here to destroy. He came in peace, he said. So much so that he brought you these gifts ..

– But what do you want in return? – cut in dry.

– That's what you say, Tata. An exchange. My master wants an exchange. It's fair – . Igboanan stood there, studying them, fearful of what the white man might do. He heard that they captured blacks, put them in stinky ships and took them to a distant land, from which they never returned. This caused him a terrible fear, and he continued:

– Why do you think he would be interested in doing business with your master?

– Because the gifts he brought are good, and you know that if you refuse, you will lose the opportunity to appropriate those delicacies. And there is much more to our camp.

Everything is yours, if you do us a little favor ...

— A favor ... I know ... But tell me, what favor would it be? What does the white man want in exchange for these ... delicacies?

Glancing quickly at the white man, the black man licked his lips, took a deep breath, as if filling himself with courage, and shot:

— Do you want blacks ...?

— Blacks? You mean, men? But how? What do you think we are ...?

— Calm down, oh! Tata, and listen to me. My master wants blacks, yes, but not blacks. We hear there are slaves here too, captured from defeated tribes. These are the slaves my master wants ...

Igboanan raised his eyebrows in surprise. The proposal was tempting. The exchange of slaves for brandy and tobacco seemed like a fair transaction. After all, slaves were part of his people. They were strangers who came to live there to work and serve. Of course, most were no longer even treated as slaves, beginning to live with the families they served as if they were part of them. But they were not, in fact, members of any clan. They were strangers and how strangers should be treated.

If anything, it was just that they were euthanized. And then...

A terrible thought came to Igboanan's mind. Suddenly, he remembered that Kandjimbo was also a slave, and he had the right to get rid of him in any way he wanted. A devilish smile appeared on his face and he started to shake his head again, showing that he agreed. The black, following the lead of the white, went on to say:

— I mean, Tata, who agrees?

— Um ... let me see. What kind of blacks does your teacher want?

— Well, he only wants men, young and strong. No women, no children.

Memories that the wind brings

It was perfect. He could exchange Kandjimbo without problems, without raising suspicions or protests. Perhaps Dallá would protest, but she had no right to express an opinion.

– "Okay," – he said at last. – Tell me how many men you want, that I will choose them myself, among the slaves of the village. After that, go away and don't come back again.

After the effusive thanks of the other black, Igboanan withdrew. He knew Dallá would despair, but that didn't matter. When he reached his hut, he was about to enter when he heard the voice of the black man again. He turned and the other, still with the white man, spoke in a low voice:

– One more thing, Tata.

– What is it?

– My teacher just wants to ask you one more favor. A special favor he need a certain slave …

– Slave? A woman?

– No, Tata, a girl.

– A girl? But didn't you say he only wanted men?

– But this is special. Just a girl, nine or ten, cute, healthy, smart, cunning. Is there no one like that? It is a special request, for which my master is willing to pay an unreasonable price.

– How is that?

The black man took another bottle from the bag and offered it to Igboanan, who carefully picked it up. He opened it and sniffed the liquid, then tasted it. The taste was indescribable. Sweet, smooth, enjoyable. He looked at the red content with an air of admiration, thinking it was the sweetest blood she had ever tasted, when the black stepped forward and explained:

– It's Portuguese wine. Even the inks didn't taste like that, right? – Igboanan agreed. – That Portuguese wine was truly unmatched. I have never tasted a more delicious drink. With the bottle in his hands, Igboanan really thought that luck was smiling at him. He had found a way to get rid of Kandjimbo and now he had a chance to get revenge on Iadalin, who had rejected his love for a young tribal warrior. Yes, Iadalin would pay him for everything she had done. He would sell his Mudima, that adopted daughter, also a slave that Iadalin raised and loved as if she were his own.

Perfect! Igboanan had the power in his hands, with which he could destroy and crush his greatest enemies.

***

Upon receiving the news that he had been sold as a slave to the white man, Kandjimbo thought that he would kill Igboanan. He wanted to strangle him, but had to hold back.

The presence of the young warriors of the tribe ended up intimidating him, and he did not dare to react. Desperate, he threw himself at the feet of Igboanan and pleaded:

– Please, Tata, have mercy! Please! In the name of our inkices, don't let me go. Please! Please!

The chief of the tribe did not reply. He stood impassive, looking cold, savoring the sweet taste of revenge.

Since his pleas were ineffective, Kandjimbo considered fleeing. He would take Dallá with him, and they would go to the forest, where they could never be found. But the vigilance on him was strict, and Kandjimbo couldn't move, fearing that he might be hit by a warrior's arrow.

Therefore, there was no other choice. With a heart full of hatred, he went to collect his things. He took his few belongings, tied them in a bundle, and waited for them to come and get him. In the eyes, tears of unbridled anger and the desire for revenge.

Someday he would get revenge, even if it took centuries. Kandjimbo knew that the spirit was eternal and that he would have all eternity to execute his revenge.

Dallá, on the other hand, nearly fainted. He cursed Igboanan, threatened to commit suicide if he did not back down in his decision, Igboanan, increasingly resentful, spoke with disdain:

– Why the interest in Kandjimbo?

– He has been our slave for many years and serves me very well. It's like a brother for me.

Igboanan looked at her wryly. She was a liar and an idiot, that was all, and she would get what she deserved.

– I think your interest in Kandjimbo is a bit exaggerated. There is no reason for all the fuss.

– How not? I have already said that I have it in mind for a brother and I would not like parting with him.

– You can join him if you want. I'm sure the white man would be happy to be entertained by someone like you.

Dallá was silent, terrified. Not that. She could never get out of there in the company of a white man. She had heard of his cruelty and was not willing to risk her life in the name of a love that was now beginning to seem impossible. Seeing the fear in his eyes, Igboanan continued:

– You know, Dallá, that is exactly what I would do if I found out that you were cheating on me: she her eyes widened and he continued. pretending nothing to notice: – But it's not like that, is it?

– No, no, of course not.

– Excellent. I am happy. And so? What do you say? Would you like to join him or not?

– Of course not, Igboanan, but what an idea! Kandjimbo is an excellent servant, a brother himself, and I really don't want to lose him. However, if it is impossible to keep it here, please be patient. There is nothing to do, right?

Without saying anything else, Dallá headed for the river. Kandjimbo hoped she would see him go, at least to say goodbye, which was impossible. She loved him, but she couldn't sacrifice herself that way. On the other hand, she couldn't bear to see his pleading, desperate gaze, his stupid attractiveness. His hands saying goodbye.

Damn Igboanan! How could it be so cruel?

Head down, Dallá wept. An immense sadness had devoured her heart, but all that was left for her was to cry. Overcome by tears, she fell onto the soft grass, sobbing in despair. Suddenly, she heard a click and raised the log, scared, afraid of some lion. But there was no lion. It was only Dalomba, who, knowing what had happened, had come to see how it was going.

– What do you want here? – Dallá asked between sobs.

– I came to see if you need anything.

– Yes. I need Igboanan to die.

– Dallá, Dallá, how many times did I not warn you that it was dangerous? But you didn't want to listen to me.

– And? Igboanan is just an old man. What do you know about love?

– You may not know anything about love. But for revenge …

– For revenge, I know. Let me wait. More day, less day, I have to finish with him.

– Don't be silly, Dallá. You know you won't do any of that. Or do you want to die?

– No, I do not want to. And so I kept quiet about what he did. But do not think that I was satisfied. And just give me time to get revenge. He will only see …

– If you want advice, the best thing you can do is forget it. Forget Kandjimbo. It was useful to you for a time, but it is not worth your sacrifice.

– But I love him!

– If you really loved him, you would be by his side, facing everything.

– I can't, Dalomba ...

– I know you don't and I really don't think you should. I just want you to understand that your love for Kandjimbo is fleeting, it is nothing more than fire, which is soon consumed and extinguished.

You will soon forget it.

– I hate Igboanan. It's cruel ...

– You were the one who was cheating on him. Remember that you are his wife and you must not betray him.

– It's old, ugly! Kandjimbo, on the other hand, is young and fiery.

– Still, you did the wrong thing with him. Igboanan did what the law allows, while you broke the law when you slept with Kandjimbo.

– Stop, Dalomba, stop! I don't want to hear anything else!

– Okay, I'm going. But think about it and make sense.

Don't risk losing your life for a man who is already lost to you. Dalomba turned her back on him and returned to the village, leaving Dallá to his own thoughts. She was right: there was no point taking risks for Kandjimbo. He was practically dead, and it was better to forget it. Then he would see.

She'd get another one and everything would be the same again.

By the time Dalomba returned to the village, a man was dragging a girl, who was still crying and kicking, not understanding what was happening.

Memories that the wind brings

The mother ran to her and, crying, told her that the village chief had sold her to the white man. Dalomba recognized Iadalin and Mudima, and was surprised.

Igboanan had told him that only men had been sold. What was that girl doing there? Suddenly, the white man came and tied a necklace around Mudima's neck, dragging her through the village. Mudima screamed louder and louder, completely stunned and terrified, begging her mother to save her. In confusion, she dropped the bundle she was carrying, probably with her clothes, and the white man kicked it, saying something she didn't understand. Mudima kicked more and more, extending her arms towards her mother, until she fell to the ground and the man, unconcerned about her suffering, tightened the necklace around her neck, dragging her across the rough earth.

Stepping back, Igboanan watched. In his eyes, an air of victory and joy. Seeing Iadalin's despair, Igboanan knew that he had managed to exact revenge on her perfectly. Hadn't she rejected him? For now, may he regret that rejection forever.

Igboanan was about to leave when Iadalin approached. Heart pounding, he looked at her superiorly and Iadalin spoke, with all the dignity of his soul:

– You are an evil man, Tata Igboanan. But the day will come when you will receive all the evil that you do today.

Dalomba watched Mudima go, feeling her heart sink as he dragged her through town like a mangy dog.

She watched as Iadalin approached her husband and accused him, and sighed dejectedly. Dalomba went to her hut, walking with shuffling steps. I was confused and shocked.

– What did you do, Igboanan, to do that with Mudima, a girl who knows nothing of the evils of the world? She asked, looking accusing.

Memories that the wind brings

– "Now, Dalomba," he replied without looking at her, "Mudima is also a slave." The white man needed a girl, Mudima was sold. There is no mystery in this.

– What you did was cruel and evil. Mudima is a girl. How do you think she must feel, dragged by a stranger to a strange and distant land, far from the affection and protection of her mother?

– It's sad, Dalomba, but it's life. Each must serve him in his own way, and the way Mudima serves life is taken as a slave by the white man. But do not worry. The girl will be fine.

– How can you know?

– I know. As I understand it, Mudima will be the company of the daughter of a very rich and powerful man. It will certainly be treated very well.

Dalomba looked at him in deep disgust. Deep down, she knew why she did it. It was for Iadalin. Dalomba remembered it very well. Right after your wedding, Igboanan had made him the offer, but Iadalin was already engaged to another and rejected his offer. He did not want to be his wife, and the spiteful and vindictive Igboanan did not miss the opportunity to take revenge on the only woman who had rejected him.

Without containing the revolt, Dalomba said:

– You did it for Iadalin, right? For revenge.

– This makes no sense! I did what was my right as head of the tribe. It was nothing personal.

– You don't have to pretend me, Igboanan. You never forgave her for rejecting him and you couldn't miss the chance for revenge. But why use the girl? That you have avenged yourself on Kandjimbo in this way, I still understand. He is a strong, tough man and knows how to take care of himself.

But Mudima is helpless. She needs someone to take care of her. And now, Igboanan, what will become of the girl?

Igboanan did not dare to face her. What she said was the truth, but he could never admit it. Without taking his eyes off the ground, he concluded:

– I'm sorry, Dalomba, but I did what I had to do.

– Don't you realize what you've done? You sold your people to the white man! The white man is dangerous; you know what it did to other towns.

– The white man is gone.

– Wbahcakt? if he comes

– He will not return.

– How do you know?

Igboanan pushed her aside and left. He couldn't take it anymore. First it was Iadalin, who pointed his finger at him and cursed that plague. Now it was Dalomba, who reproached him, accusing him of cruelty. Only Dallá hadn't accused him, but she was less interested. He had married her because she was young and beautiful, but he didn't like her. She didn't like it, but she didn't admit to the betrayal. Not that.

He left his house devastated and went to the house of the village priest. Ndombe was already waiting for him. He knew what he had done and he knew why. Igboanan feared the consequences of his actions and needed someone to tell him that he had done the right thing. He went headlong to the priest's hut, sat up, buried his face in his hands, and began to cry. The other, seeing his near despair, approached him and asked:

– Igboanan cry the pain of regret?

Igboanan wiped away his tears and faced Ndombe. He took a deep breath and considered:

– What could I do, Ndombe, tell me? I had no choice. If he hadn't sold those men, plus the girl, the white man might have attacked us.

– Are those your reasons?

– It was necessary...

– You are the boss, Igboanan ...

– "I want confirmation from the oracle," Igboanan said, barely paying attention to Ndombe's words.

– Confirmation of what?

– I want you to validate my attitude.

– Do you think our inkices will do that? What if they don't agree with what you did? You did what you thought you should, and no one can change that decision. Neither inkices nor you ... Even if you repent, you will never have her forgiveness ...

– Listen here Ndombe! Shouted Igboanan. I did not come here to hear your advice or your opinion. What you think doesn't interest me. I know that I acted correctly and it was not in search of forgiveness that I came to seek it. I just want the inkices to speak to me, give me their blessing, that's all.

Don't try to blame my actions, or I won't answer for myself! In his heart, the Igboanan knew that he had acted out of revenge and hatred, but he still wanted to try to justify himself. I needed the ngombo 5 to calm his conscience, to tell him that the enthusiasts were satisfied with his act.

1. NA: Ngombo, divination game, with sixty pieces, similar to the game of snails.

Ndombe did not want to annoy or disturb the tribal chief, who was powerful and vindictive, and had no intention of being the bearer of bad news. What if the ngombo revealed that he had done wrong? How to give Igboanan a message of this nature? Ndombe didn't want to play, but Igboanan was determined. Only the response of the inkices would appease his conscience.

– Come on, Ndombe, do your job.

Unable to refuse, Ndombe took a deep breath and replied:

– Very good. If that's what you want, I'll do it as you ask.

Igboanan felt more confident. He hoped the ngombo would confirm that he had acted correctly, which would release him from guilt. If the inkices agreed with his attitude, he could rest in peace.

Ndombe got up and had Igboanan follow him, leading him to the appropriate place for the game. He picked up the pieces, sat on the ground next to the boss, and played.

In the first crash, Ndombe realized how compromising Igboanan's attitude had been. The Inkices weren't happy about the fact that he sold his brothers to the white man, and the game tried to expose the truth. He pointed out the tortuous path of cruelty and revenge, which the Igboanan took of his own free will, and that would lead his people to lose themselves at the crossroads of suffering and pain. He spoke of the need to unite against the white man, the danger this approach posed to his people, the mistake of fragmenting his people in exchange for useless and foolish gifts. But Ndombe couldn't tell you that. If he did, the Igboanan might even turn his anger on him, and the consequences would be terrible. So, Ndombe lowered his eyes, apologized to the inked ones and began to say: – Aluvaiá 6 answer back...

6. NA: Aluvaiá, divinity of the Bantu people, who finds a correlation in Exu, in the Yoruba nation, representative of the roads and messenger of the other inkices.

– What did he say? Igboanan said eagerly, licking his lips.

– He says that his way will be one of glory and recognition, and our people will be saved by their courage to give to men in exchange for peace and security.

Another movement, and Ndombe, frowning, continued to lie:

– The winds of Matamba 7 are favorable ... They took the infidels and now they will bring peace and prosperity to our people.

7. NA: Matamba. Bantu deity, the Lansá of the Yoruba, lady of the winds and storms.

Memories that the wind brings

But Aluvaiá did not reply to any of this. Rather, he warned them about the thorny path they were traveling, and Matamba He told them they would end up in the gale of death, going abroad and suffering in the flesh the loss of life and dignity.

Ndombe did not say what he saw. Despite the inkices' warning, he pretended not to believe. This was too disgraceful to be true.

– And what else? Igboanan asked, rubbing his hands nervously.

Ndombe threw the pieces away again, and once again the Inkices showed their dissatisfaction. The response he got in the game was pretty clear. Igboanan had been carried away by the illusion of strength and power, allowing pride and vanity to override the true values of the spirit. The Inkices warned him that his mission, as chief, was to lead and guide his people, distributing justice and protection, and that he should not use his position to provoke a personal vengeance that, on top of everything, could well throw them destruction. But Ndombe, fearful, was misrepresenting the meaning of the game:

– Nzaze – Loango 8 says justice has been served. Criminals paid for their crimes – .

Igboanan exulting. It was all he needed to hear. So he had acted correctly. He could count on the support of the gods. Satisfied, he got up and gestured to Ndombe, ordering him to stop. He had heard enough. Ndombe sighed in relief.

8. NA: Nzaze – Loango, Bantu deity, associated with Xangô, the Yoruba god of justice and thunder.

He didn't know how long he could continue with this charade. Also, the inkices must have been angry. He, a priest, uses his powers and knowledge to lie and please, for the sole purpose of good graces from the chief of the tribe who, despite claiming to be his friend, would not hesitate to destroy him as well.

Memories that the wind brings

After the alert, the Igboanan continued their harmful practices. Contrary to what he had predicted, the white man revisited his village and, each time he appeared, he exchanged other slaves for more tobacco and brandy, stifling the voice of conscience within him, alerting him to the illegality of his actions. Actions. After all, it was the Inkices themselves who gave him permission to continue that practice.

Ndombe, in turn, ended up losing the gift of seeing through the ngombo. Every time I threw the pieces away, the answers came out in a different and nonsensical way. Either the Inkices had abandoned it, or weapons had taken over the game, mixing it up to confuse it.

As the exchanges continued, the day came when there were no more slaves available for the white man to take. When the Igboanan began to reject the offers that were made to him, the whites were enraged and, about a year later, invaded the village, killing and capturing all the blacks, slaves or not. Of the many slaughtered, Igboanan and Ndombe lost their lives even in African lands, shot dead by the invaders. They took many others: men, women and children, and many perished on the journey.

Of Iadalin's family, only she resisted. The children and her husband also died, some in the village, others in the tumbeiro .

Dalomba was no longer a child and was therefore killed by whites, along with other women. They were weak and light, it was not worth losing to black women who had no chance of survival and who would not make good profits.

Dallá, in turn, young and beautiful, was taken prisoner and sent to the ship. However, at the crossing, some white men chose her to serve them, and Dallá was subjected to all kinds of abuse and humiliation. Already close to Brazil, punished for the mistreatment, she ended up going crazy and was thrown from the deck, to drown and save them the hassle of having to kill her.

Thus, the prophecies of the Inkices were fulfilled, that Ndombe, out of fear and cowardice, died without revealing.

Memories that the wind brings

* * *

When Clarissa returned from that trip, she was extremely confused. Much more so than when she became the proud Louise, Archduchess of Linhares. She knew she had witnessed another of her incarnations, but she could not see herself in that lifetime nor had she identified any of her current characters. Completely stunned, she asked Toña:

- I do not understand. Where do I fit in all this horrible story?

- "You still can't see you, can you, Clarissa?"

- No. In my heart, I feel that I lived in that African village, but I cannot identify with any of its characters. I also don't recall recognizing someone from my current life ... But wait a minute. You were there! It was you, right? The girl! Mudima! It was you, grandmother Toña, before you were brought to Brazil!

- Yes, it was me.

- But how can he? I thought life was older than Luisa's.

- The story you reviewed is still quite recent. His characters disincarnated about a century ago and almost all of them are back in the carnal world.

- How is that possible? I thought it would take us longer to get back to the world.

- It depends a lot. There are spirits that do not want to wait and soon ask for a new opportunity.

- You mean they run away?

- Nobody comes into the world before their time. Reincarnation involves all planning, and the spirit that is willing to return brings everything in its spiritual baggage that it learned and was willing to do. Sometimes, you cannot reach your goal, you only reach half or only part of it.

It is a process of natural evolution, and we all have to go through it. But some are in a hurry than others, they feel different needs, they look for other ways. Each spirit is responsible for the lines it draws for its evolution, and reincarnation is just one of several options that lead to our growth. For us learning spirits, it is still the best way, because it is through reincarnation that we can experience the law of cause and effect.

– You mean we ended up going through everything we did to our neighbor, right?

– I do not understand the law of cause and effect as an instrument of revenge or punishment. The law of cause and effect shows us that we can, through experience, learn from our own mistakes. We experience the same story, go through similar developmental processes, and choose the ending. It is a reaction of life to our own attitudes, with a pedagogical and explanatory character, a weapon for our growth. We are solely responsible for everything that happens to us, and there is nothing in life that goes unanswered.

– What does all this have to do with what we just saw?

– You saw a life in which several of your acquaintances were present, people very close to you in this current life.

– Why can't I remember?

– Why don't you want to. You don't want to accept what you did. It is difficult for you to live with guilt, but you must free yourself, believing that we are not guilty, we are responsible. This difference is fundamental. Guilt weakens, responsibility teaches.

– But what am I responsible for? I feel that responsibility, but I can't remember …

– Think, Clarissa. If you really want to, you will remember. If not, you will return to the physical body and forget about tonight's dream, at least until you are mature enough to understand and accept yourself.

– Wait a minute! Now I remember ... My father, the ship ... oh! My God, this is it!

– What?

– Young Kandjimbo. He was my father, right? And Valentina? It was Dallá. Dalomba, my mother. And Ndombe?

– Probably my brother Luciano. But what about me?

– You do not remember?

Clarissa was silent in horror and covered her face with her hands. Now she remembered. I remembered everything. With tears in her eyes, she looked at Toña and said:

– Igboanan! OMG. Igboanan was me!

– Yes, Clarissa. After disincarnating as Luisa, you chose to reincarnate in the lands of Africa to try to contain and direct the pride that was even that led to mistreating the first slaves who arrived in Brazil.

– And why did I came back like a man?

– Because she was already tired of abusing her sexuality and wanted to experience the opposite side of her conquests. Reincarnating as a man, you were allowed to understand the masculine universe and value the feminine essence, not as a source of unbridled pleasure, but as the substrate of sensitivity that every woman should have.

– It was my pride that drew the destiny that I imposed on my brothers, right? I threw them into the sea, into an unknown land, and today I find myself in the same situation.

– Do not think that what happened to the blacks in your village was the work of your wickedness.

Those who were sold chose to go through that, and you were nothing more than an instrument for the realization of their destinies. Of course, no one is an instrument by chance. No one can be forced to act against their principles or their morals just to promote the growth of the other, because there would be no merit in growing at the expense of other people's commitment.

– Anyway, I did that because I wanted to, right?

– You had your free will and you could have done it differently, and life would have found other ways to fulfill the destiny of your people.

– And my father would not have sold me to Abílio to avenge what I did to Kandjimbo.

– All this is the work of life, Clarissa, and no one acts out of desire to do evil, but out of ignorance. However, when we do understand, we abandon old attitudes and change our behavior for the better. The same happens with your father, as with you and with everyone who inhabits this world.

– And you, grandmother Toña? Today I regret what I did to you. Can you forgive me?

– There is nothing to forgive.

Clarissa's eyes filled with tears and she hugged her former slave, recalling the story of her life, that she herself had told him 9. He loved her so much and could never imagine that he was the one responsible for her coming to Brazil, even in that very life.

9. NA Toña tells her story in the book: " Feeling in your own skin "

– What about Ndombe? – Clarissa answered, trying to eliminate the sad memories of Toña's life – . How is my brother with all this?

– Your brother was always a kind soul, and it was not for nothing that he reincarnated as Bertoldo, Luisa's second husband.

In Africa, he was born gifted with impressive sensitivity, and contact with spirits was extremely easy for him. However, it corrupted his faculty, distorting the warnings and truths that his inkices tried to show him, all in the name of fear and cowardice. Luciano, even today, has a good mediumship, but he has learned to develop it honestly and forever. It remains to learn from the truth.

Clarissa wept with emotion. She was happy. She had all the knowledge she needed to take on the world and herself, and she was sure she would win.

Shortly after, she said goodbye to grandmother Toña and returned to her physical body, keeping in memory only the impressions that these revelations had caused her.

CHAPTER 25

Christmas Eve dawned cloudy, with some thunder here and there. Despite the bad weather, Clarissa was willing to stay up to make the night special, especially for Angelina, who hadn't seen a Christmas party in a long time. The tree had been carefully decorated and had delicate icicles and colored balls, as well as lanterns that would be lit at dusk.

Angelina was elated. She no longer believed in Santa Claus, but she was sure that his own father had taken it upon himself to surprise her. It had been years since she had won a gift and was waiting for a new doll.

At first, Clarissa began preparations. Assisted by Jerusa, she roasted the turkey, prepared the fish, made sweets and cakes. Angelina deserved such a party. And even Vicente, who, despite his manly and arrogant demeanor, was still just a boy.

Taking advantage of a moment when Jerusa had left, Abílio entered the kitchen, approached Clarissa and said:

– Clarissa, at least today, try not to hate me.

She looked at him in surprise. She could never expect such a request from a man like Abílio. At the time, he seemed very fragile, which touched her. But he was also a murderer, a fact she had to consider. However, his face was not that of a murderer. That was the face of a tired and suffering man, not a criminal.

Clarissa was confused. Abílio had his face so close to hers that he felt her labored and gasping breath, the trembling of her hands, the anxiety and fear in her eyes. And how Vicente was like him! An almost exact replica, only a few years younger.

Vicente was a very handsome boy, and Abílio was not far behind. He already had some wrinkles, had put on a few extra

Memories that the wind brings

pounds, and had become bald that even lent him some charm. He was a handsome, mature, confident man, and Clarissa was surprised to see that. For a moment, their lips almost touched, but she, embarrassed, took a step back. What happened to him? She had married the father and was almost seduced by the son. And now, close she didn't kiss him either. What kind of woman was she?

Excited and confused, she walked away, fiddling with the pots on the stove, her back to him. Frustrated, Abílio turned to leave and was already walking away, when Clarissa interrupted:

– I don't hate you, Mr. Abílio.

He stopped, pursing his lips, but said nothing. He was afraid to say something and ruin everything. He just shook his head and left, leaving Clarissa puzzled.

Soon after, Jerusa returned and, noticing Clarissa's confused state, asked curiously:

– What did he want?

– Who?

– Now who ... Mr. Abílio. Who else?

– It may seem strange, Jerusa, but he came to make a request.

– What order?

– He asked me not to hate him.

– Strange. A man like Mr. Abílio, who did what he did, made a request like that ... Anyway, he must be really sorry.

– It is true. And then today is Christmas Eve. I think we should try to live in peace.

– You're right. The best thing for everyone is to be imbued with the Christian spirit. Who knows, we won't be able to solve this mystery?

So, they didn't talk about it anymore. For the rest of the day, Abílio was absent. He left with Vicente and Tiago, without saying where he was going.

Memories that the wind brings

At home, Clarissa, Jerusa and Angelina finished their preparations, while Luciano remained there, walking from side to side, trying to feel the presence of Leonor's spirit.

– "Come on, Luciano, stop," Jerusa snapped. It's Christmas, it's not that day.

– "Jerusa is right," Clarissa agreed.

– What things? – Angelina asked, who didn't know what they were talking about. Clarissa shot a warning look at her brother and sister-in-law and replied:

– Nothing, Angelina. Luciano's nonsense.

Angelina didn't insist, ecstatic that she was getting ready for dinner. The day came to an end, and only at dusk did Abílio and the others return.

Clarissa was already worried, afraid they would be late. They entered without saying anything, and Abílio went directly to the room, carrying a small package, while Vicente, taking a towel, went to the well at the back of the house. It was time to get ready for dinner.

Seeing Abílio go by like a bullet, Luciano felt a bit uncomfortable. He didn't know what it was about, but his intuition made him go after him. In silence, Abílio climbed the stairs and went directly to his room, entering Leonor's room. Luciano followed him and put his ear to the door, but heard nothing. What was Mr. Abílio doing there? He couldn't find anything and returned to the living room, going directly to where his sister was.

– "Mr. Abílio shut himself up in Mrs. Leonor's room," he whispered. Clarissa didn't answer.

Suddenly, she had lost all desire to deal with it.

– Leave him. It's Christmas, he must miss his wife. He turned his attention to the table he was setting.

The job done, Clarissa looked critically. It was beautiful!

Soon after, they all withdrew. The day had been exhausting and they wanted to be ready for dinner. Clarissa asked Tiago to fill the bathtubs in the bedrooms and stayed in the living room, waiting for him to finish. He took a long time on that task, and she almost fell asleep, until he appeared and said:

– There sir.

– Thanks, Tiago.

– You're welcome.

He nodded and turned to go, but Clarissa called out to him:
– We can count on your presence in the party, right, Tiago?

His face lit up with a smile. Although Abílio had already invited him, he was happy to see that Clarissa also cared for him. She was a good girl.

She could be curious, rebellious, cranky. But she had a good heart, and that was what mattered about people. Still smiling, he replied:

I wouldn't miss this party for nothing! Your delicacies smell good ...

Clarissa smiled back and stood up, waving goodbye. Silently, she climbed the stairs and went to check on Angelina first. The girl was immersed up to the neck, enjoying that cold water. Clarissa stuck her head around the half- open door and asked:

– Is everything okay with you?

– Ah! Yes. Clarissa, don't worry. I'll put on a new dress!

– Very good. It will be very nice

Clarissa pulled the body away and closed the door, looking at the pink dress on Angelina's bed. She had said it was new. Had Abílio bought it when she went to Rio de Janeiro? Upon reaching her room, Clarissa entered thoughtfully. She closed the door carefully, and when she turned, she stopped in astonishment.

Spread out on the bed, the most beautiful dress she had ever seen, ivory, with some shiny threads and, at the feet, delicate and shiny boots. Above, a three-strand pearl necklace and a pair of pearl earrings. Clarissa was surprised and took the dress, running in front of the mirror. Putting it before on her body and smiled. It was beautiful!

She dropped the dress on the bed and went out into the hall, knocking on Abílio's bedroom door. It was the first time he had given it to her, which filled her with emotion.

Other than the clothes he had bought for her shortly after the accident, he had never given her anything.

– "Come in," said a voice from within.

She entered cautiously and approached the desk where he was, still wearing his shirt sleeves, which made her uncomfortable. She had never been alone with him in his room before. I only went in there to clean it, and even then, when it wasn't there.

– Mr. Abílio, I ... – . she started, then stopped, not knowing what to say.

– What is it?

– I would like to thank you for the gifts ... The jewels ... The dress ... it's wonderful! Abílio looked at her excitedly. he wanted to run to her and hug her, but he couldn't move.

– "It was nothing, Clarissa," he said with ceremony, looking at her with restrained tenderness. It was just a pleasure. I just wish you and Angelina were beautiful tonight ...

– "Thank you," she replied, a little uncomfortable.

Then he went back to the room to get ready. She washed and dressed calmly.

When she was ready, she looked at herself in the mirror and smirked. Mr. Abílio was a good man, after all, because only someone with the most refined taste could buy such beautiful and delicate gifts. After she finished dressing, she went out and it was then that she realized that she had dressed for him, hoping that he would praise her, admire her, like her.

Memories that the wind brings

* * *

The night came pleasant, covered with stars. The thunder that broke out in the morning had disappeared, and the clouds, dispersed by the wind, showed the full moon. Only the wind didn't take a breath, blowing hard through the windows and doors. The dinner prepared by Clarissa and Jerusa was a great success. Angelina and Vicente, little used to so many delicacies, did not tire of trying those delicacies.

Tiago then tasted cakes and puddings for the first time, sure he had never eaten such delicious things.

Seeing the happiness of his children, Abílio was moved. That night brought him something he hadn't experienced in a long time: joy. He was pleased to hear the laughter of the children, especially Angelina, who, when she was a child, did not have an exact idea of what had happened in their lives.

Around midnight, Clarissa invited those present to pray together.

– We must not forget the birthday boy – she said with a smile.

– Birthday? asked Angelina

– We cannot forget that today is Jesus' birthday. It was exactly 1891 years ago that he was born.

– "It's true," Jerusa completed. Let us pray and ask Jesus to send us the best gift anyone could wish for, which are blessings of love and peace.

They all knelt down and held hands, and Clarissa began:

– Here we unite, Jesus, to offer you the best that we have in our hearts. Each of us, in our own way, experiences our own intimate feelings, and only we know what it is that warms our hearts.

Memories that the wind brings

But we are ready to offer our most genuine sentiment, asking you to accept or transform it. If our feeling is of joy, of happiness, may you receive it and multiply it, causing it to spread among all our brothers, bringing a little warmth to those defenseless souls. But if our feeling is of anguish or pain, let him take it in his hands and transform it into a valuable learning for our lives. And may we never allow the flame of your eternal love to fade within us.

Thank God.

– Thank God – they all repeated in unison.

Emotion took over the environment, and discreet tears escaped the eyes of Abílio, Vicente and even Luciano, who, still attached to the false concepts of virility of the time, were ashamed to show their emotion. Then, Abílio invited them to open the gifts, fighting to hide the strong shock he felt.

Angelina was the first to get up. She only thought of the doll her father had promised her. Seeing her anxiety, Abílio immediately took out the package containing her gift and she ripped it up in a hurry. Inside, a beautiful porcelain doll, glass eyes, hair that looked like royal, dressed in a wonderful ball gown, all gold. Angelina rejoiced, clapping her hands gleefully. She has never seen anything more beautiful. Even Tiago, who didn't care about such things, was impressed.

For Vicente, Abílio bought a solid gold pocket watch with rubies instead of numbers. He was already a young man and he no longer cared about toys. The son looked at the watch in surprise, turned it in his hands, amazed, and went to hug his father. More than a simple gift, it meant the realization of a love that had been established long ago, but that Vicente could now only discover.

Then it was Clarissa's turn. In addition to the wonderful dress and jewelry he had given her, Abílio bought her another necklace, only made of diamonds, accompanied by earrings and a beautiful bracelet. She looked like a princess, and Clarissa was deeply astonished. She knew that Abílio's fortune came from

Memories that the wind brings

jewelers days that he owned in the capital, but did not think he worked with such expensive and wonderful things.

– Its beautiful! – She exclaimed in admiration.

– I'm glad you enjoyed it.

– "You know, Clarissa," said Angelina, "Dad is the one who designs all her pieces, isn't he, Dad?"

He nodded with dislike. He did not like to expose his abilities. Clarissa, however, more and more surprised, could not contain her astonishment:

– It is true? I could never imagine it!

– "There are many things you can't imagine, Clarissa," Vicente said, looking at her ironically. At a glance from Abílio, the boy caught himself. This was not the time for provocation.

Jerusa and Luciano also received gifts, and even Tiago received a top hat and a cane, things that he silently admired. Luciano had also brought gifts for everyone, and Clarissa had placed some orders with her husband. Even children got together and bought souvenirs at the sales of the city, and the exchange of gifts took on the greatest meaning of exchange of affection.

Although the party continued peacefully until the early hours of the morning ñana. Clarissa can't help make a sad observation:

– Too bad we can't have music. I would love to play some Christmas songs ... Jerusa and Luciano looked at each other. It was from music that it all began, for that harpsichord that he received as a gift from his father, which, in fact, had seen the price of his sacrifice. However, not wanting him to be saddened, Jerusa suggested:

– Why don't we sing?

– Sing?

– Yes, we can sing.

Memories that the wind brings

– But I don't know anything about music, Angelina complained.

– "It doesn't matter," Clarissa consoled. I'll teach you myself.

As the wind whipped the outside walls, Clarissa and Jerusa taught others the songs of their land that they used to sing on Christmas night. Before long, they all learned the lyrics and melodies, and joined the group of girls, forming a beautiful, tuned chorus.

Without realizing it, countless white drops were scattered throughout the environment, resting on furniture and utensils, involving the heads and bodies of each one. As the music developed, more and more light penetrated that environment, leading to indescribable well- being. The melody is capable of awakening the purest feelings, and all those present, sensitive in their own way, let the music penetrate their hearts, caressing them with angelic softness.

Standing next to Clarissa, Toña smiled serenely. She approached the girl, hugged her and gave her a sweet kiss on the forehead, which made her feel a little chill.

– What's up, Clarissa? – Luciano asked, feeling a strange sensation in the air.

– I dont know. A good chill, all of a sudden.

When Toña hugged Luciano, the boy felt tears come to him. He knew that hug and spoke softly to Clarissa:

– I think there is a spirit between us.

– A spirit?

– It looks like Grandma Toña.

Clarissa took a deep breath, sipping that kind air, remembering the old black woman, already bent over the years, looking kind, serene. Toña, gently hugged each of those present: Jerusa, Tiago, Vicente, Angelina.

Memories that the wind brings

When she approached Abílio, she wrapped him in a warm hug, kissed his head and began to massage his heart, vibrating a crystalline green light on him. Immediately, Abílio began to cry. He did not know why, but the tears welled up in his eyes, as if he were shedding a cry that had been suppressed for a long time, a cry that today needed to go. And that was exactly what Toña had done: she had released from Abílio's heart a muffled feeling, a controlled delay, a contained sensitivity.

– Father – he called Vicente worriedly, approaching him.

– Something happened?

Dazed and embarrassed, Abílio wiped his eyes with his hands and apologized:

– Forgive me ... I don't know what it gave me ...

– "Don't worry, Mr. Abílio," Clarissa said. It is good to cry once in a while. Angelina ran to her father and hugged him, and he held her close to his chest, opening his arms for Vicente as well, who snuggled between them.

Tiago, who knew all the pain that the family intimately thanked their Orixás for that blessing and prayed gently, asking God to protect them. Clarissa, Luciano and Jerusa, faced with this moving scene, could not contain their tears and they also cried. Was Abílio really that monster they thought? It looked like anything but a monster. He seemed a sober and tormented man, but with an enormous capacity to love.

Soon after, he excused himself to leave. It was late and the night had been exhausting. They needed sleep, especially Angelina, who was still a child. They all got up and said their goodbyes, heading straight for their rooms.

When they went to bed, they soon fell asleep, while the wind was still ruthless outside: uiuiuiuiui ... But everyone was used to it, and no one paid attention to that lament.

Memories that the wind brings

Early in the morning, the moaning started again. Behind the uiuiuiuiui ... the wind, that uiuiuiuiui ... was clearly heard ... only this time with much more intensity than other times. Not that it was taller. On the contrary, it was even weaker, but much more painful and repetitive. Clarissa was the first to wake up, but she was also used to that moan, and she thought that Mrs. Leonor's soul, touched by the events of the night, must have been very disturbed, wanting to find the long- lost peace. Silently, she raised her thoughts with God and prayed for the dead, asking Jesus to support her and help her find the path to peace.

The moans, however, did not stop. On the contrary, it went on and on and seemed to increase from the noise of the wind. It was as if the gust of wind was driving it howling through the walls, and it seemed to be ringing throughout the house. In their room, Luciano and Jerusa also woke up, and the girl asked, scared:

– But what is this?

– "I don't know," Luciano answered. It seems that Mrs. Leonor's spirit is more tormented than ever.

Suddenly, they heard footsteps in the hallway, walking towards Leonor's room, and they heard a click, as if a latch was closing, Abílio, probably, went to the wife's room trying to appease his own conscience, begging her spirit to forgive him.

The moans, little by little, were diminishing, weakening, until they stopped completely. And when everyone thought that silence would reign in the house, there was a high- pitched, painful, agonizing cry, followed by desperate, high- pitched sobs.

– Nooo! Nooo! Cried the voice.

It seemed like someone was going through an unspeakable scourge, and they all ran into the hallway at almost the same time. Vicente was the first to arrive and raised his hand on the latch, shaking it violently. The door was closed and the boy began to shout:

– Dad! Dad! Open the door!

Memories that the wind brings

Nobody answered. Vicente started banging on the door, and Angelina started crying, clinging to Clarissa and moaning in turn:

– Mom!

It was a general disaster. The screams continued in anguish, and Vicente almost despaired. Tiago even showed up. He heard the screams from his hut behind the house and came running to see what was happening.

Vicente, assisted by Luciano, lunged at the door, trying to open it, until Luciano put his foot on the latch and it slammed open, throwing the door wide. Vicente shot past him and hurried inside, tripping over an opening in the side wall of the room.

Then Luciano entered, followed by Clarissa, who came with Angelina clinging to her waist and Jerusa behind. They stopped in fear, covering their nostrils with their hands. A disgusting smell invaded the room, and they, in the gloom created by the half-closed curtains, turned their faces in the direction Vicente had run and froze. The closet on the wall had been moved away diagonally, showing a passage that led to a room adjoining Mrs. Leonor's room. From there came the piercing screams that they heard, and they, trying to overcome that putrid smell, were still hesitant.

They walked in and followed the sound of that voice, terrified. Just below a skylight, where the moon casts a white light that illuminates and pales to go into the atmosphere, Abílio was kneeling on the ground and crying, rocking his body from one side to the other, holding the body of a woman, very deformed. Head back, eyes closed, pale, skin dull and flayed, covered with wounds, thin and dry hair, on the face a kind of crater in its place where the nose should be.

Beside him, Vicente, on his knees, was crying with his face hidden in his hands. Everyone stopped in horror, and Angelina took a step forward, expressing in a silent sob:

– Mom...

Memories that the wind brings

The woman, for a moment, opened her eyes and looked at the girl. Her eyes were so bright that Clarissa was startled. It was as if the eyes were the only living thing in that body that decomposed before death. The woman looked at Angelina for a long time, smiled slightly and closed them again, this time never to open them again in this life. Desperate, Abílio clung to the woman's body and began to scream, totally out of control:

– Not! Please, Leonor, no! Do not leave me! Do not leave me!

Beside him, Vicente wrapped his arms around his father's shoulders and, with tears streaming down his eyes, pleaded:

– Please, dad, let her go ...

– Not! Not! – Abílio continued shouting.

At that moment, Tiago made his way through those present, who remained still, mortified by this unusual scene. He approached Abílio and carefully placed her generous hands on his, pulling them away from the woman's now lifeless body. Abílio still tried to hold on to her, tightening his arms around the bandages, but Tiago's pressure was stronger. Little by little, Abílio relaxed until he let go of her, and the black man, helped by Vicente, lifted Abílio's heavy body. Supported by his son and friend, he got carried away. When he passed Angelina, he looked at her with deep regret, and she ran to him, hugging his waist and crying profusely. Clarissa carefully removed the girl from him and stepped aside, giving way to her. Abílio came out loaded, squeezing the hand that his son offered him so lovingly.

CHAPTER 26

Confused and outraged, Clarissa didn't know what to do or think. Everyone was amazed, and Luciano was the only one who seemed to reason more clearly.

– Come on, Clarissa – he called – let's go out. For now, there is nothing we can do.

– But it is necessary to bury the dead ... – interrupted Jerusa, horrified.

– "Later," Clarissa said. Now I have to take care of Angelina. Care is required. Clarissa led the girl back to the room. I wanted to ask her a million questions, but she stopped. Angelina was deeply sad and upset, and didn't want to talk. Clarissa asked Jerusa to make her tea, and her sister- in- law appeared next, holding a steaming mug in her hand.

– "Drink," Clarissa said, handing Angelina the cup.

– It'll be good for you.

Still sobbing, Angelina took a sip of tea and lay down, resting her head on Clarissa's lap.

– Can you stay with me? She asked, holding Clarissa's hand.

– I'm here by your side. Now sleep, you need to rest. We'll talk later.

– Please, Clarissa, don't leave me alone.

– You are not alone. I am here with you.

Clarissa lay down on the bed next to Angelina and hugged her tenderly. The girl was hot and shivering, and a few beads of sweat ran down her face.

She burned with fever and soon fell asleep. The rest of the night was busy, and Clarissa stayed with Angelina, unable to sleep. Many questions arose in her mind that did not allow her to sleep.

When dawn broke, Clarissa heard a knock on the door and got up to open it. It was Tiago who came to call her.

– Mr. Abílio asked to see you. She shook her head and replied:

– Where is he?

– In my house.

– It's okay. Tell him I'm coming.

After he left, she went to where Angelina slept and put her hand on her forehead. It was cool, which showed that the fever had subsided. Clarissa went slowly to her room, washed, and changed. Then she went to knock on Luciano's bedroom door.

– Come in – he said.

He opened the door and, seeing the two of them sitting on the bed, came in and asked:

– Already awake this hour?

– And did someone fall asleep?

– No, I don't think so. He paused and sat on the bed next to them, and added: – Mr. Abílio wants to talk to me.

Can you take a look at Angelina for me? She is very shocked, had a fever at night and does not want to be alone.

– "Don't worry, Clarissa," Jerusa assured her. I will take care of her personally.

– "Go see what Mr. Abílio says to you," Luciano said. I think the conversation will be quite interesting.

Grateful, Clarissa got up and left, heading straight for Tiago's cabin. When he came in, the black was not there. Just Abílio, sitting on the sofa, looking lost, full of dark circles. He hadn't slept either and spent the night crying. When he saw her standing in the doorway, he said softly:

– Come in, Clarissa. I think we need to talk – . She sat in front of him and looked at him, listening to him ask: – How is Angelina?

– "She had a fever at night, but she's fine." She shook her head and continued:

– Poor Angelina was the one who suffered the most from all this.

– I can imagine. The father hid the sick mother inside her own house ...

– Please, Clarissa, don't condemn me. At least listen to what I have to say.

– Very good. I'm waiting.

Abílio took a deep breath, as if filling himself with courage, and began:

– A long time ago, when we were still living in Rio de Janeiro, we discovered that Leonor was ill. Her skin had lost its sensation and a few purple spots appeared here and there. At first we thought it was just an allergy and went to see a doctor. He didn't even have to examine her to make the diagnosis.

Leonor had leprosy, there was no doubt. The shock was terrible. We had two children to raise, and Angelina was little more than a baby. We were desperate

Clarissa felt her heart sink and agreed:

– I can imagine ...

– As well. The doctor advised isolation. There was no remedy for treatment, and the result was certain death. Furthermore, the disease was highly contagious.

At that time, we learned that the only progress made by science regarding this disease was the discovery of a bacillus. Other than that, nothing else was known. The danger of contagion was so

Memories that the wind brings

great that we had no choice. We needed to get Leonor out of touch with other people as soon as possible. Especially with our children, the doctor said, since they and I would be the first to be contaminated. It was a very difficult decision, because lepers are marginalized and feared by all. And that was not what I wanted for my Leonor at all. On the other hand, the pressure was very high and the doctor threatened to tell the authorities who would quarantine our house. You have no idea how much we have suffered.

Clarissa sighed heavily and added in a weak voice:

– It must have been very painful.

– Much more than you think. I loved my wife, I loved my children. How to separate myself from her, how to deprive the children of contact with the mother they adored?

It was then that I heard about Cabo Frio. It was by chance that I was buying newspapers when I overheard two men talking. They said that there was a leper camp here and that they knew a neighbor who had been sent here.

– And there was?

– I don't know, I never tried to know. But that was not what made me decide to leave. The men said that the land was very beautiful, bathed by the sea, full of sun and, the main one, practically deserted. The city was just a town, and there were many uninhabited places. I left there more excited. I hoped that, far from the dirt and grime of the capital, Leonor would regain her strength. Everything settled, I appointed a business manager and we left. Before, however, I went to the doctor and told him my resolution.

I told him about the camp and my intention to put Leonor there. He happily agreed and promised not to tell anyone. It would keep her away and there was no need to expose her to the cruelty of others. Then one day, without saying goodbye to anyone, we left.

– Weren't you scared?

– Afraid of what?

– Contagion. You said yourself that leprosy is very contagious. Weren't you afraid of exposing your children?

– No. For a reason that I don't know how to define, I was always sure that none of us would be contaminated. And none of us have really been contaminated. But I couldn't risk it with the others. I knew that other people could be contaminated and he knew that Leonor would be publicly abused if she stayed in the capital. The rumor had already spread, and even my son suffered discrimination. Therefore, we did not participate in anything and we came here, bringing only Tiago and old Olinda, who has already died.

I had already made some trips before, looking for a place to stay, and I discovered this house. It was perfect for us. Away from the city, spacious, facing the sea.

Leonor always liked the beach and would love to go out, sunbathe and swim in the sea without risking being stoned.

– And have you lived here for a long time? Has anyone ever suspected?

– Not at first. The house is far from the city, and few people pass through here. For a few years, we managed to remain incognito. The townspeople didn't give us much thought, and we rarely appeared in public. When we needed something, Tiago went to town to get it.

– And the money? What did you live on?

– As I told you, I appointed a business manager who, to this day, comes every month to render accounts. When he came, it did not take more than a day, and Leonor did not appear. Nor did she ask questions. I paid him and I still pay him very well, and he never wanted to risk losing his job.

– But people found out, right?

– Yes they did it. And they were cruel, very cruel.

– How? You told me that no one here knew or cared about them.

Memories that the wind brings

– It is true. But fate does not forgive, and we cannot escape its web. There was a certain man, a certain Mr. Caldeiras, a prosperous merchant from the city, who used to buy products in Rio de Janeiro to resell them in his establishment. On one of his trips to the capital, he was in a farm shop, talking with the owner, when a curious man approached. This man was an acquaintance of mine who, listening to Mr. Caldeiras mention Cabo Frio, he went to ask me for news.

He asked him if he did not know any gentleman, Abílio Figueira Gomes, and Caldeiras replied that there was a guy named Abílio living near the beach, but he did not know if he was the same. From the description, they concluded that it was the same person. The man awkwardly asked if my wife was in the leper camp, and Mr. Caldeiras was startled. Why would my wife be at that camp? Hernani replied that he had heard that Leonor had contracted illness, but that I didn't know if it was true and that, as a result, I had moved with my family to Cabo Frio. Ready. That was enough. Mr. Caldeiras came back astonished, certain that there was a leper living among them, which would be a great threat to the entire city.

– But you live far away. How could they feel threatened?

– People are easily impressed, Clarissa, and fear what they cannot understand. The fact is, one day, they came knocking on my door. Olinda was still alive and came to warn me. There were some gentlemen outside who demanded that I speak to them. Ashamed, she went to attend to them, and they made their claim to me. They told me that they knew of the existence of a leper who lived here and demanded that he leave. First, I tried to deny the fact and made up that Leonor suffered from rheumatism.

Later, I tried to reflect, telling them that, despite the fact that Leonor had this horrible disease, she did not represent a threat to anyone, since she lived locked up in her house and had no contact with other people. But they were terrified. They had children who attended school. What would the other children do if they too were contaminated? No. Either Leonor was leaving, or they would be forced to hand her over to the authorities. I was desperate.

– I suppose...

– It was then that Leonor herself presented the solution to me.

At the far left of our house, at the end of the corridor, was a great room, which the previous owners used as a music room, with a large skylight in the ceiling and wide paneling. As well. Tiago and I closed the window with bricks and let the whole house fall to avoid attracting attention. Inside, we closed the door that leads to the corridor and opened another, inside Leonor's room, hiding it behind a closet, which actually functioned as a false door. With that, we intended to fool anyone who entered and searched the house.

Following the corridor, he would find nothing, only the closed wall and, in Leonor's rooms only an empty room. All set, we put our plan into action. Leonor wrote a suicide note, saying goodbye to me and the children, and disappeared. Pretending to be desperate, I went to the fishermen for help and told them that my wife had thrown herself into the sea. She was ill, with severe rheumatism pain and decided to end her life. Searches began, but no one could find the body. Until one day, at dawn, I gave Tiago orders to go alone to the beach and throw my wife's torn dress there.

The next day, they found the dress and hastily called me. I recognized the dress, I threw myself on it, I cried desperately, begging for Leonor's life.

– OMG!

– I was really crying for my pain. Even though she was alive, I had to wall up my wife so that no one would find her, so that they would not take her away, so that she would not suffer even more ...

– And your children? Did they know what you had done?

Memories that the wind brings

- They knew. I never cheated on them. When Angelina found out, she was deeply shocked, and Vicente, disgusted. He did not understand why things had to be this way and he considered me a coward, who had locked up her mother to get rid of a problem.

At that moment, Clarissa lowered her eyes, embarrassed, and ended up confessing:

- Forgive me, Mr. Abílio, but I also thought so.

I thought you were not a coward, but a murderer. For me, you had killed your wife out of pity or to get rid of a nuisance.

- You misjudged me, Clarissa. I walled up my Leonor because I couldn't leave her, because I would die fighting to save her. She would never have let them take them from me, and she knew that I would give her life in her defense. What would become of our children?

Certainly they would be taken and handed over to an interested guardian, who would only take care of them to get our money. No, Clarissa, I am not a murderer. Much less a coward. I'm just a man who, out of love, could lie and cheat, it is true, but to save the reason for his existence. I'm guilty? Yes .

Offender?

Too. But my crime is not murder. I am guilty of polygamy, because I was remarried while my first wife is still alive.

- If your wife was still alive, why did you marry me?

- The day we decided to put Leonor in that room, it was as if she was really dead to the world. She was afraid that someone would suddenly appear and surprise her. In addition, the disease was evolving and the skin, little by little, began to peel, and huge wounds opened through her body. I saw it, day by day, my beloved wife began to decompose in life, and that was a source of immense pain. However, I also needed to think about my children. With Olinda's death, our house turned into a pandemonium. It took the hand of a woman to put everything in order, to help educate the children. I thought of a maiden, but Leonor disagreed. She needed a woman, a wife.

Someone who would love me and the children, and treat us with respect.

– So you decided to buy me?

He looked at her in dismay, feeling immense remorse for what he had done, and continued:

– I know I shouldn't, but I didn't plan anything. After Leonor died, I started traveling to Rio de Janeiro, hoping to find someone to serve me. I contacted my old acquaintances, told them that Leonor had died and that I needed to get married again. It was then that I met Commander Travassos. He was talking to his father and he introduced us. When I heard that I had an unmarried daughter and needed money, the idea occurred to me. I offered him a lot of money in exchange for his hand, and he accepted. When I met you, I almost changed my mind. You were so beautiful, so young. What right did I have to ruin your life?

But my despair was greater and I carried out the plan. I married you and I stole your opportunity to be happy ...

Clarissa was crying with excitement. I was deeply moved by that man's words. She had considered him a monster, but only now did she see the wonderful man that he was.

Not realizing what was in his heart, Abílio continued:

– I confess that I even wanted you to leave. Contrary to what I imagined, you never let yourself be dominated, and it became difficult to control you. And I met you.

I suspected something, but was surprised when you told me about your suspicions. However, I couldn't give up. Leonor was visibly worse, there were nights when she cried and moaned ...

– It was the moans that I heard ...

– Yes. Especially when it was windy, Leonor gave vent to her suffering and groaned ía out loud, thinking that the wind would cover his lament. But you realized and started praying in her room, thinking that she was dead and that her soul was restless.

- Which is still true. Mrs. Leonor was really upset, wasn't she?

- Every day, her illness progressed and she felt great pain. When hearing your prayers on the bedroom wall, she often couldn't help herself and cried softly, hitting the bottom of the closet preventing her from leaving.

- And we who think it was his spirit ... poor Mrs. Leonor. How she must have suffered.

- And she suffered a lot. We all suffer And I was forced to witness her suffering in silence, taking care of her secretly, afraid even to think of her name.

- It must have been very difficult. Take care of her, feed her ...

- You can't even imagine it. After everyone fell asleep, I would go to her room and bring her enough food and water for the next day. She cried and accepted the food.

She ate that boring cold food, but she never complained or – He paused, contained by the tears, and continued: – We did everything at night, Tiago and I. We exchange buckets for her needs, drink water and bathe and wash her dirty clothes. I could not risk letting you see her dresses on the clothesline.

- And I never realized ...

- Covered by the darkness of the night, I moved the closet away and opened the window of her room, just a little, so she could breathe fresh air ... – . He stopped again, crying with excitement. How he loved her!

- Only with a lot of love to face a situation like this. And she must have loved him very much too.

– One night, unable to resist, she opened the bedroom door and ran out, running to the beach. I listened when she left the room and ran after her. She was desperate and really wanted to kill herself. She walked with difficulty and it took her a long time to reach the sand. Her body was wounded and necrotic, she had already lost some pieces. I was afraid to even touch her and cause her more pain. So I was talking, trying to call her to reason, begging her to come back to the room. But she didn't answer me and was walking towards the sea. When the waves started to hit her, I couldn't help it. I needed to stop her from doing something crazy. As gently as I could, I took her body and pulled her to me, and she moaned in pain, passed out in my arms. So I could pick her up and bring her back.

– It was the night Luciano followed them, right?

– Yes it was. Upon entering, I noticed that the jar fell and broke, and I was scared. I begged God that no one was there and walked away.

– Really, Luciano got scared and returned to the room. All he could see were two shadows fighting on the beach.

– Thank God the distance is long and it was dark. When I passed Vicente's room, I knocked lightly and he answered, following me silently. Back in Leonor's living room, I put her to bed and told Vicente what had happened, and that's when we agreed on that story. Seeing his mother's condition, Vicente was shocked.

After a few days, we had a conversation and we got along, which was a blessing from God.

However, in response to Leonor's request, I forbade my children to visit her, to spare them the terrible sight of their mother, who was rotting away in life.

– It must have been horrible.

– It was one of the hardest things I've ever done. I knew how much my children loved her and I know that I gave them too heavy a burden to bear. Especially for Angelina, who always missed her mother so much. Vicente, although he had rebelled at first, in his heart, knew that this was our only way out and he stood firm, keeping our secret under lock and key. Angelina too. Only she is still a child, more fragile, who needs maternal care. And your presence, Clarissa, came to bring a little joy to her little heart, so young and already so battered by life.

Excited, Clarissa got up and approached Abílio, and everything contracted before her approach. He loved her, but was afraid of her. She was always cold and distant, her heart leaned toward his son. At that moment, however, Clarissa could only think of Abílio and, approaching his face, she brushed her face with her lips, feeling the salt of his tears on her mouth.

Abílio closed his eyes and gently pushed her away, considering:

– Clarissa, no ... I know that you and Vicente ...

He put his finger to his lips and stood up, tugging at his hand and looking him straight in the eye. He was so moved that he couldn't speak, and she, standing on tiptoe, wrapped her arms around his neck and gave him a big hug, letting all her love flow into Abílio's heart. When he released it, He cried softly, he said with emotion:

– Thank you.

She smiled at him and said softly:

Come on, Mr. Abílio, we have to organize the funeral.

EPILOGUE

Clarissa left Abílio in Tiago's care and went to Luciano's room. Her husband was very shaken and she needed to make the necessary arrangements. She entered discreetly and recounted everything Abílio had told her. Luciano and Jerusa were perplexed. They could never imagine such a thing. Hide the woman for all those years! Who'd say?

– That is why I never felt the presence of the spirit of Mrs. Leonor ... – . Luciano considered.

– "It's true," agreed Jerusa. How to feel the presence of a soul that had not yet died?

– Clarissa, Luciano reflected, I understand Mr. Abílio's motives, but he was very wrong. I'm not even going to question the fact that he has kept the woman hidden all this time. I, in your place, could do the same. But he married you when he was still married. This is called polygamy and it is a crime under our laws. We have to tell the police, and Mr. Abílio must be denounced ...

– Why Luciano? Clarissa objected. Why do we have to tell the police? Are things not already solved like this? Don't you think Mr. Abílio has suffered enough? And children? What will become of them? What will become of Angelina?

– Can't you see? With that, we can annul your marriage. You will be free, you can remarry ...

– Who said I want that freedom?

– You do not want that?

– Before, maybe I wanted it. But not now. I can not. Mr. Abílio needs me, Angelina needs me. I can't leave them.

– But Clarissa, Mr. Abílio committed a crime. Do we have the right to cover it up?

– So what if he committed a crime? Who cares?

– Now, the laws ...

– The laws, in this case, are ineffective against human suffering. It is not fair for a man to be punished for having suffered so much.

– "Mr. Abílio was not honest with you or with anyone," Luciano objected, beginning to get angry. He lied and cheated everyone for several years. Do you think that is correct?

– And what is the right thing for you? Lock him in a cell, as if he were a common criminal? Come on, Luciano, where is your Christian spirit? Have you no mercy on their suffering?

– Is not that. It is just a question of right and wrong. Mr. Abílio was wrong. He must pay for his mistake.

– I think he has already paid enough. Don't you realize how much he suffered? He punished himself. You don't need anyone else to punish him. We do not have that right.

– We do not have?

– No. Or rather, you don't have it. If anyone should complain, it would be me. But I'm not complaining. I don't want to punish him. I don't want him to suffer anymore. On the contrary, I want him to be happy. He has suffered enough and now he deserves to be happy with his wife and children.

– What woman?

– I'm married to him, right?

Luciano was discouraged. There was no point arguing with Clarissa. She was stubborn and determined, and no one could make her change her mind.

– "Clarissa is right," Jerusa said. It is up to her to report it. But if she doesn't want to, if she intends to continue living with him after that, then that's fine.

No one better than her to know what is best for herself.

Memories that the wind brings

— That's right, Luciano. Please don't do anything. Keep this secret. In the name of my happiness, don't say anything to anyone.

— We have a duty to reveal the truth! — Luciano insisted —. It is not up to us to conceal or distort it, under penalty of agreeing with the error. Do you want to be accused of being an accessory to that crime?

— You're being uncompromising. One clings to the truth without realizing that, in this case, it will not benefit anyone.

— Isn't that why you fought so hard? To unravel all this mystery?

— I fought to discover the truth because I thought that only that could bring justice.

But what is this justice, which condemns a man who has already punished himself and suffered in the prison of his own conscience?

— I don't know, Clarissa ... I'm afraid of the consequences of hiding the truth.

— There will be no consequences. If Mr. Abílio had committed polygamy to obtain some personal advantage, he would not have said anything. But he acted out of instinct and desperation, thinking that he was doing his children good.

— But and you? What good did it do you?

— It did me good to make me learn to love him.

Luciano opened his mouth, stunned, and was thoughtful for a few minutes. He felt he had a duty to reveal the truth, but recognized that no one would benefit from it. Angelina would be an orphan, Vicente even more upset, and Clarissa would suffer. What right did he have to spoil the happiness of those people, just because he called himself a defender of the truth?

He sighed and, shrugging, finally said:

— I don't understand you, Clarissa. In an hour, you hate Mr. Abílio, and in the next moment, you say you love him —. She did not answer – . You're right. If that's what you want, your Will will be done.

I just hope you don't regret it later. Thanks Luciano! And be sure: I will not regret it!

When Clarissa came downstairs with Luciano and Jerusa, Abílio was in the living room, with his children and Tiago, waiting to hear the decision they had made.

As soon as he saw them arrive, Vicente hurriedly asked:

– So, Clarissa, what did you decide?

Luciano took a step forward, cleared his throat, and began to say:

– Well, sir. Abílio, I can't say that I agree with what you did to my sister, but I won't judge you. If Clarissa accepted it, who am I to blame it?

She asked me not to say anything to anyone, and although I cannot understand her reasons, I can only respect them. You don't even have to worry about me or Jerusa. You have my word as a man and a gentleman that we will never say anything to anyone. It will be a secret that we will take to the grave.

Abílio got up and extended his hand, saying moved.

– Thank you so much...

From there, they went to take over the funeral. It was necessary to bury Leonor as soon as possible. The body, already badly damaged, would enter a rapid state of decomposition.

Luciano and Vicente dug a grave behind Tiago's house, very close to where the thicket began, and Abílio carried the body there. Clarissa said a short prayer, asking God to receive and comfort her, and Tiago threw dirt and sand on the grave, hit the shovel well, and planted some flowers on it.

Memories that the wind brings

The next day. Luciano and Jerusa left. Luciano even tried to convince Clarissa to follow them, but she refused:

– Thank you. Luciano, but I can't. And I don't even want to. My place is here, next to my husband and daughter.

– Daughter?

– I consider Angelina my daughter, whom I must educate and take care of with all love and attention.

– That's right, Clarissa, I won't argue.

– I'm glad you could understand me. Luciano hugged his sister excitedly and spoke, his voice cracking:

– Bye, sister.

– Goodbye Love. Greetings to all –. Then Clarissa narrowed Jerusa and kissed her on the cheek, emotionally adding:

– Goodbye, Jerusa, take care of yourself and take care of my brother.

– "Don't worry, Clarissa," Jerusa said crying. Luciano extended his hand to Abílio and declared, full of emotion:

– Goodbye, Mr. Abílio. I hope you can make my sister happy from now on.

– Don't worry, Mr. Luciano. I will do everything in my power to make Clarissa happy. Even letting her go. No grudges, no pain ...

Clarissa interrupted her husband with a decisive gesture and replied:

– Why do you want to get rid of me?

He took her hand tightly, smiled at her, and didn't respond. He did not need it. His eyes had the answer.

After saying goodbye, Luciano and Jerusa left. They didn't want Clarissa to take them to the port. They would miss her very much and wanted to keep the memory of her smile, not the tears of parting. Seeing the bullock cart leaving, Clarissa waved to them and ran towards the road, speaking as she ran:

– Luciano, tell Dad that I already forgave him for what he did. Tell him I love him. Him and Valentina ...

* * *

A few days later, Vicente went to knock on Clarissa's room door, and when she saw him, she was shocked and was about to blame him:

– Vicente, please ...

– Don't be afraid, Clarissa, I won't bother you. I came here to say goodbye.

– Say goodbye? Where are you going?

– To Rio de Janeiro. Tomorrow I am going to the capital to enter the university.

– But now? So suddenly?

– I found it better. There is no reason to wait for the start of the school year. So, I'm getting used to the new winds – . She said nothing, and he murmured, `` Clarissa ...

– There is? What is it?

– I ... well ... I don't know how to tell you this, but ...

– What, Vicente, for the love of God!

– I would like you to know that I like you very much, but we could never be happy ...

– I know. I also like you very much, but I feel like I don't love you. In the past, maybe. Today, however, I know that my place is with your father.

– I'm happy for you. Nor could I build my happiness on my father's misfortune. He has suffered a lot and does not deserve to suffer more. On the contrary, you deserve to be happy, he deserves a woman like you.

Clarissa smiled contently. She liked Vicente very much, but it could never be his. Now she knew that she loved Abílio and wanted to be ready to get him back. She would know how to get him back. He loved her too.

And then there was Angelina. She was too attached to the girl to abandon her. Angelina already saw the figure of her mother in her, and after Leonor died, she began to ask for even more. Angelina liked being with her, she felt protected by her side. And what was not his amazement when she, embracing her, asked:

– Can I call you mommy?

Clarissa wrapped her arms around her, kissing her repeatedly on the cheeks. She loved that girl very much and felt responsible for her. She had not given her life, but it was as if she owed her life and she responded with emotion:

– Nothing would make me happier, Angelina.

Angelina hugged her. She was happy and excited. She did not want to replace the mother in her heart. She wanted to add Clarissa to her. Love has no limits, and Angelina was able to love Leonor and Clarissa without having to give up one to love the other.

The next day Vicente left, and Clarissa went with Abílio and Angelina to take him to the port. Toña, at her side, smiled happily, sure of the duty accomplished. She would carry out her mission and could leave, always ready, however, to answer any calls from Clarissa.

When Clarissa saw the ship standing there, she shuddered. She couldn't have gone with her brother, even if she wanted to. As long as she lived, she would never board a ship again. When the ship whistled and began to move, she flinched. Slowly, the ship crossed the Itajuru channel, assisted by a small boat, and she greeted her stepson, leaning over the railing. It was hot, but she was sweating very cold. Instinctively, she squeezed Abílio's arm, which was holding her hand.

Noting that she was cold and shivering, he held it between his own and asked:

– Are you frightened?

She smiled at him and shed tears of emotion. At that moment, close to him, she felt as if nothing could reach her, she felt safe by his side, she felt that she loved him. Lovingly, she held his chin, stood on tiptoe and kissed him gently on the lips, feeling again the salt of the tears in her mouth that he shed. She shuddered with satisfaction and held it close to her chest. When the kiss ended, Clarissa looked at him tenderly and whispered, her voice full of love:

– No, Abílio, there is nothing more to fear ...

THE END

Books of
MÔNICA DE CASTRO & LEONEL

Despite Everything

Love is not to be played with

Head on with the truth

From my all being

Desire

The price of being different

Twins

Giselle, the lover of the Inquisitor

Greta

Till Live do us part

Heart Impulses

The Actress

The Force of Destiny

Secrets of the Soul

Feeling in one's skin

Books by
ELIANA MACHADO & SCHELLIDA

Aimless Hearts

The Shine of Truth

The Right to be Happy

The Return

In the Silence of the Passion

The Strenght to restart

The Certainty of Victory

The Conquest of Peace

Lessons that Life Offers

Stronger than Ever

Without Rules to love

A Diary in Time

A Reason to Live

Eliana Machado and Schellida, Romances that captivate, teach, move and may change your life!

World Spiritist Institute
https://iplogger.org/2R3gV6

www.ingramcontent.com/pod-product-compliance
Lightning Source LLC
LaVergne TN
LVHW041618060526
838200LV00040B/1335